MESSI

The King of Camp Nou

"I, Charly Rexach, on December 14, 2000, and in my capacity as Technical Secretary for FC Barcelona, and despite the existence of some opinions against it, commit to signing Lionel Messi as long as the conditions agreed are met."

What a great signing it proved to be! (© Shutterstock)

MESSI
The King of Camp Nou

Jason Pettigrove

ST DAVID'S PRESS

Cardiff

Published in Wales by St. David's Press, an imprint of

Ashley Drake Publishing Ltd
PO Box 733
Cardiff
CF14 7ZY

www.st-davids-press.wales

First Impression – 2021

Paperback: 978-1-902719-849
eBook: 978-1-902719-993

British Library Cataloguing-in-Publication Data.
A CIP catalogue for this book is available from the British Library.

Typeset by Prepress Plus, India (www.prepressplus.in)
Cover designed by the Welsh Books Council, Aberystwyth

Contents

For Celine, Callum, Alice and Elliott

Foreword

Across the outrageous, stunning and unique career with which Leo Messi has so far delighted us, one of the things I most hated hearing, from journalistic or ex-footballing pundits was: 'There's nothing left to be said that hasn't already been said.' Complete tosh.

For the 16 years since he began to impact global awareness, Messi truly never let a week, a month – let alone a season – go by without producing something to set us on our heels again.

Whether that was his orgasmic technical skills and invention on the pitch, the career twists and turns, his increasingly enthusiastic media interviews, or his captaincy, his quest for trophies right up to his tortuous and unnecessary departure from the club he loves, Messi challenged all of us to re-appraise, to try and keep up with him. Even if you were a dyed-in-the wool Cristiano fan.

Lionel Andrés Messi supplied the joy. Our only duty was to keep watching, and keep finding ways to express our admiration at the beauty of what he achieved.

Compiling and displaying the historic stats which, in a clinical way, help establish him without any question as the greatest footballer since Pelé and Diego Maradona (perhaps he's greater than either, but that's for everyone to decide for themselves), isn't for me.

When Sir Alex Ferguson was first coming to terms with data analysis while in the latter third of his Manchester United reign, he would gather all his usual impressions of a match, honed across years and forged by his volcanic need to keep succeeding, and get ready to give one of his players a 'rocket', but then at the last minute turn to his Italian physical performance guru, Valter Di Salvo, and, on the bus back from an away game, demand short, clear data based information on a certain player.

The purpose was to either confirm or, to his surprise, correct impressions that the great man's eyes and experience had drawn from the hurly-burly of a match.

Sometimes stats and data help draw us away from misapprehensions – sometimes they underline greatness in a way that the naked eye can't calculate and retain, but, frankly, they are a side show – especially when it comes to the Galileo or Da Vinci of football, which is what Messi is.

So those who want to submerge us in his goals, assists, shots, key passes, successful dribbles and what his ratio of goals-per-match are, with and without a beard, have their place, but, I fear, they miss the beauty. They miss the anarchy, the thrill, the fear this dangerous little man inspired in rivals. How many other footballers had you on the edge of your seat, your sofa, or made you forget your pint in the pub as regularly or with as much verve? For this long?

They miss Messi's bravery, the skipping over lunges, the nutmegs, the ultra-stubborn will to bounce back like he was made of industrial rubber when another hatchet man has tried to bully him out of a contest.

They miss the tears which most recently streaked his face while he was trying to express how aghast he was to be forced out of Camp Nou, but also the sobs which overtook him, for years, when (on those rare occasions) he lost a cup final.

They miss the importance of the human drama, which became a gulf stream narrative flowing through Messi's entire career, of him 'endlessly' seeking to add either the Copa América or World Cup (preferably both) to the Youth World Cup and Olympic Gold at Beijing to which he'd already inspired his national team.

The gut-wrenching frustration of losing Copa showpiece matches against Chile, the World Cup final in Brazil weren't mere baubles denied to an over privileged 'man who has it all'. It was a spiritual quest, something which drove him to pain and distraction, before eventually experiencing deep joy in the summer of 2021.

What I know, for a fact, is that Jason Pettigrove is a man who'll tell you both versions of this story: Messi the magical man and Messi the breaker of records. I guarantee this will be the best book on Leo Messi you haven't read. Then, beauty being in the eye of the beholder, maybe it becomes the best.

There's a huge satisfaction, for me, in seeing Jason fulfil his dream and finally deliver his book to us. When I first met him, Jason helped run the London Barça supporters club which congregated, weekly, to drink and swap stories and watch football on a boat on the Thames. That, in itself, seemed a magical concept to me but, of course, Messi was the man who made the boat rock.

Listening to Mr P talk football, I knew instantly that he was a frustrated teller of stories – that he was successful in one career but that he could, with strength of ambition and daring, abandon it to become a football writer and broadcaster. It's a good long time since that prediction came true.

Jason's a notable success in his new world, but this, I'd say, is his magnum opus. Filled with detail, research, and more interviews, I'd bet, than he can remember. A wide-ranging chronicle of a great life, but also, crucially, filled with the same glowing admiration for Messi the man, Messi the footballer, Messi the bringer of joy and amazement that you and I have.

Enjoy, and Viva Leo Messi.

Graham Hunter
October 2021

Acknowledgements

The joy of writing about any subject is only surpassed by the knowledge that others are interested enough to want to read your work. It's very much appreciated and makes the long hours I've spent researching and writing this book that much more worthwhile.

Curating my own thoughts, and those of many very noteable others, regarding the footballer who I believe is the best to ever have played the game has been a hugely rewarding experience. One that took me to the depths of an Andorran bank vault – you'll find out why later in the book – and gave me the opportunity to speak to some of those in the game that have helped Lionel Messi during his career, watched him in awe from afar or who have had the arduous task of trying to defend against him.

I am very grateful and honoured that so many knowledgeable and well-regarded figures from the football world have shared their memories and opinions of Lionel Messi with me, as without them this book would not have been possible. People such as Espanyol stalwart, Moisés Hurtado; the ex-player, analyst and *Messi Tactico* author, Alex Delmas; Jorge Barraza, the former chief editor of *Magazine Conmebol*, the official publication of the South American Football Confederation; Dani Fragoso, who played alongside Leo for Barça B; and Santi Padro, the TV3 journalist behind the fabulous 'Gladiator' video that was played to the squad in the dressing room just before the 2009 Champions League final in Rome.

Mike Phelan's thoughts on the 2009 and 2011 Champions League finals from a Manchester United point of view were insightful, searingly honest and incredibly interesting to listen to. The same can be said of the recollections of commentators such as Ray Hudson and Rob Palmer, who, throughout Leo's career, had to come up with different superlatives from their vocabularic canon, week-in and week-out. Tony Watt, scorer of the goal for Celtic that saw Barça lose a game in which they'd had more than 80% possession across the 90 minutes, takes us through the lead up to that fascinating match and its aftermath.

Ex-Nigeria coach, Samson Siasia, explains his frustrations at his U20 team not being able to correctly do the basic things to stop Leo, and Horacio Gaggioli – Messi's first representative in Barcelona – recounts the whirlwind that surrounded a 13-year-old Argentine and his family during the first few months after landing in Catalonia. Josep Maria Minguella, a key figure in Messi's early career, graciously spoke to me in early 2019 about how getting Leo to FC Barcelona came about, while ex-Liverpool legends, Sir Kenny Dalglish and Jamie Carragher, explained how it felt to be a Liverpool fan on *that* night, and their own admiration for what Lionel Messi has done for the game of football.

Víctor Font, who came second to Joan Laporta in a keenly contested Barça presidential race in 2021, was more than happy to offer his thoughts on what Leo meant to him personally, as well as to Barça and all *culés*. It was particularly enlightening for me to understand the lengths he would've personally gone to, to keep Leo at the club if he'd been elected. In light of Joan Laporta's inability to stop Leo from leaving, though, Víctor would have faced the same insurmountable challenges that troubled Laporta.

Thanks to the highly respected Argentinian sports journalists, and good friends, Sergio Levinsky and Marriro Varela, I was also able to interview Argentina's national team coach, Lionel Scaloni, in the wake of the long-awaited Copa América title triumph in 2021. You'll read what it meant to him, on a very personal level, to be the coach to finally deliver a title with the national team for Leo, and how difficult it is to coach the world's best when you've only got a couple of weeks to work with him a few times a year.

In order to give a book such as this any sort of balance, it was imperative that I was able to get differing points of view, and everyone mentioned above was gracious enough to give up their time freely. I owe them all a huge debt of gratitude.

I must also give a most sincere thank you to Graham Hunter, who has kindly written the foreword to this book. Before I was able to carve out a journalistic career for myself, it was a meeting with Graham, while he was still part of the crew which delivered Sky Sports' Spanish football coverage, that set me on the path to earning a living writing about the sport I love. From that very first conversation and ever since, Graham has been a consistent source of inspiration. Despite his standing in our profession and how busy he remains, he is always available should I ever need a question answered. Graham is someone who I can never thank enough for giving me the confidence to make a leap of faith that I didn't think was possible.

My thanks also go to Adil El Khandouki. You'll find some incredible Messi stats at the back of the book. It really is quite astonishing to see the stunning regularity with which he was decisive for club and country, and Adil's hard work in compiling those stats for this book show that Leo's contributions have been extrordinary.

This is my second book and, as with the first, it has been published by Ashley Drake of St. David's Press. We had agreed at the very beginning of our discussions that such a book about Messi would need a fluid deadline and only be published when Leo retired from FC Barcelona. That was a godsend because it meant that at no point did I feel undue pressure. Well, not until an unexpected burofax in the summer of 2020, and then an actual leaving announcement that came completely out of the blue a year later. In trying to do justice to Leo's career there was an awful lot to cover and uncover. The length of the book exemplifies this.

There were certainly many other people I'd wanted to gain access to for this book, and when you're told that the highest profile stars of the game, such as Diego Maradona, have said yes to being interviewed, only to never be in a position to complete the final arrangements, it can be hugely disappointing. Despite this, I am happy with the finished result because it's been another crucial learning experience for me, and an enjoyable write from start to finish, for all manner of reasons. I'm indebted to Ashley for letting me just get on with it and offering sage advice as and when required. It's a working relationship that has flourished because of these reasons and, should I be minded to write another book in the future, it's Ashley who I'll turn to first to see if he wants to get the band back together again.

With so much already written and spoken about Leo before this book was published, some stories within these pages will be known in some form or another, but there are plenty that won't be common knowledge. From a personal perspective, this book was always intended to be an homage to Leo and a career overview as much as anything else. As a supporter of FC Barcelona, as well as a journalist working for the club between 2017 and 2021, Leo has shaped both my personal and professional life, and so perhaps my own recollections of certain matches will chime with others. They may even get you scurrying to *YouTube* to relieve the multitude of highlights that will document his career in perpetuity.

The author and Horacio Gaggioli with the famous napkin which is kept in a bank vault in Andorra and has been seen by less than half a dozen people since being placed there. (© Jason Pettigrove)

My penultimate thank you has to be to the man himself. Having had the privilege to see Messi live on many occasions, including the 2009, 2011 and 2015 Champions League finals, I had a huge amount of games and individual moments to draw upon for inspiration. Moments that will never leave me and which consistently give me goosebumps when watching them back again.

Acknowledgements

As always, having a supportive family behind the scenes is what keeps any author going. When the words just didn't flow as I'd like or the frustration at having another interview request turned down got the better of me, it was my wife Celine, and my three children, Callum, Alice and Elliott that were there to lift me up and keep me positive. It's to them, for their continued love and support, that I dedicate this book.

Jason Pettigrove
October 2021

Just Another

I guess that for Messi each goal is just another.

They come to him as sun does to summer.

Just another low drive with the right or left, or the odd lob or deft touch with head or chest.

Just another night making his rival number drift past like a ship with a busted rudder.

Just another soul left in his slipstream, by his light speed shift up from nought to sixty.

Just another free-kick from 30 yards that will swerve like the letters of his autograph.

Or another free-kick sneaked beneath the wall, or a handball that gives our praise the briefest pause.

Just another hat-trick scored. Just another home crowd's ecstatic roar.

Just another dribble that will dazzle all.

Watch this juggernaut clutch another Ballon d'Or.

Musa Okwonga

1

Rosario to Barcelona

The Journey Begins

"He would possibly have joined Atlético or Real Madrid"

Lionel Messi's time at FC Barcelona came to a surprising and abrupt end in August 2021, some 18 years after he first set foot on a football pitch for the senior side. Their union was over in a flash. An unexpected turn of events ensured that Barça were not going to be in a position to fulfil their financial objectives on what would have been Messi's last contract with the club, with the news being brutally delivered to him and his father, Jorge, on the day – August 5, 2021 – that they had expected to put pen to paper. Barça supporters the world over all knew the end had to come eventually but not in the manner it did. The 'Messi era' at FC Barcelona has ended and his Camp Nou farewell has already passed into memory. All that Barça fans are left with are their memories, the endless highlight reels on *YouTube* and grainy, unstable and often out-of-focus mobile phone footage from the stands with which to recall his other-worldly skills.

For years we assumed his departure would take the form of his yielding to Old Father Time and retiring, not moving to another club. The memories, though, live on. Many were lucky enough to see him play live, while others will have to make do with the clips and highlights broadcast on television and stored within the electronic universe. Thankfully, our grandchildren and future generations won't need to rely on tales of his magnificence from those who watched him live, as the wide-eyed descriptions that sound far too preposterous have the video evidence to confirm the sublime majesty with which he played. In decades to come children will watch and realise that time and again Messi defied logic and lifted spectators from their seats with excitement and disbelief. To see him in action was to bear witness to

Lionel Messi's childhood home in Rosario. (© Titi Nicola)

the elegant brush strokes of an artist at work: a Picasso of the pitch. Moreover, he was a problem solver extraordinaire. Just how many times did he make the seemingly impossible, possible?

Just as Freddie Mercury's extra octave gave him incredible vocal range and set him apart from most of his contemporaries, Messi's exquisite passing skills elevated his performances to virtuoso levels his opponents couldn't match. Those unable to attend FC Barcelona or Argentina's matches were left with TV or radio broadcasters in order to make sense of the seemingly implausible. Ray Hudson, an ex-professional himself, and for years the voice of GOL TV and beIN Sports in the US alongside Phil Schoen, had once described Leo as a 'Jedi knight'. His colourful commentary was always entertaining, but even he was forced to reach new heights to adequately and accurately elucidate what he had seen.

Hudson knew a top player when he saw one. In the 1970s he had played against Pelé, Giorgio Chinaglia and Gerd Müller, as well as playing alongside George Best and Johan Cruyff, who later revolutionised the footballing culture at FC Barcelona as club manager. Often ridiculed for his over-the-top verbosity, Hudson sought ever more grandiose expressions to do justice to Messi.

"Magisteeerial" was often thrown into a sentence when describing a particularly sharp passage of play and his best work mirrors one of Messi's best goals, against Athletic Club on April 27, 2013 at the old San Mames in Bilbao. After letting out a manic, almost banshee-like, high-pitched scream, Hudson's description began: "This man is absolutely main line to pure footballing magic, that belongs in a different galaxy altogether than we are living in. Absolute astonishing jaw- dropping genius from Lionel. Watch this hesitation right there. Three players inside a telephone box and he don't care. He emasculates them individually, collectively. He literally disperses his atoms inside of his body on one side of this defender and then collects them on the other. Magisteeeerial Lionel. Magnifico! Extraordinario!"

Such moments of magic were the culmination of a footballing journey whose trajectory had started on the streets and fields of Rosario, Argentina.

The story begins in a walled field just a stone's throw from where he grew up – at 525 Estado de Israel, in the Lavalleja district of Rosario – to Jorge Messi and Celia Cuccittini on June 24, 1987. Though bereft of grass and a rock-hard surface, the field gave kids from the locale hours of fun. "I remember us playing together outside my front door," said Waly Barrera in a 2018 documentary. "He came to birthdays at my house and to a fancy-dress party at school, where he went dressed as a snail. This was the first time we spent a night away from home but I remember that Leo got homesick and had to leave."

Diego Vallejos was another in the tight group of youngsters who lived and breathed football. He recalled Leo scrawling his name, which was still there when the documentary was being filmed, on a wall close to his home. "Leo wrote it when he was about eight years old. It's a living memory and we want to frame it and keep it forever. He was a shy boy but quite naughty! With adults he was very reserved, but with his friends he was cheeky. He always had a football with him and we played a lot in the street too, it felt very safe in our neighbourhood. When we were picking teams, everyone wanted to choose Leo first because he made a difference. Everyone knew he was a great footballer."

Little, aside from a mural of Messi, which doesn't do him justice, has changed there since the late 1980s. Graffiti still dominates the uneven brickwork which surrounds the area and grass still doesn't grow in the main part of the field. To anyone unfamiliar with the history, the field is completely nondescript. Mural aside, there's nothing to indicate that the future captain of the country's football team lived no more than 30 seconds up the road.

That does tend to come as a shock to those visiting the third largest city in Argentina, 'in search of Messi'. He has a limited presence in the minds of locals, most of whom support either Newell's Old Boys or Rosario Central. Guillem Balagué caught the mood in his Messi biography, writing "you breathe football everywhere in Rosario, but, curiously, the air doesn't smell of Messi [...] It's almost as if it's considered vulgar to have his face posted everywhere." Hector De Benedictis, Rosario's Tourism Secretariat, has been unable to establish a 'Messi Tour' for visitors, because the Messi family rejected proposals due to concerns over privacy. "When people ask me about a Messi tourist tour, it pains me. It's a question of ethics," he told *USA Today* in May 2018.

The district remains unchanged and dated, yet retaining an authentic charm. Leo occasionally returns, leading to the well-known story of the Swedish football fan who had made the 'Messi pilgrimage' and, waiting outside the house and immersing himself in the surroundings one Christmas Eve, was invited in for a chat by Leo himself. Though they now have property on the more salubrious side of town, the Messi family still own the Lavalleja house, built by Jorge, and it's believed that members of the family look after it for them. Although it's a world away from the life that he has led since moving to Europe, he has an understandable need to return to his roots. His early childhood gave him some of his happiest memories, before the pressures that came with the move towards a career in professional football that eliminated a normal adolescence.

He was born into a football-loving family and thanks to older brothers Rodrigo and Matias, and cousins Emanuel and Maximiliano Biancucchi, was chasing a ball almost as soon as he could walk. His skills were noticeable as soon as he was old enough to kick a ball as was his insistence on playing at every possible opportunity – either on the field at the end of the road, in the streets or at school (School No.66 General Las Heras). His older brothers marvelled at their younger sibling's apparent obsession. "When our mother sent him off to run errands, Leo always took his football with him," Matias recalled in an interview. "And if he didn't have one, he would make one out of plastic bags or socks."

Fan graffiti outside Leo's childhood home. (© Titi Nicola)

By the age of four, it was clear that Leo needed another outlet for his passion. The team coached by his father at local club Grandoli was the obvious choice. He was accompanied to almost every match and training session at their ground by the Paraná River, on the outskirts of Rosario, by his grandmother, Celia, to whom he has dedicated his goals with the simple and instantly recognisable point to the sky.

Initially at the club to watch his brothers train and play, it was not long before he would lace-up and show what he could do. Salvador Aparicio, who died in 2008, was a youth coach and needed a player for one of his sessions. In an interview with *Goal* he noted: "I looked up to the stands and saw him playing with a ball. But he was so small, so we decided to wait for the other player to turn up. He didn't, so I asked Lionel's mother if I could borrow him. She didn't like the idea and said he'd never played (in a match) before. His grandmother was there too and she said, 'Come on, let him play!' So, they let me borrow him. The first time the ball came to him he just looked at it and let it pass. He didn't even move. But the next time it virtually hit him on the left leg. Then, he controlled it and started running across the pitch. He dribbled past everyone crossing his path. I was screaming for him to shoot, but he was too small. Ever since that day, he was always in my team."

Messi was only five years old at the time, and shorter, by a distance, than anyone else on the pitch, but grainy *YouTube* videos document just how good he was. The speed from a standing start, body feints, awareness of his colleagues and positional sense all came completely naturally from that point. The only issue would be whether it could all be harnessed into a team dynamic. "Immediately he started to attract a lot of local attention," Grandoli president, David Trevez, remembered in an interview with the BBC: "He was so different from the rest. He would get the ball, go past four or five players then score. For a kid that age, it's very rare to be able to do that. People were saying Grandoli had the next Maradona, and when he was playing, people who weren't even connected to the club would come, the whole neighbourhood would watch the game."

At the point when youthful brilliance often fizzles out, Messi continued to get better and better. "Later in the youth teams, he scored six and seven goals in every match," Aparicio added. "Instead of waiting for the goalkeeper to kick the ball, he would take the ball off him and start dribbling all over the pitch. He was supernatural." He soon developed another passion; Newell's Old Boys, the team that his father and brothers, aunts and uncles all supported, and whom his siblings had turned out for at youth level. Within a year of his first match at Grandoli, he joined Newell's. True to form he scored four times in a 6-0 win on his debut for 'Nuls', and his team, which became known as La Maquina del '87 (The Machine of '87), went unbeaten for three years.

"I met him in Malvinas, one of Newell's youth football schools," Adrián Coria, a former youth coach at the club remembers. "I started seeing him in the odd game, and he really caught my attention. This little flea, darting around the pitch. He did the same things at 12 years of age as he does today, in a different setting and in different stadiums, but he was exactly the same. Leo completely absorbed everything you threw his way. I've got goosebumps, he was the real deal."

Cristian D'Amico, Newell's Vice President, agreed. "There was a Clásico match and he would've been nine or 10 years old. And for some reason, he ended up locked in the bathroom of his house. Somehow, he managed to escape through the windows, and arrived just as the match was about to kick-off. Well, in that game, he scored five goals and we won 5-0."

Diego Vallejos also looks back with fondness to Messi's time at Newell's. "I remember Leo and Newell's being like a bicycle shop," he said, "because in every tournament they played to win a bike. Every weekend, Leo turned up with a new bike!" Richard Fitzpatrick noted in a 2017 column for *Bleacher Report*. "When the club graduated to the 11-a-side format at age 11, with more space to play with on the bigger pitches, it was more of the same. They swept all before them. They won every tournament they entered, plundering fields across Argentina and competitions as far away as Peru, on the other side of the continent ... Sometimes Newell's own goalkeeper was so bored during the beatings his outfield team-mates were administering, he would sit on his backside in the box. They bullied teams so badly – racking up 10, 12 and 15 goals a game – that some opponents put a 6-0 limit on the scoreline. The game would have to stop once six goals had gone in. It was the only way to stem the bleeding. Messi was insatiable."

Leo's anger if he didn't score was legendary amongst his friends and colleagues. Team-mate Franco Falleroni recalled: "In 2000, Newell's won their championship by at least 20 points. But Messi used to go crazy when he couldn't score a goal. He was a very ambitious guy. Even if the team won 7-0 but he didn't score a goal, he got angry. Or if he didn't get passed the ball, he got angry. You could see it in his face. That's his temperament, his personality. He always wanted the ball."

Newell's Old Boys - Leo's first club. (© DACR 24)

Only one person could calm him – the love of his life Antonella Roccuzzo. He'd met her, the daughter of a supermarket owner, through her cousin Lucas Scaglia, a friend from when he was five. "We [Lucas and Antonella] used to live in the same house," Scaglia told Caracol Radio in 2013. "When we were little Leo was there all the time, to sleep there or to play ... and they [Leo and Antonella] met there."

The three, and others, would play together, often on the shoreline of the Paraná River. After a few years, and despite still being at a tender age, Leo was smitten. He knew it and so did his friends. "Leo has always liked Antonella, since forever," Falleroni continued. "Although she didn't pay him much attention when they were little, we knew he was in love with Antonella. I remember one day, we went to Lucas' house in Funes. We went there for a weekend. Antonella was there too. Every time Messi saw her, he blushed!" Scaglia echoed the same sentiments. "They became boyfriend and girlfriend when they were eight years old and, well, they are still together."

As well as Antonella, he had – unlike many of his colleagues – a close-knit family unit. As Sergio Almirón, Newell's Old Boys Technical Director, told Fitzpatrick, "Leo was given all that was necessary for a boy to grow ... Both parents were there for Messi. They supported him. They wanted what was best for their son. They sacrificed everything for him, and the result is the Messi we have today ... Often it is your family that can keep you on the straight and narrow. When he played as a child, he showed a lot of potential. He might score seven goals in a match sometimes, but no one could ever imagine that he was going to become the best player in the world. He was still so young. There are football players from seven to 14 years old who you think might be a great football player, but at 17, 18, they don't kick-on football-wise. It was impossible to know that Messi at eight or 10 or 12 years old was going to be the Messi he is today. You can't tell at that age."

Always small in stature, the early diagnosis of growth hormone disorder (GHD), a pituitary gland disorder which slows or stops growth from the age of two or three onwards, made sense of the situation and injections to treat it became a daily routine. In 2018 Messi recalled: "At first, my parents gave me the injections from when I was eight years old until I learnt, then I injected my legs once every night starting at 12 years old. It wasn't something that left an impression on me. It was a small needle. It didn't hurt, it was something routine for me that I had to do, and I did it normally."

Daily injection were one thing but without succesful treatment he had no chance of a professional career, yet monthly costs of roughly 33,600 pesos (approximately £700) were well beyond the means of the Messi family. Newell's gave some initial help, but their own finances soon made this impossible. Jorge, who was working all hours and attempting to make ends meet with the help of government handouts, started the search for a club capable of providing the necessary support for his son.

Leo excelled in a trial at River Plate as a 13-year-old, but the deal foundered on Jorge's demands for a job and house in Buenos Aires. Among those contacted by the young player's increasingly desperate father was a lawyer called Juan Mateo, who had made contacts in Spain when in exile during Argentina's military regime. Leo had already come to the attention of Horacio Gaggioli, an Argentine-born agent living Barcelona, thanks to Fabian Soldini and Martin Montero, two contacts from Rosario who ran a football school. It would take two years, however, from Gaggioli's first knowledge of Leo, until he was brought to Barcelona.

Messi's progress – potentially to a European team – required the help of Josep Minguella, an FC Barcelona scout, who had been instrumental in signing Diego Maradona for Barça back in the 1980s. After a meeting between Gaggioli and Mateo in Buenos Aires, it was decided that videos of Messi, including clips of him showing his football skills with an orange and a tennis ball, needed to be sent to Minguella. Around the same time, Messi's family had told Montero and Soldini that they had wanted Leo to be taken to a big club in an area where all the family could stay together. With Gaggioli stationed in Barcelona, it made sense for the *Blaugranes* ('blue and garnet' - the colours of the Barça shirt) to be the first port of call, however, if Gaggiolo's potential offer of work in the Spanish capital had come to fruition Leo would've been offered to either Atlético Madrid or Real Madrid.

Mateo's role in securing Leo for FC Barcelona was outlined to me by Minguella, who said:

"When he returned to Argentina he became involved in football and told me about this player that he liked a lot. With kids it is difficult to tell as usually there isn't so much of a difference but this one had to have the ball, and his obsession to have it was surprising. I arranged the transfer for them to come over, install them here [Barcelona] and sort out training."

Jorge, Leo and Fabián Soldini boarded a plane to Catalonia on Sunday September 17, 2000, and it was Gaggioli who met them at Barcelona's main El Prat airport. He took them to the Hotel Plaza de Barcelona, from where they would prepare for Leo's first training session the following day. It was a session where his feet would do the talking, leaving all concerned open-mouthed.

Gaggioli had been working with Soldini and Martin Montero since their contact the previous year, as he explained to me:

"After two or three months, they told me about a lad in Rosario. They were working closely with Newell's, and the boy was named Lionel Messi. A conversation had taken place and they'd closed a deal with the family to come to Europe for a trial with a big European club. But on one condition – it had to be the city where I lived. We started working on the matter, but we didn't offer him to any club because I had the opportunity of working for a football company in Madrid. So, we waited. In June 2000, more or less, the Madrid thing fell through. I stayed in Barcelona and asked Minguella to arrange an interview or trial with FC Barcelona. Had I been living in Madrid, he would possibly have joined Atlético or Real Madrid, that's the curious thing about his story. When I saw him at the airport, I thought I'd been conned. Messi was so tiny with such skinny legs that I thought 'this kid can't play football'. I realised my mistake the next day when I saw him training.

I was convinced. There were three of us there. Jorge Messi, Fabián Soldini and me. He super convinced me, but there were several Barça coaches there too. The one I most remember was Rodolfo Borrell, who's at Manchester City now. Jordi Roura, a chap named Guillermo and the man who is still the chief scout at Barça, Pep Boada, he was there. Migueli was around as well. Asensi had a look, Quique Costas... Soldini, who had a strong relationship with Leo said to him 'Don't you take any notice of anyone. You're here for a trial, do what you know how to do. Don't give the ball to anyone. You get the ball and off you go.' And he did! Not a care in the world. He was awesome. In a latter session, Fabián told him; 'If you score six goals, I'm going to buy you something you'll like a lot.' Leo scored five, had one disallowed, hit the post three times and the crossbar twice. It was amazing. I don't recall if he was given the gift or not!"

Carles 'Charly' Rexach, the former Barça and Spain winger who was now the club's Sporting Director, would have the final say. Legend has it that he made up his mind after watching Messi for just five minutes, but he wasn't around when Messi first arrived, since he was at the Sydney Olympics. A special game was therfore arranged at the beginning of October for him to watch Messi on his return from Australia, as Minguella explained to me:

"The decision to sign Messi was also controversial at Barcelona at that time, clearly not now. Back then Barcelona produced their own players, but they didn't bring in youth players from abroad and Leo was a first. I had to speak with the directors, with Rexach, an ex-player, coach and confidante of the president. He watched that one training session and was immediately interested, but it's never straightforward where a 12 or 13-year-old is concerned, as they are part of a group of 18 kids and the coach wants to try out different things. But Messi's ability was clear even then, and there were never any real problems or question marks over him."

Gaggioli then takes up the story, recalling Rexach's first impressions:

"Yes it's true. Charly hadn't seen Leo because he was in Sydney, so the club set up a friendly between the U14A and U14B teams at the 'bowling ground', the pitch behind the 10-pin bowling alley. When the game started, Migueli, Rodolfo and the others I named were practically all there and I was with Jorge Messi and Fabián Soldini. Charly was nowhere to be seen. Two minutes, five minutes, 10 minutes... eventually Charly arrived. He walked behind the goalposts and sat next to the wall of the bowling alley where the benches were. Leo hardly touched the ball, it was a day when things just weren't going for him. The game finished and he'd done practically nothing. Jorge, Fabián and I were gutted because we thought Charly wouldn't want Leo. With 10 minutes left of the game, Charly had disappeared. When we caught up with him afterwards, we were all dead silent. 'Didn't you like him?' I asked. 'He's phenomenal,' came the reply. 'We've got to sign him right away'."

It wasn't that simple, though, as Gaggioli explains:

> "After that game – I can't recall if it was the next day or the one after that – Jorge, Fabián and Leo went back to Argentina. Then there was a long series of meetings because I didn't have much experience. I was supported by two lawyers, Pablo Veciana and Angel Juárez, who are now my lawyers in Barcelona, and deal with the likes of Marco Asensio, amongst others. We had dealings with Joaquím Rifé, Joan Lacueva and Charly but we couldn't work things out because there were two or three coaches who had handed in negative reports on Messi – though they later admitted their mistake."

Jorge soon became irritated at what he perceived as stalling tactics, as Gaggioli noted:

> "Yes, the family were very uneasy throughout this process, though I didn't speak directly to them. They were dealing with Montero and Soldini as they were also in Argentina. By December, Montero phoned me and said; "Horacio, this is as far as it goes." He'd learned a Catalan saying during his stay – *Caixa o faixa* (Take it or leave it) – and told me to tell Charly exactly that. Otherwise, I was instructed to look at taking Leo somewhere else. The nerves were driving the family up the wall and clearly that couldn't go on. It was on December 14 when I sat down with Charly at *Reial Societat de Tennis Pompeia* and he said, 'This won't take a minute,' then pulling out a napkin and signing it as the club's commitment to take Messi."

Josep Minguella then takes up the story:

> "We [Minguella, Rexach and Gaggioli] were at the tennis club and there was no paper, just a serviette, so we made an agreement that Leo would sign for FCB, economic factors withstanding. His dad was still very keen for him to come."

Rexach confirmed the story in a separate interview with *The Sun*. "Leo's dad told me he was taking Leo elsewhere as other clubs were fighting for Leo. I told him to relax, that I was the man in charge of signing him and to prove it to him I would sign a piece of paper. Of course, I had no paper at our meeting, so I asked the waiter and he

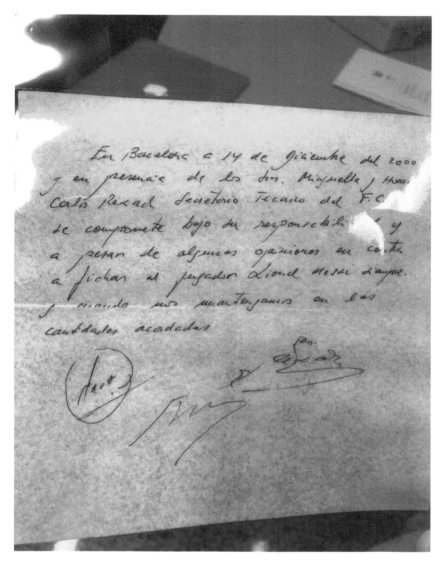

The napkin on which FC Barcelona signed Lionel Messi, on December 14, 2000. It has become one of the most important documents in the Messi story.

brought a napkin. It was because when I told the club to sign this kid, that's all I had available to write on as proof of our commitment."

Gaggioli remains in no doubt as to the importance of the napkin in the Messi story.

"For me it's extraordinarily important. I share the opinion of a journalist from Barcelona, Lluis Canut, who said that that piece of paper changed the contemporary history of FC Barcelona. The club would not have been the same without Messi."

The handwritten statement on that napkin, still locked away in a safety deposit box in an Andorran bank for security and posterity, and only seen by less than half a dozen people including this author, reads: "I, Charly Rexach, on December 14, 2000, and in my capacity as Technical Secretary for FC Barcelona, and despite the existence of some opinions against it, commit to signing Lionel Messi as long as the conditions agreed are met."

All three in attendance then signed the 'document' so, as of that date, FC Barcelona had, technically, signed a youngster who would go on to be the best in the world.

It was a relief to all three, particularly since Gaggioli had again suggested he'd take Messi elsewhere:

"I was very pleased in the end because what it said on the napkin was very significant. It showed that something would be done whatever happened. For five months we did everything we could. So many meetings, but once Charly had put that on the napkin, everyone could relax. There was still work to be done but I called Martin Montero to tell him everything was fine. We told the family and in January, Joan Lacueva got a letter saying the family was coming back to Barcelona in February."

Carles 'Charly' Rexach - who signed Leo for FC Barcelona on a napkin. (© Tuvu 13)

The club's agreement to pay for Leo's hormone treatment was a huge bonus for Jorge. Leo recalled, in *Match of the Day* magazine, that this made his decision to stay in Spain easy, even though it would split his family up: "It wasn't difficult for me to move to Barcelona because I knew I had to. I needed money for my medicine to help me grow, and Barcelona was the only club that offered. So as soon as they did that, I knew I had to go."

And so began the next stage of a remarkable journey.

2

Signed on a Napkin

Desperate Times, Desperate Measures

"That day, he showed he was willing to do anything to win"

The napkin 'contract' was transformed into something more formal and binding by La Masia (FC Barcelona's youth academy) administrator Joan Lacueva and head coach, Joaquim Rifé, on January 8, 2001. It guaranteed Messi 100 million pesetas a year (€601,000) if he made the senior side, a paid-for family apartment, image rights and the hormone treatment. Jorge would be employed by a company owned by the club.

The main issue had been resolved, but some problems and tensions remained. There was a further delay with paperwork, and Messi had a niggling injury. "I would see him at the games not even sat on the bench, but in street clothes because he wasn't allowed to play," Barça TV's Jaume Marcet remembers. "He had come all this way to play and wasn't allowed to." Jorge Messi's frustration and growing irritation was clear but understandable.

Leo's exceptional shyness meant nobody was quite sure what to expect when he finally played his first match for the *Blaugranes*, with the Infantil B (U13) side on March 7. Though he'd regularly gone to La Masia – the farmhouse accomodation behind the *Gol Nord* (north goal) section of the Camp Nou where many of the players boarded – for meals, he kept himself to himself and struggled to integrate.

He was living with Jorge in the club flat at 53 Gran Vía de Carles III in the Les Corts district. Not staying at La Masia limited his integration with other players, but meant the family could be together again. Unfortunately, Maria Sol, Leo's sister, couldn't settle. With a heavy heart, the rest of the family, including Celia, Messi's mother, and his two brothers, returned to Rosario the following summer. It was

La Masia - FC Barcelona's youth academy. Built in 1702, it was bought by the club in 1953. (© XiscoNL)

another bitter blow, but Leo's desire to reach the very top became evident at this point. Despite obvious homesickness, he stayed on in Barcelona.

When Leo was formerly introduced to his new team-mates for the first time, there was a mixture of reticence and curiosity. How could this tiny 'little boy' be anything other than cannon fodder for opponents? What on earth was he going to bring to Xavi Llorens' Infantil B (U13) side that was worth flying him halfway around the world for? They, and opponents C.F. Amposta, didn't have to wait long for their answer. It was as if he was back home on the streets of Rosario without a care in the world. Just Leo and a ball. A wonderful debut was capped with a goal.

News of his incredible talent spread through the various age groups like wildfire. "I was amazed by him," Roger Gribet, a youngster who signed for the club on the same day as Messi, told *Goal.com* in 2017. "I was conscious that my physical development had opened doors at the club. I was 1.70m at the age of 12, but he wasn't even 1.50m."

Albert Benaiges, head of football development at La Masia, set about organising an administratively vital second match for him."We had to be quick. If he didn't get to play those two games, he wouldn't have been able to play later in the national category [rather than regional] until he was 18," he noted in 2011, but bureaucratic fulfilment was accompanied by disaster. Leo played in the next match, away at Ebre Escola Esportiva in Tortosa, and no sooner had the game kicked off than the ball found its way out to him on the left, wearing the No.11 shirt. A loss of control meant a throw in for the hosts, which Escorado quickly took down the line. As Leo chased back towards his own goal, he was caught from behind by Marc Baiges.

The challenge looked innocuous enough and, with no foul given, the game continued as normal. Messi was attended to for a short period, but when the time came for him to stand up, he couldn't. His fibula was broken. Baiges apologised as Leo was carried off and was only aware of the damage he'd caused when told years later in an interview with *Libero* magazine. "What are you saying, I broke his leg? Mother of God!" Baiges exclaimed. "It's not that I didn't know that I'd broken Messi's fibula, it was that I didn't know that I'd broken anyone's leg." That the match ended 5-1 to the *Blaugranes* was little consolation.

Another few weeks of not being able to play took its toll, with Leo often forlorn and misty-eyed as he watched training. The joy that having a ball at his feet brought him was obvious, and taking that outlet away was cruel luck. "He was screwed. Imagine – three months out in his situation," Xavi Llorens recalled. "He lost the rest of the season, but [at least] we didn't have to [constantly] cheer him up like [Diego] Capel, who cried all day [when he got injured]."

Three months later, with the 2000-01 football season now over, Messi was well enough to return. He was immediately promoted to the Infantil A (U14) team, which included the likes of Cesc Fabregas, Victor Vázquez and Gerard Piqué. After a full pre-season together, they played against U15 teams for the 2001-02 campaign. Central midfielder Julio de Dios, recalled to Andrew Murray of *FourFourTwo* just how good they were: "There was such talent in that team: [Marc] Valiente was so calm in defence; Toni Calvo was a right winger with real pace; Sito Riera is now playing in the Polish top flight; Franck Songo'o had raw talent and Victor Vázquez was probably the best technician. But you could see Messi, Cesc and Piqué had something that the rest of us didn't – an extra 'plus', without doubt. We'd even smash teams older than us by seven or eight."

Exact details are unfortunately not available, since FC Barcelona did not keep full records of lower level teams, but such was the dominance of the team, questions of sportsmanship were regularly raised by opposition coaches and parents. They were, in a sense, asking the *Blaugranes* to 'go easy on them'. Such requests were understandable, as no one wants to see their youngsters humiliated. Years later, an unnamed FC Barcelona source said to *El País*, in response to CD Serranos' 25-0 victory over Benicalap C, that "competing is part of training. We shouldn't send out the wrong message. You can't tell players not to score. But we tend to move players to new positions so that the result isn't too mismatched."

It was rapidly clear that Messi needed to be promoted again, in order to play against opponents who would test him to the maximum. Before the season was out, he, Fabregas and Piqué had joined the Cadete B (U15) set-up. What was noticeable, and not really that surprising, was the ease with which they all made the step up, particularly Leo.

Players promoted above their age group face the challenge of proving to team-mates, coaches and parents that they deserve it. There can be jealousy in the air. Only the strongest survive, but without a care in the world Leo once again made an impression on his new team-mates.

"We were a very lively group, but initially he had gone largely unnoticed in the dressing room because we had been together for so long. He sat in a corner, alone and quiet," goalkeeper Roger Franch recalled in an interview with *Goal.com*." But he often made us angry [in training] because it was frustrating to play against him. You ended up asking yourself if you were good enough to do this."

Roger's brother, Robert experienced similar feelings. "After seeing that the guy was three gears ahead of us all, we decided, with the other defenders, that we would give him a couple of hits to see what happened," he commented. "But it didn't matter ... he was so quick that we weren't even able to kick him. You would go for him and when you wanted to bring him down, he had already left you behind and was taking on the next defender. He is a machine and he always was – in training and in matches. We wouldn't even get a sniff of the ball, whatever we did. Sometimes you thought that the only way to stop him was by getting out a gun and firing a shot, but even then you had the feeling that he would swerve the bullet with the ball under his control."

Any bitterness evaporated once Messi was unleashed on Barça's opponents. Team-mates knew that if they passed the ball to Leo, magic would occur with jaw-dropping displays of speed of thought and athleticism which gave them the privilege of watching a once-in-a-lifetime talent develop. Word quickly spread throughout the league and it was clear that some opponents had earmarked Messi before a match had started. Invariably, defenders would 'double up' on Leo, but it often made little difference. A slight body swerve would leave them for dead and allow him to move, with ease, into the space he had created.

Yet he remained shy and quiet off the field, rarely opening up to those around him. Socialising wasn't really Leo's thing and, in any event, his true friends were thousands of miles from Catalonia, back in Rosario. It didn't hinder him in terms of his on-pitch relationships with his colleagues, but it started to make things a little more awkward during the week when the players could take advantage of their free time. Similarly, Jorge had tunnel vision where his son's career was concerned. Eventually, thanks to a tournament played in Italy, Messi came out of his shell.

It was in Venice that the first sign of an impish sense of humour came to the fore. Socialising together as a team for a few days, Messi's shyness disappeared, and his team-mates saw a totally different part of his personality. As a result, their view of him as a person completely changed. This was a side of him that they'd all wanted to discover but never had the chance. Perhaps he had never felt comfortable enough to be himself, but in such close-knit surroundings, he could, or rather had to, let his guard down. "Even though we called him 'enano' [dwarf] for a long time [in private], we didn't start to do so until we had the mutual confidence which came on that trip to Venice," striker Roger Gribet told *Goal*."When he had made his debut for the first team, he came to see us at La Masia and we said to him: 'Enano, how did you get on with the older guys?' and we all cracked up laughing."

As Andrew Murray's article recalls, the four team captains would always play a prank on new members of the squad at tournaments. "Piqué decided to go and take everything out of his room, as if it had been robbed," Victor Vázquez recalled: "They took out the bed, his PlayStation, kitbag – literally everything. After we had eaten, everyone went back up to their rooms and Cesc and a couple of other players recorded Messi going into his room. He stood stock-still. His face was a picture! He didn't know what to say, because he was quite a shy lad, and so he just put his hands on his head. Then we told him it was something that we did to every new player. He really opened up after that."

Barça won the Maestrelli Tournament with Messi, wearing No.14, named man-of-the-match in the final against a Parma side that included Giuseppe Rossi. Those few days away forged a lasting bond with the rest of the team, as Julio de Dios recalled: "He was making jokes, and I think he got Piqué back with some prank. 'Now Messi's arrived!' we'd say, patting him on the back. From that moment he became one of us. We were a cohort of brothers."

His mood may have been helped by completing human growth hormone treatment. It was still 18 months before WADA (World Anti-Doping Agency) began testing for HGH as a banned substance, although it is believed to have been on a prohibited list earlier than the first recorded testing date of 2004. His case appears never to have been investigated, and there has been no official comment from WADA. Will Carroll's 2013 column in *Bleacher Report* recorded that a Therapeutic Use Exemption (TUE) should have been sought, covering him under Section 46 of FIFA's anti-doping code.

Freed of his shyness, Messi enjoyed himself more. He and his team-mates had to undertake learning tasks during the week in order to play at the weekend, a carrot-and-stick method of ensuring they kept up their education, but the match was where he truly expressed himself. "All of us that knew him and played with him were not surprised by the wonderful technical ability he had, but by his ability to adapt so quickly to any given situation," Gribet recounted. "Messi was able to accelerate and get up to speed in a very small space without losing the ball and as the years have gone by, he has readapted his game to carry on being decisive but with other qualities, such as his finishing or that ability to give the final pass, which he has shown more recently. In every stage of his career, he has been able to determine what his best virtue is and adapted that for the collective, to keep on being the best for more than a decade. Because, from the youth teams until now, he has always been the best."

At the Willem II tournament, which always featured the best young pro club academy football teams, they met a physical Rangers side in the final, winning 2-0. In 2015, speaking about the game, Rangers midfielder Paul Paton said: "We performed well in the tournament, playing against Brugge, Willem II and Arsenal. We defeated Feyenoord, who had De Guzman, in the semi-finals, but the Barcelona team were a step up in class, physically bigger, stronger, fitter and faster. At the time, I didn't realise their players would go on to be some of the best players in the world, but it was obvious they

The proximity of the original La Masia to Camp Nou, the home of FC Barcelona, illustrated the importance of the youth academy to the club. (©Barçelonista)

were a special side. Almost every player in the team has gone on to carve out a career in Spanish football."

The 2001-02 team became the first under-aged squad to win the Preferente Catalana (regional league) title, ahead of local rivals Espanyol Cadete A (U16). The challenge this set Barcelona was how best to handle Messi, Piqué and Fabregas. All three were well ahead of their colleagues, themselves no slouches, and Benaiges realised that in order to fulfil their exceptional potential he would have to move them up again to a level where they'd need to start thinking about the way they played, rather than easing through games on autopilot. They'd be up against more physically demanding and athletically superior opponents once more. The question was, did they have what it takes?

They began the 2002-03 season with the Cadete A team amid a strong sense of expectation. Jorge Messi was, by now, delighted with his son's progression, and the season would really showcase his talents to their fullest, leaving no doubt as to how good he could become. Tito Vilanova, later to become Leo's coach in the first team, was incharge of the team, alongside Alex García. They soon realised the group would be something special as opposing sides were routinely dismantled and Vilanova, speaking with Martí Perarnau for his book *The Champions' Way: From La Masia to Camp Nou*, said; "I remember a game in which we were winning 3-0 after only three minutes. It's almost impossible mathematically. I turned to my assistant and said 'And now what do we tell them?' What can you say at the break when they're winning 8-0?"

Before long they were nicknamed 'The Baby Dream Team'. "It was a question of how many goals we'd score, not whether we'd win," Victor Vázquez told *FourFourTwo*. "We'd win games 10 or 15-0, and Messi and I would have competitions between the two of us to see who could score the most goals in each game. Piqué and Cesc would keep themselves occupied by trying to outscore each other. It was the most interesting way to keep ourselves motivated." Some results have been lost, but Fabregas says one match was won 32-0, a remarkable performance for any team, let alone one including under-age players.

With Messi banging in the goals (36 in 30 games), Piqué helping stop them at the other end and Fabregas orchestrating the midfield, an unprecedented treble of the league and both the Catalan and Spanish cups became a foregone conclusion. "It was such an extraordinary group, with born winners," García said in 2015. "That generation will never be repeated. You had the best mixture possible: incredibly talented players with very good players, who had all played together from the U11 side upwards. It was an armada of talent."

One match has gone down in club folklore. 'El Partido de la mascara' or 'The Game of the Mask' was the Copa Catalunya final played on May 4, 2003 against Espanyol. Just one week earlier, when Barça had won the league against the same side, Messi had his cheekbone broken, some said deliberately. It put his participation in jeopardy, but there was no way he was going to miss it. Eventually, after lengthy consultation with club staff and the medical services team, it was decided he would play on the condition he wore a mask. The pre-match line-up picture shows him on the left of the front row looking like a *Blaugrana* super hero.

The match was fierce even by derby standards, with tackles flying in and Messi bearing the brunt of the opposition's aggression. Within five minutes he'd had enough of the mask and threw it off, allegedly telling García that he would come off at half-time. By then Barça were 3-0 up, courtesy of a Messi double and one from Piqué. It finished 4-1, with García seeing a significance well beyond completing the treble. "At *el partido de la mascara*, I found out that Messi understood football not only as a game but as a collective effort. That day, he showed he was willing to do anything to win."

It was the last time, until Fabregas re-joined Barcelona from Arsenal in 2011, that the trio would play together. Messi did not play in the Spanish championship final victory over Athletic Club, and Fabregas was soon on his way to Arsenal. Breaking up the spine of their best ever youth team sent shockwaves through the club. They genuinely believed they'd done enough to keep their best young players, but footballers who feel their path to the senior team is blocked are always likely to look for an escape route. Money was incidental. Arsene Wenger immediately had Cesc training with the first team and soon gave him his debut, a much more intoxicating prospect than having to fight for minutes here and there at FC Barcelona. That summer was a period of contemplation at the club, to ensure nothing similar happened again, though unknown to them Piqué was already talking to Manchester United. Messi had no intention of leaving the club that had given him his chance, and that at least was a source of pride and optimism. As previously, however, his excellence had set Barça a real conundrum.

3

Five Teams in One Season

A Debut for the First Team

"He just loved playing football. He didn't mind what level he played at."

Cesc had moved to north London, whilst Leo and his colleagues had a relatively quiet summer, free from too much distraction. Arsenal wanted Leo as well, but baulked after being told they'd need to buy the Messi family a house, so he was able to enjoy some downtime, and his 16th birthday, before getting back to business for what proved to be a momentous 2003-04 campaign.

This was the year of one of his earliest and most spectacular records, one yet to be repeated. Rising through the ranks, he played for five different FC Barcelona sides during the season. "Messi was a kid to whom you could say, 'Look, there's a ball, let's play a match'," Albert Benaiges said in a 2011 interview. "He just loved playing football. He didn't mind what level he played at because he just wanted the ball at his feet. Some kids play in the A team, but when you ask them to play for the B team, they pull a face. With Messi, he always gave everything and he was always the best."

He was in spectacular pre-season form for Barça's U18 (Juvenil B) side, winning the player of the tournament in every competition in which he appeared. Once the season started it took only one match for him to be promoted to the U19s (Juvenil A).

Some thought this might be the level which put the brakes on that continuous accelerated progression. How wrong could anyone be?! Juan Carlos Pérez Rojo had taken over the side at the beginning of July 2003, from Jordi Roura, later to temporarily manage Leo in the first team. In Messi's first 11 games, he scored 15 goals, including one in the 3-0 win on his debut against Hércules, four away to Gimnàstic de Tarragona (7-0) and a hat-trick against Granollers (8-1) on

Manager Frank Rijkaard gave Leo his first start for Barça on October 16, 2004, against Espanyol. (© NASA)

November 15. The following day he made his first-team debut.

He had made an impression earlier in the season when called up to the senior squad by coach Frank Rijkaard. An international break had depleted the first-team's ranks and he took his chance with both feet. *"Messi was only 16, but he destroyed us all in a training session,"* former Barça player Ludovic Giuly vividly remembered in an interview with the Catalan daily, *Sport*: "They were kicking him all over the place to avoid being ridiculed by this kid, but he didn't say anything. He just got up and kept on playing. Every play he made was dangerous, it was incredible. He would dribble past four players and score a goal. Even the team's starting centre-backs were nervous. They would go in hard on him, but he took it in. He was an alien. He killed us all."

Deco echoed Giuly, speaking to *Soccer Laduma*'s David Minchella. "In that very first moment on the training pitch, he was exactly the same as today. He did a move when the ball came to him and 'wah' – it was brilliant! Everyone was amazed and said, 'Wow, who is this guy?' We – and I'm talking about guys like Xavi and Andrés Iniesta too – knew how special he was from the very first moment we saw him. He looked like a normal player, but he did something unbelievable. He just kept amazing us."

Rijkaard and his staff knew his reputation, but now saw the reality of experienced professionals being bamboozled by a 16-year-old. That performance in training doubtless earned his promotion to the squad for the friendly to mark the opening of Porto's new stadium, the Estádio de Dragão, on November 16, 2003. He was 16 years, four months and 23 days old.

Leo was joined on the subs bench by Tiago, Jordi Gómez, Expósito and Oriol Riera, while the starting XI were; Jorquera, Óscar López, Oleguer, Rafa Márquez, Fernando Navarro, Xavi, Santamaría, Luis

Enriqué, Luis Garćia, Ros and Gabri. Porto's manager, José Mourinho, the former assistant to Bobby Robson at Barça, was fresh from guiding his side to a treble of UEFA Cup and Portuguese league and cup triumphs, and *en route* to a famous Champions League triumph. His side that night consisted of Vitor Baía, Jorge Costa, Ricardo Carvalho, Secretário, Derlei, Maniche, Mendes, Fernandes, Moraes, Evaldo and Tiago, with an extensive subs bench of Emanuel, Jankauskas, Nuno, Almeida, Mário Silva, Barbosa, Ribeiro, Vieirinha and Machado.

There was little memorable about the 74 minutes before Messi, in the taupe coloured away kit resplendent with horizontal blaugrana pinstripes, replaced Navarro, wearing the no. 14 shirt. Within a minute he was upended on the edge of the penalty box by two converging defenders. This was followed by two more runs into enemy territory that ended disappointingly with weak, ineffective shots.

In the 86th minute he was thwarted only by a covering defender forcing him to cross rather than shoot after he had rounded Baía. Porto won 2-0, but Barça coaches including Henk Ten Cate knew they had seem a remarkable cameo from their debutant. "It seemed as if he had been playing with us all his life," Ten Cate recounted to Guillem Balagué for the Spaniard's own book on Leo. "His movement was so natural. The first time the ball came to him, he created a scoring chance. The second time he nearly scored. If you are 15 or 16 in a game like that against Porto, at the opening of a new stadium full of people, and you do all that, it is because you are something special. Frank and I looked at each other and I said: 'What the fuck? Did you see that?'"

Messi watched a re-run of his debut the following day with his parents Jorge and Celia, and described his thoughts for Barça TV. "My father told me the night before that it could happen [make his debut], and then it was confirmed," he said. "I was sent to warm up and I was a little nervous, but I wanted to play. It went well and there are many players who would want to play alongside Luis Enriqué, Xavi and Marquéz. You always want to play in the first team, and I've fulfilled my dream."

As a result of his impressive performance in Porto, Leo was moved up to train with the club's reserve side, Barcelona B, while also being brought into the first team set up once a week. It was the only way to keep him competitive because, even in training, he was far too good for anyone in his own age group. Rafael Carbonell, in his *El País* column 'El Último Salto de la 'Pulga" [The Last Jump of the Flea], noted that around this time Ronaldinho, the star signing from the previous summer, took Leo under his wing, referring to him as 'little brother'. This genuine friendship would in time become problematic, but at this point it was to Messi's great advantage.

As well as playing for the U19s, Leo started appearing for the third team, Barcelona C, later scrapped in 2007, making his debut against Europa on 29 November. He scored a hat-trick in the 3-2 win over Gramanet B on January 4, 2004 and exactly a month later, February 4, signed his first professional contract with Barça, tying him to the club for eight years with a buyout clause of €30m.

There was a further appearance in a first-team friendly, playing the second half against Shakhtar Donetsk on February 18, followed by an extraordinary 13-day spell in which he appeared for the U19s and both the C and B teams. His B team debut against Mataró on March 6 completed his record of five levels in the space of seven months and automatically raised his buyout fee to €80m.

The B team was now his home and former team-mate Dani Fragoso, at the time playing for Real Jaén, aged 37, told me what an extraordinary force Leo had been at the lower age group levels:

"Leo was so explosive when he arrived with us that it was amazing to have him as a team-mate. We saw him grow and it was clear from the very beginning that he would be as great a player as he became. From the first day we saw him, and in every subsequent training session and game – every single one – it was a privilege to be alongside him. After one away game, on the bus home, he was sleeping on the floor of the bus and we all said 'Look, the best player in the world actually sleeps!!'"

Fragoso played in central midfield and he was integral to the way in which Barça B were playing at the time, getting Messi in on goal as early as possible.

"The coaches told us all, in general terms, that all the balls went through Messi. We knew the importance he had in the team and that he would win us the game if he was inspired. That's exactly what happened the majority of the time – we gave him the ball and he won the matches. I particularly remember games against Osasuna and Espanyol B where we just let him do his thing. The opponents

Camp Nou, the cauldron of Catalan passion. (© Ayman Anrar7)

couldn't get anywhere near him! As a midfielder, whenever I had the ball, the first option was to pass the ball to Leo and from there the team played. I was alongside him for a year and a half until he moved up to the first team permanently, and it was an education for us all, to see his evolution in the time he was with us. At the beginning he was very quiet off of the pitch, but as time went by, he let go a little more and we became great friends. For me, there's no argument that he's the best player in history because he's shown it week after week, month after month, year after year. He's reached an incredible level, and to be at that level week-in and week-out for the best part of 15 years is nothing short of astonishing."

Yet it was an under-19 game which assumed legendary status, Barça at home to Sevilla in the first leg of the Copa del Rey, Round of 16, on May 15. Messi told Barça's TV channel after the game: "In the first half they were very well organised. I think in the first 20 minutes of the second half we wore them down a lot. We had great rhythm with the ball. That was when they got tired and we scored the first goal … and then the rest came." 'The rest' referred to his four-goal haul inside 18 minutes, a taste of things to come for his marker Sergio Ramos, who had not long made his debut for Sevilla.

Turning 17 that June, Leo had little time to celebrate. Performances like his commanded attention a long way from Barcelona. Aware of consistent Spanish overtures, Messi always made it clear that he

Leo in action against Málaga during the 2005-06 season. (©Josep Tomàs)

wanted to play for his native country, with Argentina calling him up for an under-20 friendly against Paraguay. Paraguay were already 4-0 down when Messi, wearing 17, entered the fray in the second half. He first floated a free-kick for Pablo Vitti to head home, then set up Federico Almares with a trademark run and slide-rule pass into space. Then, with 10 minutes left, came the archetypal Messi moment. Receiving the ball just inside the Paraguay half, Leo ran straight down the middle of the pitch, leaving four players in his wake. Both centre-backs were left for dead and, as the 'keeper advanced, he was sold an expert dummy as Messi stroked the ball into an empty net. An international debut, with a goal that hinted of his still developing genius and two assists, wasn't a bad 17th birthday present!

There were two more goals in just 11 minutes after coming on again as a second-half substitute in the next match for Argentina U20, a friendly against Uruguay, helping transform an even contest into a 4-1 romp. Then at last came the chance of some summer rest after a season which had started with his name being whispered in football circles, but ended with it being shouted from the rooftops.

The question was no longer whether he would make it as a professional, but when. From the start of the 2004-05 season, he was permanently upgraded to Barcelona B, with some involvement in the first team's pre-season friendlies. The first team had started well, winning eight and drawing one of their first nine games, while the B team's start to the new campaign was mediocre – three wins, three losses and a draw in the same time frame. At this time, senior colleagues who'd been exposed to Messi's brilliance in training, and Ronaldinho in particular, were urging his promotion to the first team. The upgrade, and his league debut, came in the derby match against

Espanyol, at that time in exile at the Estadi Olímpic Lluís Companys on Montjuïc.

A lot of the pre-match narrative had surrounded Messi after Rijkaard had decided to name him on the bench, but he was not expected to play any part in the match. With nine minutes to go, and Barça leading 1-0 from Deco's early goal, Rijkaard decided he would. He motioned to the bench for Messi to get ready, and after the briefest of warm ups, the 17-year and 114-day-old Argentinian made his way to the touchline.

Deco's number was held up, the Portuguese by now looking a little leggy after his recent international exertions. What's interesting was his reaction to coming off. We're so used to seeing players eyeballing their managers, shoulders slumped, muttering under their breath as they walk off. Not Deco. He walked off with a rueful smile, high-fived the kid wearing the number 30 and kissed him on the right cheek. He understood the significance of the moment – Leo was now the youngest player in Barça's history to represent them at senior level in an official game. Deco was only 27 at the time, and in his footballing prime. Most players of a similar age would baulk at being hooked for someone 10 years their junior. That he accepted it with good grace spoke volumes. Rijkaard was clear in his post-match press conference why Messi had been given the chance too. "Putting him on was not a prize [for good work in training]," he said. "We put him on for his quality and because I saw Deco was a little tired. Messi is a lefty, he is a very good dribbler coming inside, and he can shoot with his left foot."

Young Leo was soon in the thick of the action, but as a cameo it was fairly nondescript. However, it marked the beginning of yet another chapter in Messi's meteoric rise. An unused sub in the Champions League group game away at AC Milan the following week, the Camp Nou would finally get their first glimpse of this wunderkind just eight days after his debut as Rijkaard handing Leo another 20 minutes against Osasuna. Samuel Eto'o and Ronaldinho had given the hosts a 2-0 half-time lead, and it was the Brazilian who had made way for Messi when the game was put to bed. The column inches that greeted that particular passing of the baton were extensive too. The fact that Ronaldinho's goal was his first of the season in what was Barcelona's 10th game in all competitions seemed to almost pass by unnoticed. Messi didn't make a major impact on the day, but his presence was still notable. Why? Less than two months after the Osasuna match,

Ronaldinho won the FIFA World Player of the Year award and, well, a teenager just doesn't replace the best player on the planet...!

Three days later, Messi attained another significant marker, his first start. He made, for once, only a limited impact on the Copa del Rey, Round of 64, clash with Gramenet, which Barça dominated but somehow contrived to lose in extra time to Segunda B (third division) opponents and was replaced by Samuel Eto'o after 73 minutes. Even so, 102 cumulative minutes over three first-team games in 11 days was, perhaps, more than he expected.

If a return to Barça B duty disappointed at one level, the need to play doubtless outweighed this, with his first-team role largely that of unused or cameo substitute. Six matches with the first team – all as an unused sub and which included an El Clásico against Real Madrid and a couple of European fixtures – were interspersed with a handful of Barça B games, of which he played a full part. On 1 December, he played and scored in a 4-3 friendly victory over a UEFA All-Stars XI featuring Mauricio Pochettino, Michael Owen and Hidetoshi Nakata.

Another (brief) taste of the big time, 10 minutes against Málaga, was followed by another landmark, his European debut and first full 90 minutes. It came in a 'dead rubber' Champions League group stage tie away to Shakhtar Donetsk. Barça had already qualified, so their 2-0 defeat was academic. Rijkaard fielded an experimental front line with Messi, playing for the first time as a central striker, flanked by Gio Van Bronckhorst and Javito. It didn't really work. Leo was constantly having to drop deeper to receive the ball and was either fouled when in possession or crowded out by two, three or four covering defenders. There were, however, flashes of brilliance and enough in his all-round play against experienced opposition for Rijkaard and his team to know there was plenty more to come from him.

Two minutes against Albacete on December 11, and just over half an hour against Levante in the final fixture before Christmas were his last first team action until he played six minutes against Getafe in April 2005. His absence from the first team in early 2005 wasn't due to a loss of form. It was because he was on international duty in Colombia at a keenly contested South American U20 championship where 10 nations were chasing four qualification places for that year's Under20 World Cup.

Argentina dominated their opening group matches and remained undefeated, but a series of draws in the final group of six condemned them to third place behind Brazil and winners Colombia, whose Hugo Rodallega was leading scorer with 11 goals. Leo's five included the winner in their final match against Brazil, and there was the substantial consolation of qualification for the U20 World Cup.

Returning to Spain, where Barça's senior side had consolidated their lead at the top of La Liga, he was reintroduced briefly against Getafe. Finding himself back in the B team for their match at home to Figueres, Leo played the full 90 minutes, and then came the next big step in his trajectory...

4

Making History Against Albacete

The Goal That Started It All

"We knew we were seeing the birth of a superstar in 2005"

May 1, 2005 has gone down in FC Barcelona's history, but with just three minutes to go and Barça leading Albacete 1-0 thanks to Eto'o's 66th-minute goal, there was little hint at what was to follow. After some final instructions from Rijkaard, a tense-looking Messi replaced the Cameroonian for the briefest of cameo appearances. Fouled by Santi within a minute, he would exact his revenge on the full-back just 30 seconds later as the clock ticked into the 90th minute. Some typical Ronaldinho trickery saw him work enough space to be able to loft the ball into Messi's path and with one touch to set himself, Leo expertly chipped the 'keeper with the coolest of finishes to deftly deliver the ball into the empty net, only for the linesman's flag to rule it out. TV replays would show Messi was, in fact, onside, but in those pre-VAR days the decision stood.

Not to be denied, 30 seconds later he fired in a cross which Andres Iniesta just failed to connect with and then, 10 seconds of injury time having elapsed, the Ronaldinho-Messi partnership worked its magic again. Receiving a long ball from Deco, Messi headed it over the right-back and was strong enough in the tackle to keep Albacete's covering centre-backs at bay, playing a short ball to the Brazilian in the centre of the pitch. In the same movement, Ronaldinho controlled and flicked the ball over both central defenders and left Messi with only 'keeper Raúl Valbuena to beat. Allowing the ball to bounce once, and with Mingo closing in and ready to clear any shot, Messi leaned back and calmly slotted another lob into the net with Valbuena stranded outside his six-yard box. This time there was no offside flag and the noise from Camp Nou was almost primal. A huge roar erupted –

MESSI *GOLEADOR*
En tres minutos
metió dos, uno de
ellos anulado.

May 2, 2005: 'Messi Goalscorer - Scores two in three minutes, one disallowed' is the comment in the player rating section after the Albacete match.
(© Mundo Deportivo)

more in the knowledge that it meant Barça were one step closer to the league title, as for the significance of the strike.

Messi ran towards the corner flag, pumping his arms as he did so. As he turned back around, his beaming smile captured by the worldwide TV cameras, Ronaldinho was there to greet him. Arms outstretched, Leo hitched a ride on the Brazilian's back and the entire stadium rose as one to acclaim a new hero. This was the person they'd been reading all about and, clearly, the column inches were justified. The 17-year-old had done more in four minutes than some players do in an entire match. Van Bronckhorst and Puyol soon arrived to join the party, quickly followed by Iniesta, Oleguer and Márquez. The joy on their faces as they bounced up and down in celebration was a sight to behold. For a moment, the *Blaugranes* players were in their own little world, experienced professionals temporarily taking leave of their senses. Deco and Belletti also came to offer their congratulations, with the locals still on their feet and ensuring Messi was given a sustained ovation.

As the group of players returned to their own half, Ronaldinho, Messi's 'big brother', high-fived the player who would, eventually, take his crown at the club, and embraced him with the kind of extended hug that you just know really means something. In that one iconic moment, everyone else knew too. A special player from the La Masia production line was coming of age, and the following day's news coverage emphasised the point. "Oé, oé, OÉ!" screamed *Mundo Deportivo*'s headline. "A crowded Camp Nou unleashes the euphoria to the cry of 'Champions, Champions.' Eto'o breaks the wall of La Mancha, Messi scores and Barça choke Madrid." Inside the paper, reporter Begoña Villarrubia noted: "It's difficult to imagine a better crowning jewel for a season in which he has always been training with the first team, although he has played almost all the youth team games. Messi now feels the La Liga title, which with all probability Barça will win, as his own. Naturally, Messi did not hide his satisfaction after the game ... 'I've been almost all year working with the team and yes, I think if we win the title, I'm going to feel like it's mine' ... Because of his talent, he is a player very valued in the dressing room. 'They all treat me very well, but Ronnie has a special affection for me.' Messi is one of the academy players with a great future and, for the moment, he's satisfied with being on the bench although he admits that 'you suffer more than in the field'."

It was, though, his last action of the season for the first-team. He was an unused sub for two of the last four league matches which saw Barça win La Liga, and played twice for the B team before heading off for the U20 World Cup finals (FIFA World Youth Championship) in the Netherlands. The tournament took place from June 10 to July 2, meaning that Messi would celebrate his 18th birthday during the competition. He also had something else to celebrate that day, and it wasn't just that Argentina had been drawn in Group D alongside the United States, Germany and Egypt.

With it now beyond any reasonable doubt that Leo was a huge star in the making, Barça tied him down to a new contract on his 18th birthday, June 24, 2005. On that day he signed his first contract as a first-team player and though the length of the deal was two years shorter than the previous one, his buyout clause had been raised to €150 million, unheard of for a player of that age. Various media outlets speculated that the club had lost its collective mind, but president Joan Laporta was in no doubt that if the board didn't act quickly, another club would come in and acquire his services.

At the U20 World Cup Argentina got off to a poor start, losing their opening game 1-0 to the United States at the Arke Stadion in Enschede. Messi, to the surprise of many, started on the bench. Coach

Francisco Ferraro later explained his reasoning for the decision: "Everyone asks me why I left Messi on the bench in that game. The truth is, in the last training session before the match, Daniel Martinez told me, 'Pancho, Leo has discomfort in the back,' and that's why I decided to put him on the bench and play him if I needed to at some point. Many things were said about that game until I put him on."

Replacing Emiliano Armenteros after the first 45 minutes, Leo overshadowed everyone on the pitch in the second half, but his bursts into the US half were not enough to breach a backs-against-the-wall defence. Nor was there any great shame in defeat. The US would go on to win the group without conceding a goal, and DC United's Freddy Adu attracting the attention as major household name at the tournament. Post-match comments from supporters included 'Freddy looked like a young Ronaldinho out there', 'Messi was great, but Freddy was a heck of a lot more entertaining' and, 'I saw nothing Messi did that would make me think he is any better than Adu at this level', while a banner at the ground read 'Adu – The new Pelé'.

Argentina qualified from their group along with the Americans, but without creating much excitement. Messi scored in the next match against Egypt, but it took a lung-bursting run and wonderfully chipped finish from Zabaleta in injury time to finally secure the win. Then a goal just before half-time from Boca Juniors' Neri Cardozo settled the win-or-bust clash with previously unbeaten Germany.

The same pattern followed in the Round of 16 against Colombia, just two days before Messi's 18th birthday. Much to Ferraro's chagrin, his side were unable to puncture their opponents' defence in the first-half. TV pictures showed the pent-up anger he directed at a capable squad who seemed incapable of dominating in the first 45 minutes. He needn't have worried. Harrison Otálvaro's 52nd-minute opener for Colombia was soon cancelled out by Messi, who smashed home at Arenas' near post after a swift one-two with Cardozo. The relief was palpable on Leo's face, as he celebrated wildly. Just as they had done against Egypt in the group stage, Argentina would win in injury time. Surrounded by six defenders in the D on the edge of the penalty area, Julio Barroso contrived the sweetest of strikes into the top corner.

It meant that Messi would be pitted against Cesc Fabregas and a talented Spain squad in the quarter-finals, the day after his 18th birthday. With the likes of Raúl Albiol, Juanfran, Fernando Llorente,

José Enrique and David Silva also in their ranks, *La Roja* were not to be taken lightly.

It was in this match that Messi began to stamp his authority on the tournament. His early goal from a free-kick was ruled out when Barroso, who argued furiously that he was not interfering was play, was given offside but Argentina had just taken a 2-1 lead with goals from Zabaleta and Oberman when, with 17 minutes left, he produced a moment that referee Benito Archundia would describe as 'sheer poetry, incredible'.

Picking up Francisco Molinero's poor clearance on the edge of the Spanish area, Leo somehow flicked the ball over his shoulder with one touch from his right foot, and before it had even hit the ground, manoeuvred it beyond Miquel Robusté's covering challenge with his left. Having opened up the space beyond the back four, he slid the ball expertly under Biel Ribas as the goalkeeper came out to narrow the angle. It was Leo's third goal in five matches and allowed Argentina to see out the remainder of the game with ease.

Messi had no time to celebrate his birthday or his new contract because a semi-final against arch-rivals Brazil was scheduled three days later, but thanks to youth coach Miguel Ángel Tojo's idea of making the youngest members of the squad room-mates, he was forming a friendship with team-mate Sergio Agüero.

Daniel Fresco, the author of *Born to Rise*, Sergio Agüero's autobiography, recalled in an interview with *Goal.com* that Miguel Ángel had told Kun [Sergio Agüero's nickname] that he'd share a room with Leo because he believed Sergio was destined for Europe, and Messi's experience in Barcelona would be of value to him: "They had already met, almost by chance, earlier that year at the national team's training camp on the outskirts of Buenos Aires. Leo had been summoned for the U20 team and Sergio was playing for the U17s. Kun hadn't met him before, but both of them had heard of each other. Sergio knew there was an Argentine teenager playing for Barcelona, who, according to the local press, had an extraordinary career ahead of him. He wasn't able to put two and two together until that meeting. The thing that had given Messi the most lasting impression [of Agüero] was watching a game on TV where he heard the broadcaster proclaim it a historic day, that "the youngest player in Argentine Primera Division history will set foot on the pitch at only 15 years [and 35 days] of age [on July 3, 2003 against San Lorenzo when playing for Independiente]. They got along very well during those 40 days in Holland. They were two really extraordinary players, two guys who shared everything. It was a great success to have them placed in the same room and to train together. They had a lot of fun."

It is worth remembering, though, that the home-based Argentinians still knew little about him. "We didn't know Messi," Zabaleta confirmed in a later podcast interview. "Nobody knew Messi. Eighty or 90 percent of the players were in the Argentinian league. We knew each other from playing in academies, but nobody knew Messi. When we first met him he was so quiet. He was sat in the dressing room, not talking to anyone. He was very thin. Then he started to talk on the pitch. He was amazing."

The semi-final against Brazil was played at Stadion Galgenwaard in Utrecht, in front of 16,500 fans, most of whom were on their feet within seven minutes. Taking possession in the inside-right position, Messi cut inside two defenders and shot from 25 yards. The ball was in the net before goalkeeper Renan had completed his dive. GOLAZO! Even the Brazilian supporters had to acknowledge the brilliance of what they'd witnessed.

Brazil equalised with 15 minutes left, but Messi continued to tie their right-back Rafinha in knots and struck the decisive blow three minutes into injury time. Taking the ball from Cardozo on the left, he beat his man and crossed. The ball fell kindly to Zabaleta, whose mishit shot struck Fábio Santos and deflected past Reman and over the line.

Brazilian coach Rene Weber felt the goal was "More of a lapse of our concentration than Argentina's superiority," but the Argentinians were naturally ecstatic, the entire squad including substitutes diving on Zabaleta in celebration.

Argentina's opponents in the final, Nigeria, had beaten tournament hosts, the Netherlands, 10-9 on penalties in the quarter-finals, before swatting aside Morocco 3-0 in the semi-final. Captained by 17-year-old Isaac Promise and with 16-year-olds Daddy Bazuaye and Dele Adeleye in the team, Nigeria certainly were not overawed and had plenty of support in the capacity 24,500 crowd at Utrecht. It was goalless until Messi took advantage of Adeleye's inexperience as the game approached half-time. Taking possession on halfway, he motored away from Sani Kaita and into the area that Adeleye was patrolling. The youngster did the hard part by forcing Messi wide, but then cleaned him out with a wild swing. Referee Terje Hauge had a clear view of the certain penalty.

The Nigeria coach, Samon Siasia, speaking about the incident, told me:

> "I remember telling the boys 'don't foul anyone in or around the penalty box.' We talked about it in every conversation but the boys never listened. Not playing the right structure in the end, not listening to instructions, going in too hard inside the 18-yard area. We lacked discipline at the back, but that sort of thing has always affected us, at every level – the same problems over and over again. We'll never get anywhere if we continue making those same mistakes."

Messi calmly converted the spot-kick, sending Ambruse Vanzekin the wrong way. Running towards the nearest camera, he lifted his shirt to expose a t-shirt with the message 'Para Mari, Bruno, Tomi, Agus'. Leo would later go on to explain that it was for "my sister [Mari], my cousin [Bruno], my nephews [Tomi and Agus] ... at the time they were the youngest in my family."

Nigeria equalised with an incredible flying header from Ogbuke eight minutes after the break, but the final was settled by another penalty with strong echoes of the first. Again Nigeria protested volubly, with 'keeper Vanzekin earning a yellow card, after Monday James was judged to have upended Agüero with 17 minutes left. To a chorus of whistles and boos, Messi once more fooled Vanzekin, this time to the opposite side, for his sixth goal of the tournament. Siasia believed his team had the ability to combat Messi's influence, but collectively weren't good enough.

> "My players just seemed to stand around admiring him, rather than trying to take the ball from him and give Argentina a game. And of course he scored the two penalty kicks. Plenty of times Messi would pick up the ball and run with it, beating defenders easily. Only problem was, as I've said, our players not doing what I asked them to do; 'Don't start slide tackling or committing fouls.' But my words fell on deaf ears. I'm still proud of the players though."

The goal knocked the stuffing out of Nigeria and the final 15 minutes were comfortable for Argentina. Messi was awarded the Golden Boot and Golden Ball to go with his winners' medal, and a tribute on FIFA.com: "Bagging both penalties in the final against Nigeria and top scorer and top player honours, the baby-faced Messi earned comparisons to none other than Diego Armando Maradona. His rip-roaring form in Holland was arguably the most individually influential since 'Dieguito' left fans gasping for air at Japan 1979. And as the team only won two of their seven matches by more than a one-goal margin, they needed every inch of their young talisman's inspiration."

Siasia acknowledged he and his team had witnessed something special:

> "We knew we were seeing the birth of a superstar in 2005 because it was like he was already a senior player but at that young age. What we didn't know in advance was that he was going to be as great as he was for as long as he was. Lots of kids can look good at 17 years of age but none have made it like Messi. The things he has done individually and collectively... wow! He's been wonderful. Ronaldo has always tried to catch up with him or be better than him, but there's no competition as far as most of us involved with football are concerned. We're happy to have Messi in this world. He made all of us happy. He showed to the world that he's the best player to have ever played the game, and we appreciate him. I'm very happy to have been part of his 'working life,' having my teams play against him once in a while. We have to appreciate what he has done for football. A superstar from an early age who blew the world away with his talent and his good behaviour. There's never been anything bad about Messi, he's just wonderful. A good role model that anyone would want to have on their team."

While Messi needed rest before the new season, the clamour for him to make his senior debut for Argentina persuaded coach José Pékerman to include him in *La Albiceleste's* friendly against Hungary at the Ferenc Puskás stadium in Budapest on August 17. "I couldn't believe what I was seeing when I first worked with Messi," he said years later. "I had no doubts about what Lionel would become and I always dreamed he would go on to achieve what he has. We knew then that we were looking at a player who was going to be the biggest star for the next few years."

Leo was a sub, with Pékerman naming as starters: Leo Franco, Roberto Ayala, Gabriel Heinze, Lucas Ademar Bernardi, Andrés D'Alessandro, Lucho González, Maxi Rodríguez, Lionel Scaloni, Juan Pablo Sorín, Hérnan Crespo and Lisandro López. They were expected to win comfortably, but the game didn't exactly go to plan. Sándor Torgelle's goal equalised Maxi Rodríguez's opener before Gabriel Heinze bagged the winner just after the hour mark.

Nor could Messi's debut have been much shorter or unhappier. Within 40 seconds of replacing Lisandro López he was shown the first red card of his career. Receiving the ball from Bernardi – his first touch – midway between the half-way line and the Hungarian penalty area, Messi turned and looked to immediately push forward. As he did so, Vilmos Vanczák tugged at his shirt, but in trying to escape Vanczák's clutches, Leo threw out an elbow which connected forcibly with the defender's chin, knocking him to the ground. Referee Dr. Markus Merk, just six yards away from the action and with a clear view, had only one option. After ushering away four Argentinians pleading for mercy he first yellow carded Vanczák for the shirt pull then, to cheers from the terraces, showed Messi the red.

Messi was shell-shocked. Throwing his right arm in the air, he turned his back, untucked his shirt and walked off, straight down the tunnel. "He came through me, had a hold of me and I wanted to break free," Leo said after the game. "But the referee interpreted it as though I had tried to shove him away. I went on with a lot of time left in the game, but then what happened, happened. It was not like I had dreamed it would be."

For his part, Vanczák later told *FourFourTwo* that he didn't believe Messi should have been sent off: "Everyone was looking forward to Messi stepping onto the pitch – it had been speculated that he would make his international debut and although it was still very early in his career, he was already very much in the news. As soon as he entered the pitch as a substitute, I fouled him: I pulled him back, but he was sent off for lashing out at me. It wasn't a dangerous or strong example of aggression and truthfully not in a bad place as he only touched my throat, so I don't think he should've been given a straight red card. I felt a bit sorry for him as I'm sure he never dreamt of this kind of introduction to international football."

Cue the inevitable headlines about Messi's immaturity and lack of readiness for the international stage. Just as predictably, he bounced back, within a week dominating Barça's traditional curtain-raiser, the Joan Gamper Trophy, against Juventus. On his first start at home he overshadowed giants like Patrick Vieira, Alessandro Del Piero, David Trezeguet and Zlatan Ibrahimović on a balmy August night in front of 90,000 adoring *culés*. Famously understated Juve coach Fabio

Capello was inspired to superlatives: "This guy is a phenomenon," he told reporters. "In my life I've never seen a player so young do the things he did to us ... I didn't see a thing like that since Maradona was in Naples."

Capello acted on his words in a way which confirmed Laporta's fears about Barça's ability to keep Messi. Some years later he told *Sport* that "at the end of the game I went to Rijkaard and said that he already had three foreign players in the squad, could he loan us Messi for one season ... I asked to sign him, but we couldn't buy him because Barça didn't want to sell." Inter Milan were also willing to pay the €150m buyout during the season. "It was 2006 when Inter made an offer," Laporta told Sid Lowe of *The Guardian*. "They were prepared to pay the €150m buyout clause, which is why we [later] raised it to €250m, but I always felt reassured by my relationship with his dad, Jorge. I told him: 'They'll have to pay the clause because I won't sell. He'll be happy here, he'll get glory. There, he'll only win financially. Your son's destined to be the greatest in history and here he'll have a team to help get him there. He'll enjoy it'."

Barça were still sufficiently perturbed to reassess his contract, and on September 1, 2005, extended the deal until 2014. There was simply no way that the *Blaugranes* were going to countenance losing their prized asset.

5

The New Maradona

Time to Shine

"I have seen the player who will inherit my place in Argentine football and his name is Messi"

A second Argentinian cap, for 12 minutes against Paraguay, was – on a personal level – happier than the nightmarish first, although Argentina lost 1-0, but questions over his nationality had created problems at club level after the Royal Spanish Football Federation had queried his status as an 'assimilated player'. FC Barcelona had assumed he was, having joined them as as a 13-year-old, and with Samuel Eto'o, Rafael Márquez and Ronaldinho already taking up the three squad berths permitted for non-EU nationals in La Liga games, Messi had to apply for Spanish citizenship before he could play again in the league. He was, though, still able to play in the Champions League since UEFA considered him an assimilated player.

Cameo Champions League performances against Werder Bremen and Udinese came before his first league start of the season against Zaragoza on October 1. His Spanish League status had been clarified the night before the Udinese game, putting to bed fears that he might have to be loaned out while the issue remained. He told UEFA.com: "It all happened very quickly. I signed, I swore allegiance and it was all over. I have always said that I want to triumph here and stay at the club for a long time. I read about offers for me in the press, but I never took any notice because I never considered leaving. It's not been easy to wait for this moment though. I said that I was calm and patient, but on the inside I felt bad because I was being prevented from doing what I love most."

While waiting, he had trained harder than ever and his 27 minutes at Zaragoza were followed a week later by his first 90 minutes for Argentina in a World Cup qualifier against Peru. Coach José Pékerman told reporters: "He's phenomenal, a jewel. Let's hope that we can look after him and avoid the problems which can sometimes happen. It looks as if we've found someone who is going to give us a lot of happiness. The fact that this lad is already playing this type of match says it all." Striker Hérnan Crespo agreed: "Messi is a promise that is turning into reality. It's not easy to play in the Monumental [River Plate's stadium] when it's full, in the way he did."

Watched by up to 30 family members, he put on another jaw-dropping performance, drawing seven fouls from desperate opponents and managing five shots on goal. One of Leo's incisive bursts led to the first goal, a penalty converted by Juan Román Riquelme after goalkeeper Leoa Butrón was red-carded for flattening him. Luis Guadalupe scored an injury-time own goal for Argentina's second.

Fulsome praise dominated the following day's headlines. Leading conservative paper, *La Nación*, went with 'The freshness of Messi, a great appearance' and a sub-headline of 'With his talent, the kid of 18 years seduced everyone'. Those headlines evoked the national longing for a hero comparable to Maradona to lead Argentinian football back to greatness and the hope that Messi might be the man. At the same time *La Nación* sounded a note of warning: "The first thing that comes to mind is the imperative need to care for the treasure driven by the national team shirt, and who, in the Youth World Cup, shone in all his glory. Every time Messi dazzles with his devilish left-foot, everyone is expectant. No one knows what's about to happen, neither opposition defenders or spectators ... The fear of exaggeration is always latent, but there is one point that must be taken into account: many within football circles agree that Messi is different. One of them is Pékerman, and Maradona himself recognised his magic. On the field of play he has no limits. His achievements have surrounded him so quickly that he didn't even notice, but Lionel Messi's life has changed completely in the last 365 days. To think that at the start of 2005, he was taking his first steps in the U20 side. He's achieved important things thanks to his talent, which has been wrapped in youthful freshness and humility."

Before long there was another personal milestone, his first Champions League goal. Greek side Panathinaikos came to Camp Nou on November 2 planning another defensive masterclass after holding Barça to a 0-0 draw in Athens, but were behind to a Mark van Bommel lob within 40 seconds and two down to an Eto'o header soon after. Messi's moment came in the 34th minute. With Filippos Darlas and Igor Bišćan only succeeding in getting in each other's way, Messi nipped in between the pair and pounced on the loose ball as Darlas attempted an ill-advised diving header back to 'keeper Galinović. As Galinović came out to narrow the angle, a perfect dink over his sprawling body meant Messi could round him with ease and open his Champions League goal scoring account.

If Camp Nou had had a roof it would have been blown off. The noise, a pit-of-the-stomach release of energy that sent shivers down the spine, was deafening. Messi could have been forgiven for milking another momentous moment in his career but limited himself to a couple of fist pumps – a muted celebration at odds with the madness unfolding in the stands.

A 23-minute workout against Getafe was followed by another Argentina cap for an otherwise inconsequential friendly in Qatar, but what followed was far from inconsequential – his first Clásico, at the Estadio Santiago Bernabéu. Though the match is chiefly remembered for the standing ovation that the Madridistas afforded Ronaldinho after two fantastic second-half strikes, Messi's virtuoso performance still lingers in the minds of *culés*. His penetrative run set up Eto'o for the opener, and he carved Madrid apart every time he entered their half. It took a linesman's flag to deny him his first Clásico goal, a shot from outside the area that was greeted by Sky Sports' Rob Palmer as "just a warning as to what he can do".

A Real XI including Zidane, Ronaldo, Robinho, Beckham and Raúl Tamudo was outshone by Messi's darting movements, quick change of pace and total lack of fear. The normally raucous Bernabéu plunged into an awed hush as Leo took possession with space to run into. This was a taste of what was to come over the following years when the little magician came to Madrid. Providing space to Leo was an open invitation for him to bomb forward at every opportunity, and he didn't need asking twice. Casillas thwarted him on at least two other occasions, and when he was substituted on 70 minutes, in between Ronaldinho's wonderful efforts, the smiles on the faces of Frank Rijkaard and his assistants said everything. If this wasn't a coming-of-age performance for Barça, then it was mighty close to it. There he was, strolling about in one of the finest football stadiums in the world, playing in exactly the same way as if he was back in Rosario, over the park in Lavalleja with his mates. The roughhouse tactics often employed by Madrid only succeeded in bringing out the best in him, as he toyed with an opponent over whom he knew he would eventually reign supreme.

Leo scored his first league goal of the season, one of eight in all competitions, in the next match against Racing Santander, but would only play 90 minutes on three more occasions before the end of the campaign. Two were against Zaragoza in a home and away 5-4 Copa Del Rey aggregate win, while the third, in the Champions League against Chelsea at Stamford Bridge in late February 2006, announced him to a whole new audience.

There was already some needle between Rijkaard and Chelsea coach Jose Mourinho from their meeting the previous season when Mourinho's allegation that Rijkaard had visited referee Anders Frisk at half-time created a furore that ultimately led to Frisk's retirement.

In the pre-match build up Rijkaard did his best to calm matters ahead of the reunion: "In the end every coach wants the same and that's to win. Mourinho is very intelligent, he knows what he's doing. He has the right to act like he wants to act and he's very successful with it, so who am I to criticise him? It's no problem for me. I can separate these things perfectly. We are opponents. Both teams want to win, both coaches want to win but it doesn't go further than that. As a sportsman I like the way he creates something to make a winning team. Sometimes he's looking for those kind of moments – he's a little bit conflictive, challenging a lot of people. I always said right before the game and after the game that I have the highest respect for Mourinho and what he's doing at Chelsea. He's a great coach, I'm not thinking about last year. Let's hope it will be a pleasure to watch these games."

It proved a pleasure for Barça fans as Messi ran rings round established opponents like John Terry, Frank Lampard and Claude Makélélé, and drew a foul which earned Asier del Horno a red card. It earned Messi one of Mourinho's textbook post-match whines: "How do you say cheating in Catalan?" the Portuguese asked. "Can Messi be suspended for acting? Barcelona is a cultural city with many great theatres and this boy has learned very well. He's learned play acting."

The outburst may have achieved its purpose, to neatly deflect the shortcomings of his own XI, but Messi was unimpressed and commented: "I don't do theatre, I don't attach any importance to that because we know what he's like. That he likes talking, he likes to say things and heat up the atmosphere. I got past Arjen Robben and

Del Horno charged at me with bad intent. Luckily, I saw him coming and I jumped, because if not he would've hurt me much more."

Privately, Barça were seething but Rijkaard continued to take a more considered tone in his own press conference. "I see fouls on Messi all the time and he's not a player to overreact," he noted. "We created enough chances to win but Chelsea's goal helped us in a strange way."

Referee, Terje Hauge explained his decision: "I feel it's important to see the situation live. When you see it in slow motion, you can be fooled by how he got into the situation. I have got a good feeling myself, but the red card was a key moment for how the match would develop. The incident will probably get discussed in the coming few days. It was expected that it would be a tough match and it was."

Del Horno, unsurprisingly, backed Mourinho in the *Sunday People*: "Messi is too young for these tricks. They are obviously teaching him bad things at Barcelona, negative things for his career. I won't let them get away with accusing me of deliberately going for him. I have always been a controlled player and I've never gone in to hurt anybody. I think the referee was wrong but, as always, I accept his decision."

Largely ignored amid the arguments over the red card was the wonder that Barça and Messi had played so well on a dreadfully threadbare pitch, and an earlier 'studs up' challenge from Del Horno which caught Messi on the inside of his knee, which was worthy of a red card on its own. Booed incessantly after the red card Messi had revelled in his tormentor-in-chief role, and was denied a late goal only by the width of the crossbar.

There was, as *MARCA* noted, no doubt who the star of the evening was: "In a rarely seen shown of skill, intelligence and courage, Messi tore Chelsea apart to astonish the English fans who reacted as always when a player causes panic. Beyond the boos every time he touched the ball, there was worry. Worry at his overwhelming demonstration of class. You shouldn't be able to dominate a game of such calibre at 18 years of age."

Diego Maradona was moved to proclaim Leo as his true successor: "I have seen the player who will inherit my place in Argentine football and his name is Messi," Maradona told the BBC. "Messi is the best player in the world, along with Ronaldinho. I see him as very similar to me. He's a leader and is offering lessons in beautiful football. He has something different to any other player in the world."

Argentinian Football Association president, Julio Grondona, agreed. "Messi is brilliant, different, with a strong mentality. Let's hope he doesn't change. He's playing at the level Diego was in 1979, maybe a bit more."

Argentina already had a classic playmaker, Juan Román Riquelme, but Messi strengthened his claimed for a place at that summer's World Cup with his first goal for *La Albliceleste* (the 'white and sky-blues', the nickname of the Argentia national team), a low left-footed drive, in a 3-2 friendly defeat by Croatia in Basel. Then came the second leg against Chelsea at Camp Nou on March 7, and another setback.

A 5cm tear to his right hamstring during the 1-1 draw which sent them into the quarter-finals ended his season with Barça. There was the consolation of a league winners' medal, but the injury could not have come at a worse-time for his World Cup hopes. Clamour for his inclusion grew after the Croatia match, but Pékerman refused to be influenced by anything other than Messi's fitness and prowess. "We're not going to have our progress determined by public opinion or the press," he argued. "If it [Messi's return to fitness] went badly, the only one to pay the price would be the boy – because Messi is still only a boy. We can't predict anything. We have to make the decision according to what happens."

A more immediate concern was getting fit for the Champions League final against Arsenal in Paris. Messi aggravated the injury in training in the lead up to the final, and an unnamed member of Barça's medical team was quoted in the May 3 edition of *El País* as saying: "If he's in too much of a hurry, he'll miss the World Cup too. There are no miracles with this type of injury." Two weeks before the game, the Spanish daily only gave him a 'two percent possibility' of playing any part in the match. Leo continued training until the last possible moment but Rijkaard wasn't convinced and didn't name him in the starting XI, or as one of the subs. Messi was furious and made it very obvious. He later acknowledged to Graham Hunter that he quickly regretted his refusal to celebrate with his team-mates once they'd overturned 10-man Arsenal's 1-0 lead, given to them by Sol Campbell.

Two goals in four minutes from Eto'o and Juliano Belletti sealed Barça's first European Cup win in 14 years, but it was of little consequence to Leo: "I'd been central to the team in an important stage of the tournament and all that happened was that I had a rush of blood to the head and made a decision I'd take back if I could," he

May 17, 2006: Captain Carles Puyol lifts the Champions League trophy after Barça had defeated Arsenal 2-1 in Paris. (© Shutterstock)

told Hunter. "I feel completely different about my La Liga medal compared to my Champions League medal. I feel champion of Spain much more than I do a champion of Europe but, God willing, I'll be back to win this tournament again."

Included in the World Cup squad on condition he proved his fitness, he made his case a fortnight after the Champions League final when replacing Riquelme in the 63rd minute of the international friendly against Angola in Salerno. Already 2-0 up through Maxi Rodríguez and Juan Pablo Sorín before his introduction, it was a chance for Pékerman to assess his No.19's form and fitness. Instead of his usual club position on the right, Pékerman deployed him in a more central role where he'd be involved in virtually every attacking move. It would test his ability to cope with physical opponents and be a barometer of his own personal level of fitness. It worked like a charm. Only the woodwork denied him assists after Rodríguez and Pablo Aimar hit the posts from his passes. A shot on goal, on 88 minutes, bookended an inventive, bright showing and convinced Pékerman that Leo could contribute in Germany.

He was a spectator for Argentina's opener, a 2-1 win over Ivory Coast with goals by Hernán Crespo and Javier Saviola, but on June 16 against Serbia and Montenegro he became – at 18 years and 357 days – the youngest player to represent Argentina at a World Cup.

He came on in the 75th minute with Argentina leading 3-0, as the crowd and spectators around the world were still gasping in awe at the stupendous move that led to Esteban Cambiasso's goal – a 25-pass move which took 54 seconds to unroll. It was sheer football poetry that expressed the principles Pékerman had drummed into his players and is remembered to this day as one of the great World Cup goals.

Messi seized his chance with a vengeance. Within three minutes he provided an assist to Hérnan Crespo, drilling the ball across goal to find his colleague at the far post. A superb individual effort from fellow sub, Carlos Tevez, made it five and two minutes from time Messi completed the scoring with a collector's item – a right-footed goal. It made him the youngest Argentinian to score at a World Cup and the sixth-youngest goalscorer in the history of the competition. "Despite only playing 15 minutes, it was a dream [World Cup] debut," *Mundo Albiceleste*'s Roy Nemer recalled. "Maybe it was the difference in class between both teams, but Messi tormented the Serbia and Montenegro back line. Quick dribbles, change of pace and just Messi doing what Messi does." In a further foretaste of the two figures who would dominate football for the next decade, Portugal's Cristiano Ronaldo was scoring his first World Cup goal, a penalty against Iran.

Rewarded with a place in the starting XI against the Netherlands in the final group C game, Messi was kept well shackled until replaced after 69 minutes of a tough, tight contest which ended 0-0. He then found himself back on the bench on his 19th birthday – June 24, 2006 – when Argentina played Mexico in the Round of 16. Barça's Rafa Márquez, gave *El Tri* (the nickname of the Mexico team, 'the three' colours of the national flag) an early lead which was quickly cancelled out by Crespo. It was still 1-1, with just six minutes left, when Leo was given his opportunity and he almost made it a dream substitution for himself and the manager. He appeared to have scored the winner, but Aimar was incorrectly ruled offside and the game went into extra time.

He did, though, have a hand in the winning goal, playing a sweet one-two with Riquelme before passing the ball out to Sorín who was wide on the left. His cross found Maxi Rodríguez on the edge of the area, and after one touch to control the ball with his chest, the striker unleashed a terrific dipping volley which remains one of the all-time great goals at a World Cup tournament. In the second period of extra-time, Messi had the Mexican's chasing their own shadows and almost set up Tevez for another goal with some exquisite skills. In spite of the win, and Argentina's 'favourites' tag, many journalists asked, post-match, why Messi had been kept on the bench for so long, when it was clear he could change the game, questions which would resurface once Argentina had exited the tournament.

Hosts Germany were always going to be a tricky proposition in the quarter-final, and their coach, Jürgen Klinsmann – who had spent his two years in the job calling for a quicker, more attacking style of play – was in bullish mood, saying: "Going out in the quarter-finals would be a catastrophe".

That Germany won only on penalties did not spare Pékerman huge criticism for not playing Messi for a single minute in a match which cried out for his industry and creativity. The coach's options were also reduced by having to replace goalkeeper Roberto Abbondanzieri. Cambiasso replaced Crespo but would go onto miss Argentina's first penalty, meaning that once Roberto Ayala also failed from 12 yards, Pékerman and Co. would be catching an early flight home.

"We always had that option [Messi] in mind ... but it wasn't the right moment," Pékerman explained after the match. "I'm very sorry for the coaches and the fans and the players. This team deserves to go further but we couldn't make it [...] It was a very exciting match. Argentina played like favourites and gave of their best although they lost. This has come to an end and I will certainly not go on. You have to make a decision and I'm convinced I've done everything in my reach. It's time to look for something else." The press and Argentinian public weren't impressed. They wanted to know why, with 20 minutes left and Juan Román Riquelme tiring, he was replaced by 31-year-old Julio Cruz – who'd only scored three international goals in a decade – and not the energetic young goalscorer, Messi.

The widespread sense of a golden opportunity having been missed was shared elsewhere. The distinguished English football journalist, Brian Glanville, summed it up in his column: "Pékerman's error [of replacing Riquelme with Cambiasso] was compounded by the failing, in that game, to make any use of the precociously incisive 19-year-old-winger, Lionel Messi." Had Pékerman not immediately resigned, he would have been hounded out of the job. It was Leo's first taste of disappointment at major tournaments with Argentina, and it wouldn't be the last.

6

A Clásico To Remember

Barça's Hat-Trick Hero

"He's been the most decisive player on the planet and undoubtedly the best, those who enjoy football can't say otherwise"

After playing 32 matches for club and country during the season, as well as having to deal with his injury concerns, Messi had a limited post-World Cup respite. Less than six weeks after Argentina's defeat by Germany he joined Barça for the third match of their tour of the United States, a 4-4 draw with Club América at the Los Angeles Coliseum. Still, he looked in sparkling shape and was a willing participant in the photo opportunity when the team visited NASA's Johnson Space Centre in Houston where Puyol, Ronaldinho and Xavi presented *Blaugrana* shirts – each numbered 13 – to the Russian Pavel Vinogradov, NASA's Jeffrey N. Williams, and the European Space Agency's Thomas Reiter, the crew of Expedition 13 to the International Space Station.

After the Joan Gamper Trophy match with Bayern Munich came the more serious business of the Super Cup clash with Espanyol, the previous season's Copa del Rey winners. Even so, the Estadio Olímpic Lluís Companys, Espanyol's home from 1997 to 2009, was less than half-full for the first leg, which Espanyol won 1-0. As a second-half substitute Messi found himself in opposition to his international team-mate and friend, Pablo Zabaleta.

In the return, the following Sunday, Espanyol were already two down to early goals by Xavi and Deco before they made the error of angering Messi, when Eduardo Costa's elbow cut the bridge of his nose in the 23rd minute.

With no sanction forthcoming from the referee, Messi set about inflicting his own punishment and ran at Espanyol's defence at every given opportunity. Just before the 30-minute mark he ran from deep in his own half, evading one sliding tackle before swivelling his way past another at full tilt, then laying the ball off for Eto'o to find Ronaldinho. The Brazilian's shot with the outside of his right foot went just wide, leaving Sky Sports' Rob Palmer to opine; "You want them to score, it's so perfect. They've proved they're human, after superhuman, super-skilled football." Co-commentator, Gerry Armstrong, quipped "Messi is a dream unless you're playing against him. He skips past players so easily, the creativity of this young man!" Deco's fine second-half volley completed the victory, but it was a totally different story against Sevilla five days later when the Andalusians ran away with the UEFA Super Cup 3-0. Despite enjoying almost two thirds of possession and having more shots, Rijkaard's men couldn't impose their will on a well-drilled Sevilla side for whom Dani Alves, later to join Barça, was man of the match. By now moving from the margins to become a regular starter, Messi scored in the league opener, a 3-2 win at Celta Vigo, before playing for Argentina in a 3-0 defeat to Brazil, but the Barça event most remembered from this period happened off the pitch. On September 7, 2006, the club announced that for the first time in their 107-year history, FC Barcelona were going to have a

August 2006: Leo in pre-season training. (© Rafael Amado Deras)

name on the front of their shirt, something they had resisted as other heavyweights had sold their shirts to sponsors since the mid-1980s.

In New York, Barça president Joan Laporta and United Nations Children's Fund (UNICEF) Executive Director Ann M. Veneman unveiled the *Blaugrana* shirt with 'UNICEF' and their logo emblazoned across the front. Furthermore, far from having the charity swell the coffers of the club, FC Barcelona were paying for the privilege. "Barcelona shows us that sports can be a powerful, positive force for children," Veneman noted. "The team has opened a door of hope to thousands of children." The club pledged $1.9 million per year to UNICEF over five years, with their first year donation to support programmes in Swaziland aimed at preventing mother-to-child transmission of HIV, providing treatment for paediatric AIDS, preventing HIV infection among adolescents and providing care and support for children orphaned and made vulnerable by HIV/AIDS. It was a powerful statement by the club, and in stark contrast to the standard practice of clubs selling shirt sponsorship to the highest bidder.

"At FC Barcelona, we are aware of the global dimension of soccer," Laporta said. "The increasing number of FC Barcelona supporters and fans around the world in the last few years has been spectacular. The club has an obligation to respond to this enormous positive wave. The best way to do so is by using football as a tool to bring hope to millions of vulnerable children in need." The press release at the time also noted that "through the work of its foundation, FC Barcelona has an extensive philanthropic history. It has committed itself to social, cultural, educational and humanitarian activities in Catalonia and has expanded internationally during the last few years under the motto 'More than a club' [*Més que un club* in the original Catalan]."

Més que un club had been coined by the then club president Narcís de Carreras on January 17, 1968, in a speech that was as much about Catalan identity under the Franco dictatorship as it was about football: "Barcelona is more than a football club. Barcelona is more than a place of leisure where we go to watch the team play every Sunday. More than those things, it is the spirit that is so ingrained within us." It had subsequently been used to portray Barça as different from other clubs, a claim epitomised by the UNICEF deal.

Many fans had already bought the usual unsponsored shirt, but there were numerous UNICEF replicas in the stands when it appeared on the pitch for the 5-0 defeat of Levski Sofia in the Champions League opener on September 12, and at Racing Santander's El Sardinero stadium five days later, where Barça won 3-0. The welcome for the UNICEF deal wasn't universal, with local radio phone-ins and newspaper columns being filled by *culés* complaining of a 'sell-out' by the club, but the general mood of the fans was positive.

Paolo (now Nicky) Bandini of *The Guardian* summed up the mood well: "For over a century, club bosses stubbornly resisted the march of time and capitalism to keep their team strip sponsor-free, at a time when every other club from football's upper echelons right down to your average Sunday League side had given in to financial expediency. To be fair, this may have profited them, with their logo-free red-and-blue-striped tops taking on something of an iconic status worldwide, and it was always assumed that when they did eventually sell out, they would be all set to command unparalleled sums for the taking of their sponsorship virginity. Instead, quite without warning, Barcelona's top brass have gone in a very different direction. Last Thursday, president Joan Laporta signed a five-year collaborative agreement with UNICEF that will see Barcelona not only sport the children's charity banner on its shirts, which they did for the first time yesterday night against Levski Sofia, but also contribute just over £1m to its humanitarian projects each year ... The conspiracy theorists will paint this as just another cynical marketing ploy by a club that is doing a fine job of casting itself as 'everybody's second favourite team' but with the sort of popularity and worldwide appeal they already had, I find that argument hard to swallow."

Antonio Giralt was one of many *culés* who initially found the notion of having a 'sponsor' an anathema, but was swayed by the uniqueness of the branding. As he explained to me, it captured the essence of the club for many, and the decision was lauded around the world.

"Like many other supporters of the club, the idea of staining our sacred shirt with any name was unacceptable but I admit that the deal with UNICEF was one of the two or three best decisions taken by Barça since our foundation in 1899, the credit for which goes to Joan Laporta. The UNICEF logo marked a milestone. I have travelled a lot, especially in 2nd and 3rd world countries, and I can tell you that such a decision had a huge impact. I might not be neutral, but I swear that in all the countries I've visited the number of people wearing the Barça shirt now easily outnumbers the second, probably Man United."

Craig McGeough, a Scot living in Newcastle but a member of Penya Blaugrana London, the only fan club based on a boat (on the River Thames), echoed this view:

> "I came to support FC Barcelona later than some, around 2007-08, so UNICEF were already on the shirts. I always found it warming that a club were using arguably one of the most valuable marketing canvasses in the world, never mind football, as a force for good. I certainly didn't have the same feelings of 'tarnished *Blaugrana*' that others did."

Leo scored against Osasuna and Sevilla in La Liga, and Werder Bremen in the group stage of the Champions League before suffering the injury that denied him the chance of wearing the UNICEF shirt for three months. Barça were 1-0 down to Real Zaragoza, although Messi had been running them into the ground, when he was challenged by Alberto Zapater and former Barça player Albert Celades. The FC Barcelona website reported: "Messi has broken the fifth metatarsal in his left foot. He will need surgery and the estimated time out will be three months." Eto'o was also out, until the New Year, after knee surgery and Saviola was unavailable for a month after tearing a thigh muscle later in the Zaragoza game.

Due to his injury Messi was to miss 11 league games and the Club World Cup in Japan, where Barça were overwhelming favourites but lost the final to Internacional. They still led La Liga, with Real Madrid down in fourth place, when he returned against Racing Santander on February 11, 2007, but had suffered the double blow of being overtaken by Sevilla and knocked out of the Champions League by Liverpool by the time the second Clásico of the season came round on March 10.

Massive animated crowds packed the Les Corts district three hours before the game, many jumping and chanting the playful call to arms of "*Boti, boti, boti, Madridista qui no boti*" ("Jump, jump, jump, you're a Madridista if you don't jump)." The game attracted 97,823 fans and the sound from within Camp Nou was deafening. The exhuberant Catalan crowd and television viewers across the world were privileged that day to see the next stage in Messi's ascent to greatness.

Ruud van Nistelrooy switched off the cacophony of noise when he put Madrid 1-0 ahead after only five minutes, but Messi's equaliser just six minutes later restored the high-decibel party atmosphere, when he placed his shot low, past Iker Casillas. Van Nistelrooy immediately silenced the crowd again with a well-taken penalty, but just before the half-hour, Messi fired his second into the roof of the net after Casillas had parried a well-struck Ronaldinho effort.

Barça defender Oleguer's deserved red card right on half-time resulted in a more defensive outlook from the home team, and the second-half was a little less fraught until a late headed goal from Sergio Ramos had a similar effect to van Nistelrooy's opener. Heading into injury time, 3-2 down, large numbers of supporters had already decided to make their way home, a decision they'd quickly live to regret.

Barça pushed forward in one last gargantuan effort to save the game. Ronaldinho managed to evade the close-marking Míchel Salgado long enough to find Messi cutting across the defensive line just outside the Madrid penalty area. Three touches later and he was in on goal. Ramos' last-ditch challenge was in vain as Leo buried the ball past Casillas' outstretched left hand. Whether it was relief, celebration or a mix of the two, the Camp Nou erupted. Strangers hugged each other as they were drenched in the beer being thrown high into the air, and many emotionally drained fans resembled the character in Edvard Munch's *Scream*.

March 31, 2007: Leo scored in the 44th minute as Barça beat Deportivo 2-1 at Camp Nou. (© Darz Mol)

Messi had already arrived, in terms of his escalating imprint on the world game, but his first professional hat-trick, against Barça's fiercest rivals no less, represented a further huge step forward.

The memorable Clásico hat-trick was followed a month later by the goal, in the first leg of the Copa del Rey semi-final against Getafe, that was voted, in 2019, as Barça's best ever. It remains an epic work of art. Known colloquially as the 'Maradona goal', 53,599 fans saw it live but millions have enjoyed it on *YouTube* ever since. Leo had assisted Xavi for an early opener, and the midfielder returned the favour just before the half hour with an inoccouous pass to Messi who was lurking close to the right touchline.

Leo, still in his own half and with a defender in close proximity, took himself past the first challenge with a quick drop of the shoulder before nutmeging another, which opened up acres of open space to run into. Motoring towards the penalty area with intent, he was faced with three defenders, all within five yards of each other, but he only needed two touches to evade them all. As 'keeper Luis García came out to narrow the angle, Messi took the ball around him and then had the presence of mind to lift the ball slightly as he aimed for goal, instinctively knowing that the defender getting back to clear would slide in and clear it if were it played along the floor. As Messi wheeled away to bask in the congratulations of his astonished team-mates, Eidur Gudjohnsen just stood there with his head in his hands. It was an understandable reaction. Was there nothing that this player couldn't do?!

Captain Carles Puyol led the applause as the supporters waved their white hankies in deference to the youngster. The Spanish papers would talk about it for days afterwards, dissecting every twist, turn and swivel. Could the defenders have done any more? Was their positioning to blame? Should the 'keeper have come off of his line earlier than he did? What part did Messi's team-mates play in opening up the channels for him? One element in the debate was disbelief that a 19-year-old could score such a goal, schooling experienced professionals. A truly magnificent goal, of that there was no doubt, it was ultimately in vain. After winning the first leg 5-2, Barça went down 4-0 in the return and were eliminated 6-5 on aggregate.

That disappointment paled beside the drama of the penultimate day of the season, and topped anything that had gone before. Espanyol were at Camp Nou while Real Madrid played in Zaragoza. Both had 72 points, but Madrid had the vital tie-breaker of a superior head-to-head record. Each knew a slip would probably hand the title to the other. Espanyol captain, Raúl Tamudo, gave the visitors the lead on 29 minutes, and two minutes before half-time Messi powered home a cross from the right-hand side. TV images would clearly show that he'd palmed it in with his hand, and though Espanyol's protests were vehement and sustained, referee, Julián Rodríguez Santiago, wasn't for turning. In fairness to the official, his sight line directly behind the Argentinian gave the impression that a perfectly legitimate goal was scored. The *blanc-i-blaus* were incensed and they would get their revenge in the most dramatic fashion.

Messi fired Barça ahead just before the hour mark and, with Real only drawing at Zaragoza thanks to a van Nistelrooy equaliser, the league title appeared to be heading towards Catalonia. Word spread quickly around Camp Nou that Real had fallen behind again as the Barça faithful joyfully anticipated another title, and even when van Nistelrooy scored again to bring the teams level with a minute to play, the party atmosphere at Camp Nou wasn't dampened. Then calamity struck in the final minute when, in a lapse of concentration down Barça's left side, Espanyol's Tamudo received a well worked pass and found himself in on goal. As Víctor Valdés advanced, the attacker simply slid the ball underneath him, kissing his badge as he wheeled away in celebration. In an instant the the atmosphere changed from unbridled joy to funereal. The 'Tamudazo' as the goal came to be known, would deny Messi and his team-mates the title, and the Barça fans knew it.

Playing alongside Tamudo that day was Moisés Hurtado, a defensive midfielder noted for his aggression on the pitch. It was the first time he'd come face to face with Leo and, as he outlined to me, he remembered it well:

> "Of course I kicked him! We were close to the bench and I remember everyone shouting 'Ooooohhhhh'. He stopped and then suddenly started running like a hare, zig-zagging so fast that it was harder to kick him after that. To be honest, at that time the reality was that we were more concerned with Ronaldinho rather than Messi. Xavi and Iniesta were also there so we had to pretty much all be together for the 90 minutes, avoid leaving any gaps, help, be supportive and kick someone else haha!! It was a strange game in the end because Messi could've gone down in history ... but that match is only remembered because of his handball and because we prevented FC Barcelona from winning the league."

Looking back over later meetings with Messi, he concluded:

"It was a privilege to have played against him and it was very difficult to stop him even though he wasn't then at his peak. We were nothing but spectators. I have always maintained that Ronaldinho was more spectacular, but Messi was always more efficient and with clearer ideas. His physical condition and speed in reduced spaces made Messi different. He evolved his performance levels and became more of a passer than a scorer.

Messi forced us to have three or four players watching him and the area he covered. The full-backs, the pivot, the centre-backs and sometimes the winger had to help out with defensive tasks. We all knew that once Leo got in possession of the ball he was very dangerous. He's been the most decisive player on the planet and undoubtedly the best, those who enjoy football can't say otherwise. Although he's never won the World Cup, he is the player who has provided the best performances most consistently. What I liked about him too was that I always thought he was a very calm person. I remember one day that Dani Jarque was on the Castelldefels highway, and in front of him he had a car that was going at about 20km per hour and he couldn't understand why. As he overtook the car, he realised that the driver was Messi, in a world of his own. He only thinks about football, nothing else."

7

Olympic Glory

A Golden Memory

*"One single player couldn't stop him, so it was a case of being aware
of him and hoping that he didn't have one of his great games"*

A two-goal haul in the final game of the campaign, a 5-1 win away at
Gimnàstic de Tarragona, was of little comfort to Leo and his colleagues,
who were still smarting from the 'Tamudazo' and the lost title. It is still
trotted out at Catalan derby time every year. Raúl Tamudo himself
said to the Spanish daily *AS* a decade later that "I should charge every
time they use that word [Tamudazo]!! It's a beautiful story which I
will always tell my children, and was a unique moment."

Nor was there any rest for Messi. Within 11 days he was playing
for Argentina in the 2007 Copa América tournament. New coach
Alfio Basile had learnt from Pékerman's misfortunes, and Leo would
play all six matches.

While the tournament ended in yet another disappointment,
winning Young Player of the Tournament served to elevate Leo's
status in the game further, and one exquisite moment of skill
underscored all of his incredible performances. It came in the semi-
final against Mexico. To that point Leo had only scored once in the
competition, Argentina's third of four in their quarter-final romp
over Peru. *El Tri* were expected to provide a sterner test, and until
Gabriel Heinze's opener on 45, they did. Once Messi and his team-
mates got into their stride after half-time, there was, though, only
ever going to be one winner. The *coup-de-grace* came just after the
hour mark and left Ray Hudson scrambling for superlatives. Taking
a pass from Carlos Tevez just inside the area, Messi saw that Mexico's
'keeper Oswaldo Sánchez was just off of his goal line, and with the
most delicate of touches he chipped the ball into the opposite corner.

"How do you describe magic?" Hudson asked in his familiar maniacal Geordie tones. "How do you describe this? It's virtually impossible. The ball is fizzed from Tevez who's begging for it back and Messi says, 'I see you mate, I don't need ya.' Watch it. Perfect pass by Tevez who's on for the square ball, for the tap-in. Leo says 'nah, I fancy a little bit of Román in the night. He picks one out of Riquelme's genius book. Messi produces the rainbow and there's a pot of gold at the end of it. It's absolutely pure class in a glass."

Coach Basile obviously agreed, telling reporters post-match that "only a genius could do this." Five minutes later Riquelme himself rounded off the scoring with a penalty. TV pictures showed that Tevez was on his way down before any contact was made, but the game had already been won. Leo almost went one better in injury time, curling his shot just wide after beating two defenders in typical style.

Just four days later, *La Albiceleste* would do battle with *La Seleção* (the nickname for Brazil, meaning 'the national team') in the final. *The* Brazilians were missing several players so were regarded as the underdogs when they took the field at the Estadio José Encarnación. Seven yellow cards were brandished by Paraguayan referee, Carlos Amarilla, as Brazil took the lead with their first attack and Julio Baptista fired an unstoppable rocket into the top corner past the badly positioned Abbondanzieri. They then thwarted Argentina with a tight defensive performance.

Argentina's best chance came when Riquelme fired against the woodwork after a typical Messi run, but they couldn't break through. Brazil extended their lead when a superb cross for tournament top scorer, Robinho, was turned into his own net by Roberto Ayala just five minutes before the break.

Dani Alves, involved in everything after replacing Elano in the 34th minute, completed the scoring after a stunning counter-attack with 20 minutes left. When Robinho received the ball, he was only just outside the box, but with one pass, to Vágner Love, Brazil already had a two-on-two situation on the halfway line. Such criminal defending was always going to be punished and Brazil just needed the right ball to be played. With Alves scampering forward to his right, Vágner Love simply slipped the ball between the two covering defenders and, such was the precise nature of the pass, it allowed Alves to bury it first time past Abbondanzieri.

With 20 minutes left to play, the game became an exercise in restoring pride, and Messi managed to get ball into the net, only to be denied by the offside flag. Brazil's deserved victory exposed the Argentinian players to yet another firestorm of vitriol and abuse from supporters and media alike, but Leo at least was able to return to a relative haven in Europe while his age and his own performances exempted him from at least some of the abuse.

Back in Catalonia, Barça had signed Thierry Henry from Arsenal to join Leo and Samuel Eto'o in a new-look front three. Fellow *Alibiceleste* Gaby Milito had also joined, along with Eric Abidal and Yaya Touré, while prolific youth team goalscorer Bojan Krkić was elevated during the season, Camp Nou's 50th. Yet although Messi's star continued to ascend, it was a campaign with all the hallmarks of the end of a natural team cycle, proving to be the last for Ronaldhinho, Lilian Thuram, Giovanni van Bronckhorst, Ludovic Giuly and Gianluca Zambrotta. It would take a year for the 'freshening up' of the squad to begin and in the meantime, Frank Rijkaard was backed to continue, with the brief that titles had to be won.

There were few hints of decline during the seven straight pre-season victories which saw Messi score another of his most remarkable goals, beating Bayern 'keeper Michael Rensing so completely that the ball was in the net before he had moved. However, there was also a warning of the stop-start season to come when he suffered a hamstring contracture in the 91st minute of Argentina's friendly against Australia in Melbourne.

Though he was back in action within a week, playing in the Champions League against Lyon then scoring six times in seven league matches, before a quieter run of two from eight, he suffered a more serious thigh injury after creating two goals against Valencia in the run-up to Christmas. He would not return until the match against Racing Santander on January 20, 2008.

His absence was keenly felt because, according to the former player – now author and football analyst – Alex Delmas, who shared his thoughts with me:

"No one could take his place, and neither should it have been so. Barça had to learn to live without him and little by little reformulate themselves. He would eventually become indispensable as no other player could contribute the same things. The club needed to balance around the collective (what it had always done to ensure success). Leo didn't have a style but created his own style: an unstoppable dribbler, but a successful dribbler nonetheless."

By the time he returned, the *Blaugranes* were well behind in the title race, and only one goal in his next six league games wasn't really enough from the player fast becoming their talisman. Leo did manage a brace against Celtic in the Champions League, but disaster struck again in the return at Camp Nou on March 4.

With no one close to him as he bore down towards goal just before the break, Messi pulled up sharply and immediately put his hands to his head before collapsing to the floor in agony. Deco understood the gravity of the situation but his attempts at getting Leo up again were doomed to failure. Another (left) thigh injury meant he wouldn't be back in competitive action until April 12, a further six weeks out of competitive action. Little was expected of him when, with only two league games under his belt, and from 62 minutes into a 0-0 draw against Manchester United in the first leg of their Champions League semi-final, Barça headed to Old Trafford for the second leg, but he confounded expectation and the team were denied victory only by Paul Scholes' first-half howitzer, and an incredibly dogged 90 minutes from United.

Just like at Chelsea two years previously, Messi ran the show. United had been warned by Leo's Argentinian team-mate, Carlos Tevez, a summer capture from West Ham, what to expect every time he received the ball. Whenever he was in possession, a fearful hush fell upon Old Trafford and there was a real sense of when, not if, Leo would either score or create one for a team-mate. Along with Xavi and Iniesta, he ran United's midfield ragged. Paul Scholes in particular was routinely bamboozled by Messi's quick feet, and no one could get near him, unless it was to bring him down. Edwin Van der Sar needed to be at full stretch to keep him out on more than one occasion and Leo was also to be denied a blatant first-half penalty which would certainly have changed the complexion of the tie. The pattern continued throughout the second half, and though Barça's dominance was, ultimately, unrewarded, no supporter could be unhappy with the level of their application.

Astonishingly, despite being aware of his brilliance, United didn't have a game plan for Messi for that key 2008 encounter, their assistant manager for that game, Mike Phelan, told me over a decade later:

"There was never, in those big games, a specific role to counter anything that Barcelona had. We were aware of all of their strengths and obviously you analyse individuals, and he [Messi] was the high-quality performer. What we did talk about was how we could stop him from operating in certain areas of the field. So it wasn't a need to stop him playing so much or a need to man mark him, it was more about how do we stop the supply and what sort of areas will he take up positions in. That was more of the talk that we always had before big games because a lot happens in the different phases of a game. He conserved energy really well, we'd noticed that, and when he was on the ball he was electric, but in everything else we knew he'd be quite passive. We'd also noticed that he would drift into certain areas of the field but they were where we didn't believe he'd be a threat. He'd take himself wide, right out onto the touchlines, and drop into areas where you don't necessarily observe because he normally does it when the opposition are in possession of the ball, so you'd probably take your eye off of him a little bit. That was going to be the disastrous part for us! We knew we had to make sure we were secure and that someone within the unit was aware of that space because the space was going to be our biggest enemy. There were certain patterns of play we knew Barcelona would execute and certain ways in which they'd utilise Messi, and deep down we knew all about his quality. He was world class and we knew that one single player couldn't stop him, so it was a case of being aware of him and hoping that he didn't have one of his great games. We had to take that into account too, that he might be having an off day and just not quite at it, or the service into him wasn't quite as great. If we were aware of it as a possibility, we could look to capitalise on that. But the guy's a genius."

With Real already champions and nothing now to play for, Rijkaard was clearly in jeopardy. He said after the United defeat that he had no intention of leaving: "It would be different if the players were saying it's time for me to go, but that's not the case." The Dutchman was sacked a week later after a crushing 4-1 Clásico defeat at the Bernabéu.

The morning headlines in the Catalan papers were no more forgiving toward Rijkaard than Real had been. 'You dishonour the Barça shirt' was probably the politest. By the end of the day Barça B coach, Pep Guardiola had been appointed for the start of the following season. The news was received with a mixture of incredulity and excitement. The club had previously talked to José Mourinho, who made a tremendous pitch for the top job. Marc Ingla,

New Barça manager Josep 'Pep' Guardiola was a club legend and had achieved success with the B team, but not everyone was convinced he had what was needed for the club's top job. (© Tsutomu Takasu)

the vice-president, and sporting director, Txiki Begiristain, were believed ready to offer him a contract, but were less than impressed with his attitude after the meeting.

"In considering him we were also dealing with the Mourinho brand," Ingla told Graham Hunter for his book *Barça: The Making of the Greatest Team in the World*. "I said to him, 'José, the problem we have is you push the media too much. There is too much aggression. I added, 'the coach is the image of the club, you cannot start fires everywhere, this is against our style.' Mourinho answered, 'I know, that is my style. I won't change.' He was to be No.1 but wouldn't listen."

Guardiola was revered by everyone at the club but had no prior experience at the top level. Surely it was a risk in appointing him? He'd won promotion to the Segunda División for Barça B through the play-offs, but the season hadn't been without its low points.

Reports of incredible attention to detail, unheard of preparation before a game and the nurturing of academy talent had the powers-that-be pondering his possibilities. "It was definitely the best time of my career," Barça B player Gai Assulin told Sky Sports. "Everyone enjoyed his style of play, he gave us a lot of freedom. He expected a lot from us but he never put us under too much pressure. He wanted us to show our quality and we knew that the results might not come sometimes. But that's football. The way of playing was perfect for us because it's about having the ball for most of the minutes in a match."

The big question on Catalan lips was could Pep transfer his methodology and way of working to the elite level? It would be a few months before the questions were answered and, in the meantime, Rijkaard had a season to finish. The final home match, against Mallorca, attracted only 39,298 fans and the eerily quiet atmosphere allowed the faithful *culés* to hear every word from pitch level, leading some to suggest that it wasn't only fans who had had enough. That the crowd were more excited by the paper aeroplanes raining down onto the pitch says much about the insouciance from those who had bothered to turn up. The bad atmosphere at Camp Nou was compounded when the visitors were allowed back into the game after Barça had led 2-0, and when Mallorca's Dani Güiza's scored a 93rd-minute winner there were more resigned guffaws than cheers. There was no anger as such, just acceptance that a season that had started with such dreams and aspirations had ended in failure.

The season had ended but Leo still had international duties that summer at the Beijing Olympics, which conflicted with his club's pre-season preperations and resulted in a club v country battle. Argentina had been lobbying for a while to include him in the men's Olympic tournament in China but Barça had refused, citing the first leg of their Champions League qualifier in spite of the FIFA directive that clubs should release players aged under 23 for the tournament. Their refusal had Messi seething and in no mood to play the dutiful employee at Barça's pre-season camp at St. Andrews in Scotland.

"We have a great squad, but Messi is an important player for us, one of the best in the world," captain Carles Puyol had told the media after one of Guardiola's intense training sessions. "What's happening with his situation is a theme that we can't really get into since we can't control it. Let's hope it's resolved soon and that we can count on him being with us." While Messi scored in a a 6-0 win over Hibernian and bagged a hat-trick two days later in a 5-1 demolition of Dundee United, his body language told another story.

Barça, citing support from the Royal Spanish Football Federation, won an appeal in the Court of Arbitration for Sport (CAS), but thanks to an intervention by Guardiola, Messi still went to Bejing. Recalling the coach pulling him aside after a pre-season friendly away to Fiorentina and saying "You want to go, don't you?" Leo explained to *Estudio Futbol*, "I said 'yes' and he replied: 'Well, I'll give you permission and the only condition is that someone from the club will accompany you and follow you everywhere.' I told him that that wasn't a problem, as long as I left. When I am frustrated I can't hide it and they realised it. At some point I wanted to show them that if I stayed for the pre-season, I was going to be that way. I really wanted to go as I was talking all of the time with my team-mates on the national team and they told me that they were waiting for me until the last minute."

It was a significant moment in the relationship between the coach and player. A novice in his role Guardiola may have been, but he held sway and authority and commanded instant respect. Getting the board to trust him on the issue immediately bonded him with Messi, despite Leo not having played a competitive game for his new coach at that point. "Pep was phenomenal with me as nobody wanted me to go, but he understood why I wanted to go."

It was the best decision Pep could've made. Leo was happy, and Sergio Batista's team were a wholly different proposition with him in the side. He scored in the opener against Ivory Coast and, with the absorbingly tight quarter-final against the Netherlands finally settled, his old foes Brazil – with Ronaldinho as one of their over-age players – were lying in wait. The Brazilian had also been told by Barça that he couldn't compete at the Olympics, but his new club, AC Milan, were more relaxed. Guardiola had sold him and Deco because he felt they were having a negative influence on the lifestyle Leo was leading and the company he was keeping. Argentina triumphed with two goals from Agüero and a Riquelme penalty, with Brazilian frustrations culminating in two red cards within three minutes for Lucas and Thiago Neves.

Argentina's opponents in the Olympic final at Beijing's 'Bird's Nest' stadium were very familiar, the 2007 U20 World Cup finalists Nigeria. Ridiculous scheduling to benefit prime time audiences in Europe meant a midday kick-off, with conditions so hot that there was a formal time-out in each half when players and officials could take on liquid. It meant the ebb and flow of the game was interrupted and may have influenced the result. As it was, Nigeria missed chances in both halves and Messi made them pay. He tormented the Super

Eagles all game and, just before the hour, a defence-splitting ball from well inside his own half sent Di María scampering away.

All but one of Nigeria's centre-backs had pushed forward, giving Di María the freedom to run unchallenged to the edge of the area. Goalkeeper Ambruse Vanzekin had come well off of his line to narrow the angle, and he was past the penalty spot when the No.11 simply dinked it over him, into an unguarded net. Once referee Viktor Kassai had blown for full-time, the celebrations began in earnest, with Diego Maradona jubilantly dancing for joy in the stands as the youngsters embraced on the pitch.

That title remains the one that Leo treasures above any other, telling *Esquire* some years later: "The Olympic gold in 2008 is the win that I value the most because it is a tournament that you may only play once in your life and involves many athletes from different disciplines. The fact that we have been to the athlete's village and met famous sportsmen … it's all an experience that we will not forget quickly." In a separate interview with *ESPN*, he cheekily added: "The World Cup is great, but the Olympic Games are something special."

But for Guardiola's intervention, Messi might never have had the chance to experience the highs which the 2008 Olympic Games gave him, and that wasn't going to be forgotten in a hurry.

8

'Tiki-Taka'

Poetry in Motion

"It's like his brain operated at a different speed. Everything happened so fast and it's only with the assistance of slow-motion technology that you saw the subtleties of his movement."

It comes as a shock to be reminded that Barça fans ever wanted Guardiola fired, but it came almost immediately and was due to the unease at the extent of change at the club. Giovani dos Santos, Edmílson, Deco, Ronaldinho, Zambrotta, Thuram, Oleguer, Santiago Ezquerro and Marc Crosas all departed, and Dani Alves, Seydou Keita, Martín Cáceres, Alex Hleb and Gerard Piqué were brought in, the latter repatriated from Manchester United. Further personnel changes included the promotions of Sergio Busquets, Pedro and Jeffrén from within.

Samuel Eto'o, having scored 16 goals in 18 games during the previous season, was unamused to learn he was surplus to requirements: "I firstly reminded Guardiola that he was never a great player, he was a good player," the Cameroonian told *beIN Sports*. "And I said if it was coach Luis (Fernandez) who told me, I would've said ok. As players, we know. We also knew Pep. Especially as a coach, he hadn't shown anything for him to be able to walk into a dressing room like Barcelona's. He didn't even know the story of the dressing room."

Yet no queue formed for Eto'o's services, one surprising offer apart: "I had a very, very good offer to go and play in Uzbekistan. I would've made $26m in six months. Pep was sitting in his office with Txiki Begiristain and he told me, 'Oh Samuel, that's gonna be good for you, go there.' I told him that the one who will make the team win will be Eto'o, not Messi, and you will come and ask me for forgiveness. And I stayed there. I kept training, and we went to the United States. We were in Houston, in the dressing room, and he said before the game; 'OK, we are going to change numbers.' Everyone looked as if to say 'oh, the coach does this now? Surprising.' He said 'Titi [Thierry Henry], you take Samuel's No.9 and Eto'o will wear No.14.' Everyone was surprised, and that was a total lack of respect. I couldn't accept that. I had written a beautiful story, and even if it had to stop at Barcelona, I had done a lot for the club. Whether it was on the field, but foremost off the field, I was always there for my team-mates, for the club."

By the end of the season, Eto'o had responded in the best way possible. He delivered from the very beginning of Pep's reign with a brace against Wisla Kraków in the Third Qualifying Round of the Champions League, Guardiola's first competitive game in charge of the *Blaugranes*. The second leg loss was incidental, but then came the first league match of the 2008-09 campaign, Messi's first competitive game under Pep. It was also his first setback as newly-promoted Numancia declined their designated role as cannon fodder and sent their 9,300 fans into ecstasy with a 1-0 win from a goal by Mario Martínez, reportedly the worst-paid player in La Liga.

Racing Santander, the first opponents that season at Camp Nou, proved similarly undeferential. Messi was on the bench after travelling back from two more games for Argentina in South America and the expected procession turned into another baffling evening. Boos echoed around a sparsely populated stadium long before Messi, introduced after 58 minutes, dispatched a 70th minute penalty. Racing equalised through Jonathan Pereira five minutes later and the 1-1 draw left Barça in 15th place.

Even though Guardiola praised the attitude of his players afterwards, saying that he "wouldn't reproach them." *MARCA*'s Santiago Siguero did: "One point from six. Barcelona haven't even started. After the defeat against Numancia, the match against Racing presented itself as an occasion to scare off the fear. It should've been easy for Barça because their opponents totally gave up the game and were willing to settle for a 0-0. Guardiola's side were a team without gunpowder and, what's worse, without a spark to blow it up. Very predictable and easy to disable. Many teams will play like Numancia and Racing, Muñiz's side were ultra-defensive and with the eleven behind the ball."

Compared to some opinions amongst the grandees of Spanish football journalism, Siguero's was almost polite. Vox pops conducted on the streets of Barcelona were scathing, and 'Guardiola out' was, unbelievably, a common theme. It was left to the usually undemonstrative Andrés Iniesta to sound a rallying call. Recalling the tricky period in his autobiography, *The Artist: Being Iniesta*, in 2016, the midfielder recounted a conversation he'd had with the new manager: "Don't worry mister. We'll win it all. We're on the right path. Carry on like this, okay? We're playing brilliantly, we're enjoying training. Please, don't change anything. Vamos de puta madre (Let's go mother fuckers)! This year we're going to steamroller them all!"

Iniesta was right. Starting the following weekend with a 6-1 hammering of Sporting Gijón at El Molinón, Barça won 19 and drew two of their next 21 league games, scoring at least three goals in 13 of them. Something just clicked. The team were unstoppable and Messi was unplayable. It wasn't long before the phrase 'tiki-taka' – short, sharp passes and movement while dominating possession – was applied to them. Spanish broadcaster, Andrés Montes had used during one of his *La Sexta* commentaries on the Spanish team during the 2006 World Cup – "Estamos tocando tiki-taka tiki-taka" (we play tiki-taka tiki-taka), but the Guardiola style represented a fresh development of the style previously preached by Johan Cruyff and Rinus Michels. The baton at FC Barcelona had been passed again, into safe hands.

Messi had claimed 16 league goals and 10 assists by the last match in the run, a 2-2 draw at Betis on St Valentine's Day. There were also five goals and three assists in the Champions League group stages, and three assists plus four in the Copa del Rey. Pep was getting the best out of Barça's talisman and Leo was loving it too. How could he not? While ostensibly the left-hand side of a front three with Eto'o and Henry, he was allowed to roam the pitch as he saw fit in order to help construct Barça's delicious passing carousels. TV rights deals now allowed fans across the world to peer in through the window at this phenomenon, and they weren't often left disappointed. It meant Barça and Messi were celebrated globally for the unmatched panache of their play.

As Sky Sports' La Liga commentator, it was Rob Palmer's voice that described many of Leo's goals. Speaking to me about how he juggled the professional requirements of his role as a broadcaster with the sheer amazement of witnessing the brilliance of Leo, Rob commented:

> "I was in the fortunate position and experienced enough to claim a few firsts. You are generally given a heads up when a club thinks they have someone special about to break through. I could retire if there were royalties for the commentary on Steven Gerrard's introduction as an unknown Anfield substitute – luckily, I'd done my homework, and Wayne Rooney's first-ever goal carries my voice. The first of millions of David Beckham interviews was conducted by me in a cold Preston North End changing room and last week Robbie Fowler had me choked when someone asked how he knew me, and said 'Rob did my first interview when I got into the Liverpool team.'

> When there's a buzz at a club like FC Barcelona about a youngster, you know that the words on his first-ever goal are going to be used for posterity. Some commentators script such moments. I try to speak from the heart. You are there as a verbal bookmark in history, to capture the moment and significance. Commentating on Messi is like defending Messi. When he gets the ball, you sharpen your senses. It's like handling a poisonous snake. If you don't concentrate, he'll bite and you won't notice. Normally when a player takes possession of the football you may have a glance at your notes or survey his options ahead. When Messi gets the ball there's none of that. You have to focus and be prepared for any eventuality. Like the defender or goalkeeper, you need all of your dexterity and wits. As we reached the Guardiola era, Pep worked on tactics to maximise the talents of Messi. I remember analysing one performance with the great Michael Laudrup. He pointed out that Messi's starting position was often just in front of the right back position. His team-mates would clear the stage, giving him a clear 10 yards to work in. Each would offer an outlet if needed for a quick one two but keep a respectable distance away to allow him to dribble past the opponent."

As a former professional himself, Rob was able to enjoy Messi's talents from a more technical standpoint.

> "I never reached the top level but was part of a squad that was in the top English division so witnessed what it meant to have special players in our midst. I remember Charlie George returning to Derby County

and the clamour of everyone to see him just try things in training and then see it come off on a match day. Messi was at another level. He did things no other footballer can do. It's like his brain operated at a different speed. Everything happened so fast and it's only with the assistance of slow-motion technology that you saw the subtleties of his movement. It was like watching the wing movement of a hummingbird. Even the most accomplished and talented footballers were, and are, aghast at what he could pull off with natural ease. I think most professionals marveled at his calmness and humility. He would be on an amazing run, having left several opponents in his wake and suddenly he'll be hacked down. The natural reaction is to be angry, to complain and feel pain. He just bounced back up, rarely showing that it bothered him - the greater the standing of the offender, the less reaction. He must've thought 'X is world class and even he resorted to hacking me.' It seemed to merely fuel him."

The unbeaten run ended against local rivals Espanyol, who were bottom of the league, winless since November and 42 points behind Barça. Referee Carlos Delgado Ferreiro issued 14 yellow cards and one red as Espanyol parked the bus and prepared for a battle. Barça seemed oddly unprepared and and offered little, even before Seydou Keita was sent off in the 37th minute.

Former player Ivan De la Peña, the 'Little Buddha', scored twice in four minutes for the visitors and, for all of their underhand tactics and time wasting, one couldn't but admire their resolve. Yaya Touré's swift riposte and Messi's prompting would normally have rescued Barça, but there was nothing normal about this game. Pep was philosophical afterwards, telling reporters: "It's been a good test for us. We've lost the game but I don't want to focus on the distance we have now [Real Madrid had closed to within seven points], we're going to Lyon and we'll move on. Nobody said that it [winning the league title] would be simple. It was a very demanding match, I'm sorry we didn't get the win because of the people who came to the stadium. We lacked a bit of rhythm ... but I congratulate Espanyol, we have to get back up and, in the end, the league will put us where we are. We can lose many games but we will continue until the end."

Pressed to talk about the referee, Guardiola shut down the debate and the press conference. "I will not talk about the referees. To this day I don't like to talk about the referees. If we lose, it's our fault."

The following game, a Champions League Round of 16 match at Lyon, is most remembered for Juninho producing a moment of genius. When he placed the ball not too far from the corner flag with seven minutes played, a simple cross into the box may not have been expected, but nor was the incredible, arcing shot that flew over the heads of Eto'o and Messi in the wall and continued its upward trajectory before completely bamboozling Valdés and nestling in the net. Juninho's invention inspired Andrea Pirlo who, in his autobiography, *I Think Therefore I Play*, wrote: "That man made the ball do some quite extraordinary things. He'd lay it on the ground, twist his body into a few strange shapes, take his run-up and score. He never got it wrong. Never. I checked out his stats and realised it couldn't just be chance. He was like an orchestra conductor who'd been assembled upside down, with the baton held by his feet instead of his hands." Thierry Henry's stooping 67th-minute header salvaged a draw for Barça.

An epic 4-3 defeat by Atlético at the Vicente Calderón after 90 minutes of stunning attacking play, with Sergio Agüero grabbing the winner, was seized upon by journalists who had nonsensically been calling it a 'must win for Pep'. It was a mixed day for Messi, who scored Barça's second goal but committed the foul on Florent Sinama-Pongolle that enabled Diego Forlán to equalise, at 3-3, with a penalty with 10 minutes to play.

Nonsensically or not, Barça's season appeared to be on the line. A third successive league game without a win meant that any goodwill Guardiola had built up with his friends in the media was beginning to evaporate. Now things were getting serious and the kingdom was beginning to crumble. In the second-leg of the Copa del Rey semi-final a few days later, Mallorca took the lead, to bring them to within one goal of levelling the tie. Awarded a penalty in the second half after Martín Cáceres was red carded for bringing down goalscorer Castro, FC Barcelona's season almost hinged on what would happen in the next minute or so.

Although they still led the league, many *culés* felt that the title was slowly slipping away. Reserve 'keeper José Manuel Pinto in goal for the semi-final, hardly inspired confidence. Mallorca seemed about to take control. It was then that TV cameras caught one of the iconic images of the season, Pinto motioning to penalty taker Martí that he was going to dive to his left. You had to admire his courage. Barça's participation in the competition was on the line and the 33-year-old was playing high-stakes football poker. Martí nodded his head as though to say 'of course you are mate' and promptly fired it straight down the middle. True to his word, Pinto went left but managed to kick the ball away with his right foot as he dived.

Messi was a spectator for all of this, but with Barça below par Pep was forced to bring him on. He was hacked down at almost every opportunity and soon the on-field numbers were evened out as Josemi received a red for his second yellow. In the last few minutes a simple long ball from Gerard Piqué left Messi a free run at goal. As 'keeper, Lux, advanced, the Argentinian flicked it over his outstretched palm. Game over. Messi would play in his first cup final.

Speaking after the match to *Sport*, Pinto was keen to downplay his part in the win: "I hope that little quirk is understood to just be part of my personality. I've never liked to be the main man and I don't want to be now. I believe that we are in the final due to everyone's performance. It was fortunate that I could save the penalty, but I don't think it should mean that I'm given more attention than any other player. These tricks are learned on the street. I was fortunate but it's just something small that happened. In football you have to be crafty, and these are things I picked up on a day to day basis in my area."

That draw, and the aggregate victory it delivered was a pivotal moment too. Though Barça's participation in the domestic cup final has since been taken for granted, their 2008-09 appearance was their first since 1997-98 – coincidentally a 1-1 draw against Mallorca, that Barça won 5-4 on penalties. Any hint of a slump was over. They were 90 minutes away from their first silverware under Pep, still holding their own in the league and a 5-2 hammering of Lyon a week later put them into the draw for the Champions League quarter-final with a performance so dominant that the narrative turned again.

At least four presentable opportunities were passed up before Henry slid the hosts into a 24th-minute lead. A wonderful pass from Xavi three minutes later split Lyon's defence wide open and the Frenchman buried his second to put Barça firmly in control. Six minutes before half-time, Leo evaded three tackles as he weaved his way into the heart of the French team's defence and executed a delicious one-two with Eto'o before placing the ball out of Hugo Lloris' reach. The move was so characteristic of Messi – majestic in its construction and finish. There was still time before the break for Eto'o to rifle one into the roof of the net, and by now the Camp Nou was

April 11, 2009: Leo taking a corner at Camp Nou during the 1-0 victory against Recreativo Huelva. (© Rafael Amado Deras)

rocking. The poor recent form was forgotten and not even the two goals from Lyon before 48 minutes had been played were enough to dampen the atmosphere. Deep into injury time, Seydou Keita's goal gave Barça five – what Spaniards call a *mano grande* (a big hand).

Barça were definitely back in the groove, and Guardiola was in good spirit at his post-match press conference: "We played very well. We played a good positional game, we were brilliant ... We've played other good games, but maybe because of the importance of this one, it is one of our best. I want to highlight Sylvinho, who hasn't played much until now and has done very well, and I can't deny that Piqué is having a great season. He's young and he has to keep growing and growing, but I congratulate him for the match he has played. Even if Eto'o hadn't scored, his attitude would've remained the same. I think the eight teams left [in the Champions League] are at a very high level, and I would like to be back at home [for the quarter-final first leg]. The important thing is that we are in the draw and we will be able to enjoy a great game at the Camp Nou again."

Pep got his wish and Jürgen Klinsmann's Bayern Munich came to Camp Nou for the first leg of the quarter-final. Since the Lyon game, Barça had once more looked an unstoppable juggernaut, winning four league games without conceding a goal, and the home fans was treated to another epic four-goal first-half. Playing down the right wing, Messi claimed the first and third, played Eto'o in for the second with a reverse pass and was handed a booking for diving in the box which so incensed Pep that he was sent off.

The fourth, by Henry, sent Barça in at half-time with the game – and possibly the tie – already won. The second-half passed without incident or further goals, and Bayern's legends were furious in their condemnation. Franz Beckenbauer told Premiere Television: "This is a catastrophe. It's schoolboy stuff. The first half was quite the worst I've ever seen Bayern play. It was a demonstration, almost a humiliation. Barcelona gave us a lesson in football." Nor did club chief Karl-Heinz Rummenigge, hold back. TV pictures had shown his icy stares as he sat in the box alongside Barça president, Joan Laporta. "One should not take any decisions today," he told CNN. "It was a disgrace but it's best if you sleep and then deal with these issues rationally. The question to know is whether to be angry or sad at what took place. It was undoubtedly an enormous humiliation which was hard for everyone." German tabloid *Bild*, by contrast, predicted one decision, headlining: 'Klinsi close to the exit door'.

Laporta was understandably cock-a-hoop, commenting in a post-match interview with the Catalan daily, *Sport*: "It was a great football night before a big team in Europe, and with all due respect for Bayern, today Barça were superior. We played a magical football match and in the second half we were more serious. I think we have an important lead to take to Munich." Henry, who'd lost the 2006 final to Barça when with Arsenal, knew a place in the final was within touching distance. "I want to win the Champions League," he said after the mauling of the Bavarians. "It's a competition that I'm passionate about and I've never won it." Even the official FC Barcelona website called it: "One of the best opening 45 minutes of football ever seen at the ground." Barça's place in the semis was confirmed the following week by a 1-1 draw in Munich, and Messi looked an ever more compelling candidate for this first *Ballon d'Or* for the world's best player.

The biggest 11 days of the season now loomed – Valencia at home and Real Madrid away in the league, as well as yet another home and away Champions League clash with Chelsea. Much of Guardiola's success with the team owed a lot to his attention to detail, though his practice of spying on players was taking things to a whole new level.

"The Método 3 detective agency spied on FC Barcelona players under orders from the then director of security and now director general of Penitentiary Services for the Generalitat [autonomous government of Catalonia], Xavier Martorell," a report in *El Confidencial* noted. "Pep has developed a good understanding and friendship with Martorell, who willingly helped Guardiola to be informed at all times." That practice would only intensify a year later when Piqué found himself falling head over heels in love with Colombian pop princess, Shakira.

A 2-2 draw at Mestalla in which Messi scored wasn't the worst result in the world, nor was a goalless Champions League semi-final first-leg at home to Chelsea, even if Barça's 18 shots at goal – compared to just three from Guus Hiddink's side – left the players disappointed that at least one hadn't gone in. They had, though, stopped the Blues from scoring and knew an away goal at Stamford Bridge would really put the cat amongst the pigeons. Before heading to London, however, there was the small matter of the second Clásico of the season, which would go into Barça legend as *La Chorreo* – loosely translatable as 'stream', as in 'a steady stream of' – in this case, goals.

Los Blancos had kept up the pursuit of Barça in second place, winning 15 matches and drawing one of the last 16, and could pull to within one point of the league leaders with a win. The celebrations when Gonzalo Higuaín put Real ahead on 15 minutes showed genuine belief that this would be their night against a team who possibly had one eye on the following midweek's Champions League semi-final date with Chelsea. Within two minutes that thought had disappeared when Henry fired level and, after two more he won a free-kick when Fabio Cannavaro was yellow-carded for an overly aggressive challenge. The free-kick produced another of the images of the season, as shaggy-haired captain Carles Puyol – after heading his first goal for two years – ripped off his distinctive Catalan flag wristband and raised it aloft to a deeply unappreciative Bernabéu crowd. Barça, behind four minutes earlier, led 2-1.

As Barça seized the initiative, Messi began to dictate every aspect of the match. He was unplayable again that night – and with good reason. It was the first time that Pep had played him in a role of 'false nine'. In Graham Hunter's book, *Barça: The Making of the Greatest Team in the World*, Messi described how the strategy evolved: "Pep called me a day before El Clásico and he made me come to the Ciutat Esportiva to tell me that we were going to change the position. He had been watching matches with Tito Vilanova and they had decided to do something new. It was something new for Real Madrid too. They had studied us very well, but we had freedom when I pulled back and the central defenders had to try and cover Samuel (Eto'o) and Henry." Xavi also referred to this in a later interview when commenting; "The coach put Leo in as a 'false nine' because knew that Madrid's defenders wouldn't follow Messi when he dropped back into midfield, which meant that Messi, Iniesta and I could play a three-on-two in the middle of the pitch. Pep said to us: 'And that is where the game is! That is where the game is!'"

Pep was right. Time and time again Messi carved open Real's defence and his own personal reward came 10 minutes before half-time. Xavi seized on a mistake by Lassana Diarra and played Leo in. Only Casillas stood between him and a potential title-winning goal and as good a custodian as 'San Iker' was, he had no chance with Messi bearing down on goal with an assassin's look in his eye. At 3-1 up going into the break, and having put on an exhibition of passing football, the game was Barça's to lose.

The start of the second half didn't go to plan and, as in the first 45, the hosts scored first. Sergio Ramos was unmarked in the six-yard box and rose highest to head Real back into it. Lightning struck twice, however, because within two minutes Henry had scored again. As Real's already dangerously high line pushed still closer to the centre circle, Xavi lofted a perfectly timed ball into Henry's path. Casillas, inexplicably, had raced 25 yards out of goal and had to get to the ball first but was nowhere near it. As he jumped, Henry pushed the ball under him and into a gaping empty net.

It was as if the life had been sucked out of the Bernabéu at that point, but worse was to follow. Real had not lost in the league since the previous Clásico, Juande Ramos' first game in charge, a run of 20 games, but they looked like cannon fodder, with Barça threatening to score with every attack. Enjoying such dominance, it was a surprise it took until 15 minutes from time for the visitors to claim their fifth. Messi received a ball from Dani Alves 35 yards from goal and aside from Xavi he had eight Real Madrid players closer to him than any team-mates. A short pass to Xavi, followed by a pirouette from the midfielder and a pass back to Messi's feet and, no more than five seconds after Alves' initial pass, the Argentinian was one-on-one with Casillas. Sitting the 'keeper down was a little cruel but it was all too easy. Goal number 36 for Leo and to add insult to injury, there was still time for more.

Passionate Catalan Piqué, in a move that would later come to be seen as a different aspect of his game, set off on a lung-bursting run into the heart of Real territory. Denied at the first attempt, he outfoxed the Real Madrid's back line with his second shot from an acute angle. It was the first time Real had conceded six or more to Barça since September 24, 1950, and began a run of five consecutive defeats which ended both their league title hopes and Juande Ramos's tenure. His contract up, he was replaced by Manuel Pellegrini.

MARCA called it 'a practically perfect game' from the visitors, with Casillas philosophical in defeat. "When you play against a steamroller, you can't do anything," he said in the immediate aftermath of his most embarrassing defeat to that point. Guardiola might have crowed, but instead paid tribute to Real as well as his own players. "I would like to congratulate Madrid," he said to reporters. "A month and a half ago, we could've been champions, but Madrid ensured we had to show our faces tonight. Today we've taken a great step, an immense one, but we had to come here and get a result in order to put the title to bed. We had talked about a small detail, putting Messi as centre-forward and Eto'o on the wing, but it's the quality of the players that caused the imbalances. It's the players that make everything work and it's easier with these players."

If there was a concern, it was the possibility that it had taken too much out of them ahead of the away meeting with Chelsea, but the mood of optimism among fans gathering in West London was strikingly upbeat. Odd as it may now seem, Barça's history of big game failures meant *culés* were generally pessimistic before them, and many supporters were surprised at feeling so positive.

Pessimism may have been restored when Michael Essien put Chelsea ahead with a volley so astonishing that many away fans applauded it. Barça were now behind in the tie, and Chelsea threatened to overrun them, but they stuck to the style which had served them so well. Pep had given the team specific instructions and to change them now would be a risk in itself. With limited goalmouth action, the game remained finely poised and both sets of fans were increasingly nervous, knowing that a late away goal would seal the tie for Barça.

Aside from the goal that did send Barça through, the 'Iniestazo', the game is always remembered for referee Tom Henning Øvrebø's decision not to award Chelsea a penalty despite there being at least four reasonable appeals, two fairly blatant. By the time he'd waved away the last of those, Guardiola was left with a conundrum. Dani Alves would be ruled out of any final after receiving a booking, whilst Eric Abidal had been red carded when Nicolas Anelka tripped over his own feet. It was one of many decisions that the official got wrong on the night, admitting in 2018: "It was not my best day really. Some days you're not at the level you should be. I can't be proud of that performance. There were several errors and everyone will have their opinion of those plays. There were handball situations. I understand that people think different to the decisions I made at the time." Within a year he'd retired from refereeing altogether, his performance in that game ensuring he'd not be handed any meaningful fixtures again. English media reports that he had to be smuggled out of the country were quickly rubbished by Rune Pedersen, a Norwegian spokesman, who explained Øvrebø's change of hotel had already been pre-planned.

Messi had been quiet by his standards, but in no way poor. He had linked well all night with Alves, Xavi and Iniesta, and the passage of play where he would prove his worth once more just happened to come after 90 minutes. With Chelsea's legs tiring and thoughts surely turning to a second successive Champions League final, Xavi found Alves bombing down Chelsea's left side. His deep cross was headed out of danger by Terry, who lived up to his 'captain fantastic' moniker on the night, but when Eto'o's heavy touch on the edge of the box dropped to an exhausted Essien, he failed to clear the ball and it rolled past him to a lurking Messi. With three opponents closing quickly, Messi had the presence of mind and foresight to find the only unmarked Barcelona attacker on the pitch. A right-footed pass found Iniesta in the D on the edge of Chelsea's area and he didn't even need to break stride. BOOM! No stopping that one. As the ball bounced down from the roof of the net, all hell broke loose in the Barça end, on the pitch and inside the Barça dugout.

Pep took temporary leave of his senses as he sprinted down the touchline quicker than he ever did as a player. Iniesta led his team-mates over to the corner of the ground behind the goal, where the away fans were going berserk, windmilling his shirt over his head. Barça had done it, with just 90 seconds left. The image of Didier Drogba at full-time screaming, "It's a fucking disgrace" into the TV cameras was an enduring one for those watching at home and, in fairness, he had a point, but the *culés* didn't care. They were on their way to the Champions League final.

Meanwhile, there was still the matter of a Copa del Rey, and with it a domestic double, to win against Athletic Club at Mestalla. Another astonishing team performance had Messi at the heart of everything. Athletic Club scored first, but didn't really stand a chance. Yaya Touré's stunning solo effort made it 1-1 at half-time and three goals in nine second-half minutes – Messi firing the first through a crowd of opponents, Bojan passing home the second via a post and Xavi's unstoppable free-kick – enabled Barça to win at a canter. With the domestic cup and league now settled, thoughts very definitely turned to the Champions League final against Manchester United.

9

A Deserved Ballon D'Or

The First of Many

"With his intelligence and his football ability, he would adapt to anything"

At the Stadio Olimpico, Pep had one pre-match ace up his sleeve. Once the warm-ups were complete, the players returned to a pitch-black dressing room. Guardiola stood in front of a screen that was about to play a short film which would have an incredible impact on his team.

May 27, 2009: Leo shared the pitch on many occasions with Cristiano Ronaldo. On this occasion it was at the Stadio Olimpico in Rome for the 2009 Champions League Final against Manchester United. (© Shutterstock)

He'd hatched a plan with Catalan journalist, Santi Padro, to produce something that would make the players feel 10 feet tall when they stepped out on the pitch. It worked a treat. To the strains of the theme from the film *Gladiator*, Padro had curated a video presenting the highlights of the season, and ensured every player in the squad was featured. As a motivational tool it couldn't have worked any better, Thierry Henry latterly noting that "It was so powerful ... I would also say it was too powerful! After the video, Pep just said, 'Guys, at the end of the game I want people to say we can play football. Have a good game'." Victor Valdés, like many of his colleagues, was also blown away. "The boss was very sentimental, and after warming up I went to the dressing room but was told I couldn't go in because the boss was preparing something. When I finally got in, I had no time to prepare properly and it was sweltering hot. Then he showed us the video that had all of us in tears."

I spoke to Santi Padro about his part in the triumph, a moment of which he is still rightly proud. His friendship with Pep was the starting point for the idea.

"I'd known Pep since he started playing in the first team at FC Barcelona. I recorded a report for TV3 and that's where our relationship began. He was only 19 years old. That was another era, when you could have friendships with Barça players, but now it's very different. We're still friends now though. Pep was and is curious, very intelligent and has a great quality; he knows how to listen and also to ask. He's a sponge that talks to many people, collects many opinions and, in the end, he, as a leader, decides. We had talked a lot about the videos and montages that I made for television. The first one that he asked me to do was in 2008, for the decisive game of Barça B's promotion from the Tercera [Third] Division to the Segunda B [Second]. With the one in 2009, he sent me a message just after Andrés Iniesta's goal against Chelsea at Stamford Bridge. He told me: 'I need your help to win the Champions League.' We had a meeting at the Ciutat Esportiva Joan Gamper [Barça's training facility], and all he asked me was to keep the video short, that all of the players appeared in it, and that he wasn't seen in it at all. The idea for 'Gladiator' came from Pere Guardiola, Pep's brother. He worked for Nike and had used that movie in a motivational talk. I watched the film and then needed to find some footage that might fit into the video, for example: 'There was a dream that was Rome.' Together with the team of usual collaborators at TV3, we searched for the images and goals that I thought I would need. To assemble the video, we stayed from 11pm on the Sunday night before the final until 7am in the morning. On the Monday afternoon I went to deliver the video to Pep and on Wednesday the final was played."

The decision to make the video was also top secret, with only a handful of people knowing of its existence before it was unveiled. "The first person to see the video was Pep, in his office at the Ciutat Esportiva," Santi continued.

"He and I alone. Afterwards, Pep showed it to Tito Vilanova and Manel Estiarte. We ended up watching it again in the video room [where Pep would explain various tactical ideas to the players and look over footage of previous matches], with almost all of Pep's technical staff. It was, for me, an unforgettable day. I still get goosebumps when I remember it. My bosses at TV3 didn't know anything about the video because I did it as a favour for a friend who asked me for help. I didn't think that the video would be broadcast, until Pep told me after seeing it: 'If we win the Champions League, you must put the video on TV3.' My bosses, afterwards, were more than satisfied by the great reaction to the video broadcast. It was such a powerful video that it made some of the players feel unbeatable and I was very excited that a video montage could affect them so deeply. The truth is that after all these years, I have spoken to many of those players who were in the dressing room that night and what's most important to me is that the video worked very well for them. I therefore have the feeling that I was part of the eternal team that ended up winning the six cups. I contributed my knowledge and my experience to help a friend, and he gave me the gift of being able to showcase my work and that of my entire team of collaborators on TV3. As Johan Cruyff always said; 'Gallina de piel' [goose bumps]."

Despite the Barça players striding onto the pitch feeling like Catalan gladiators, United completely dominated the opening 10 minutes. Cristiano Ronaldo went close and was clearly in the mood, but he and the rest of his team-mates were completely deflated when, against the run of play, Iniesta was allowed to run deep into the heart of enemy territory before finding Eto'o who, after cutting inside, poked Barça ahead. The goal changed the game. From that

May 27, 2009: Leo's goal in the Champions League final was his first against an English club and secured a 2-0 victory. (© Shutterstock)

point onwards, Pep's men took control and outplayed United for long periods. By the time Messi claimed the second, killer, goal – his first against English opponents – with 20 minutes left, rising high to guide Xavi's cross beyond an open-mouthed Edwin van der Sar, the game was up.

The flip side of Barça's shared joy was the abject misery for anyone connected with Manchester United, such as their first-team assistant manager, Mike Phelan, who spoke to me about that unforgetable night in Rome:

> "Eto'o's goal didn't automatically alter anything. In a game of football of that magnitude, scoring early isn't necessarily the be all and end all. Ten minutes into a game you feel as though you've still got a little bit to offer. The problem was it became a key moment, because when Barcelona got in front, even though we knew we'd get opportunities, it was going to be very difficult to wrestle possession from them. That was going to be a real issue. When someone is leading in a game and they're of the magnitude of Barcelona, you think 'ok there's still 85 minutes left in the grand scheme of things' but 75 minutes of that could be controlled by them. Opportunities for us were always going to be few and far between but one goal was never going to be the end of the world either.

We went behind and Sir Alex and I were looking at how our players were going to react to that, what were the areas on the field where we could hurt them, and so our game began to change as the minutes ticked by. That last 20 minutes was when Barcelona had us really, because we had to open up a little bit more, we had to take more risks. Some games you see Barcelona play and they punish you in that final period with three or four goals. With Messi's goal, there were elements of errors on our part for sure, but they put us in those positions. I think Messi himself finished it the way Messi does. There's a lot you can get away with out on the field if you're at a certain level, where it might take two or three opportunities before the opposition are clinical, but certainly in Messi's case, give him one opportunity and he is clinical – that was the difference. We hoped he wouldn't get that one opportunity but it was very difficult to stop it, and it didn't help that we were making mistakes. Barcelona as a team, as soon as you make an error, they're in your face and at you with their superior movement. It's exactly what they do to teams. We were more than aware of those facts but it was still almost impossible to deal with them. They dominated us."

Ronaldo, overall, had a poor game by his standards, and completing the treble – the first time it had been achieved in Spain – meant that it wouldn't be long before Messi took the Portuguese's Ballon d'Or crown. With so many comparing the two prior to that 2009 showpiece, and innumerable times since, Phelan was simply happy to recall what both had brought to that final, and to the game in general.

"The one thing about Messi and Ronaldo is that both had an extreme desire to be the best. They've been at the pinnacle of their careers for years now, and done it at the top level consistently. That's what they both had in abundance. I can only observe Messi because I never worked with him, but they are challenging individuals, both to themselves and to the people around them. They've maintained that challenge for a long, long time. The differences between them from my point of view are certainly not attitude and application, they've both got loads of that, but they have different styles. Ronaldo's all-round game is probably more robust, more dynamic from the point of view of power and speed, whilst Messi is down to technique, skill and awareness. An awareness of players around him, and an understanding of space.

Ronaldo was the real deal as far as him and football goes. Could he develop the team ethic along the way? He ended up being a far more capable player than when he was at Man United, and he was brilliant for us, but he took a lot of things from his journey in football which was different to Messi's. Leo was at one club for god knows how long, since he was a kid, an association that's been unbelievable really, but Ronaldo's journey was different. He experienced different things at different clubs and, as such, had a different perspective and understanding of the game. As to the question of whether Messi could do it on a wet Wednesday in Stoke (laughs), he would've adapted. With his intelligence and his football ability, he would adapt to anything. He's a footballer that wants to play football and football is played all over the world in the same way. Same rules, same regulations. He would've found a way, just like Ronaldo found a way from Portugal to England, England to Spain, Spain to Italy. They were driven enough to find a way, and Messi was one of the best ever, in any division in any part of the world. Talent like that is for everybody to see and he used it wherever he wanted to play football."

The conundrum facing Guardiola ahead of his second season was how to improve on 'perfection'. In the end, everything had fallen into place in 2008-09, but surely it was going to be impossible to replicate? If the team needed regenerating, how were new players going to be assimilated into the best team in the world? Some tough decisions needed to be made and so Eto'o, Aleksandr Hleb, Eidur Gudjohnsen, Martín Cáceres, Henrique and Sylvinho were dispensed with. Dmytro Chyhrynskyi, an imposing 22-year-old centre-back from Shakhtar Donetsk, proved to be a terrible purchase, though the intriguing hire was Zlatan Ibrahimović in a swap for Eto'o (+ €46m). "Ibrahimović is a fantastic player, is very powerful and can do everything at the greatest level," Pep noted at the press conference for the Swede's unveiling. His 11 goals in his first 14 games, including the winner against Real Madrid, appeared to justify this assessment.

Ibrahimović's arrival forced a slight change to the way Barça played. Big target men had rarely been part of their game. Though there was some logic to having a more physical, aerially dominant centre-forward in situ, it would still take some getting used to.

Two early trophies were claimed. Messi scored twice, one from an Ibrahimović assist, as Barça claimed the Supercopa de España title over two legs against Athletic Club. Then, on a dreadful pitch

August 19, 2009: FC Barcelona beat Manchester City 1-0 in the pre-season Joan Gamper Trophy match. (© Tsutomu Takasu)

at Monaco's Stade Louis-II which prevented much football being played, Pedro's stabbed 115th-minute finish from Messi's pass won the UEFA Super Cup against Shakhtar.

Ibrahimović's incredible start helped keep Barça unbeaten in the league in the first half of the campaign. A goal against Sporting Gijón marked his league debut, and goals in his next four league games made him the first Barça player to score in every one of their opening five league appearances, and by the time Real Madrid came to town at the end of November, the Swede was really in the groove. "I was clear in front of the goal and shot a volley with my left foot," he recalled in his autobiography, *I Am Zlatan*. "Bang, boom, goal, and the stadium woke up like a volcano. I felt in my body that nothing can stop me now. We won 1-0. I was the man of the match and was praised everywhere. At that moment no one questioned my price of almost €70m. I was on fire."

In other weeks, his heroics would have dominated the headlines, but his luck was out. Just two days later Messi claimed his first *Ballon d'Or* by a record margin. Cristiano Ronaldo, the previous season's recipient, was beaten into second place by 240 points, as the 96 journalists from around the world awarded Messi an incredible 473 points from a possible 480.

Given his and Barça's dominance, there was never any doubt about it. "Honestly, I knew that I was among the favourites because Barcelona had a fruitful year in 2009," Messi told *France Football*. "But I didn't expect to win by such a margin. The Ballon d'Or is very important to me. All the players who won it were great players, and some great players never won it. For me, it's a big honour to win. I dedicate it to my family, they were always present when I needed them and sometimes felt even stronger emotions than me." He was also named FIFA World Player of the Year in the award's final year before being merged with the Ballon d'Or in 2010 to become the FIFA Ballon d'Or – a far glitzier and more professional event befitting the best players on the planet.

In spite of the awards and the unbeaten league run, not all was well with Messi at Barça. He was used to being the main man, with the team dynamic tailored to his game, and his awards only strengthened his position, but accommodating Ibrahimović meant he was shunted out to the wing most weeks. In nine games leading up to their semi-final in the Club World Cup against Mexico's Atlante in Qatar, he neither scored or assisted, evidence of a more peripheral role he was never going to accept for long. Writing in *I am Zlatan*, the Swedish striker noted that his Barcelona career "started well but then Messi began to talk. He wanted to play in the middle, not on the wing, so the system changed from 4-3-3 to 4-5-1. I was sacrificed and no longer had the freedom on the pitch that I needed to succeed." There appeared to be no love lost between the pair, and the drop off in Zlatan's form in the new year was marked.

Against Atlante, a side which featured future Real Madrid coach, Santiago Solari, Messi was instrumental despite not playing the first 53 minutes. Though comfortable for the most part, Guardiola's side were only drawing 1-1 thanks to Sergio Busquets' equaliser just before half-time. Within two minutes, Messi gave Barça the lead and 12 minutes later Pedro made the game safe. Argentina's Club Estudiantes de La Plata stood between Barça and the historic feat of winning all six titles possible in a calendar year. Their captain, Juan Sebastián Verón, was confident ahead of the game, and with good reason. Their manager, Alejandro Sabella, who would later manage Messi at national team level, had built a side who were not only able to handle themselves physically, but could play a bit too. As Graham Hunter recounted in his book, *Barça: The Making of the Greatest Team in the World*, Guardiola was philosophical about the result, whichever way it went. "The most important day of our lives?" he'd opined. "I hope not, because we all have wives, children or other family at home. But the future is bleak because there is no way we can improve on what we've achieved so far."

Sabella had clearly done his homework, and Estudiantes more than held their own in the opening stages of the match played at the Zayed Sports City stadium, ensuring that the supply line into the forwards from Xavi, Busquets or Keita never operated smoothly. When the opening goal came, in the 37th minute, it was the Argentinians who were celebrating. Mauro Boselli got in between Carles Puyol and Eric Abidal to thump a header home for a lead they held until the final minute of normal time. Far from the dominant force many expected, Barça had controlled the game at some points but ceded control at others. Had the score stayed at 1-0 in favour of their opponents, it's unlikely there'd have been too many complaints. The fat lady was clearing her throat as the clock ticked over into the 88th minute. Estudiantes were so near and yet so far. Pedro, who'd scored in every competition that Barça had played in 2009, was in the right place at the right time – and completely unmarked – to guide a looping header over Damián Albil and into the net. The short break before extra-time started gave Guardiola the chance to exercise his oratorical gifts, and Barça looked a different proposition in extra-time.

With 10 minutes left Dani Alves received the ball out wide on the right and in acres of space. Allowed far too much time and space to deliver a cross, he picked out Messi just outside the six-yard box, but the ball dipped too low to be headed. Flinging himself at the ball, Messi scored with his chest, the only one of his hundreds of goals to be scored with that part of his anatomy. It proved to be the winner. Guardiola was overcome, breaking down post-match in floods of tears. "For me this was a great year," he said after the match. "We have achieved something that no one has achieved before. I'm lucky that I have such quality players in my squad. The success that we've had has been down to them and I'd like to thank them for that. To win six successive titles is unthinkable. So many things contributed to it; having few injuries, a squad made up of players who play because they like to, mental strength ... everyone should be happy and congratulations to the club and everyone associated with Barça. We've had the best year in the history of the club."

Verón, though defeated, was unbowed. "We were so close it hurts," he told reporters: "But unfortunately football's like that. Sometimes it gives and other times it takes away. We set our stall out intelligently, we all ran our socks off and we gave it everything. They couldn't find a way past us and then, right at the end, they levelled via an odd passage of play, with a high ball into the box. Perhaps our only regret is that the game didn't finish earlier! The sheer strength of our opponents must be taken into account too. For many stretches of the game, you couldn't tell which side had all the star names and at no point did they ever feel that they had the game under control. What's more, I dare say that if we'd been a touch more clinical, we could even have scored another goal. We gave everything we had and came into this tournament with the bare bones. It's been a long year with a small squad. Though I'm aware that Barcelona have also played a lot of games, the respective substitutions the teams made during the game underlines the point I'm trying to make. I'm very proud of this squad and this club and I think the other lads should be too. We had Barcelona on the ropes in the final of a Club World Cup. I think that sums up what we did at this tournament. Our minds should be at ease because we gave our very best, and over the pain of losing and the sadness we're feeling, we'd like to congratulate Barcelona on their victory."

Losing to Sevilla in the Copa del Rey Round of 16 first leg ended the run of consecutive trophies, but only two more games would be lost in all competitions that season as Guardiola continued to press for more running, more intensity and more goals. There was only one league loss, in week 22 to Atlético Madrid, and Barça were never lower than second. Messi hit a purple patch in March scoring 10 goals in four games, including two hat-tricks, but Zlatan's output tailed off significantly. He didn't score in the league again until February, and managed only four more league goals towards the tail end of the season. Messi had got his wish at the expense of shunting the previous summer's signing out of the limelight. Their mismatch was evident in the Champions League quarter-final against Arsenal. Zlatan's double secured a 2-2 draw in the first leg at the Emirates Stadium, with Messi unusually off colour, but with the Swede missing for the return at Camp Nou just under a week later on April 6, Messi had another night when everything turned to gold.

Nicklas Bendtner gave the Gunners an 18th-minute lead, but their dreams were dispelled within three minutes as Messi rifled the equaliser past a helpless Manuel Almunia. With eight minutes to go before half-time, Pedro played in Messi for his second after a marauding run by Eric Abidal. His pièce de résistance wasn't far behind, a simple clearing header from Seydou Keita putting Messi through on goal despite starting his run just inside the Arsenal half. Almunia stood tall, but the Argentinian's sweet caress and chip into an empty net had the whole stadium purring. He rounded off his, and Barça's, evening with a fourth in the second half, setting up a semi-final clash with José Mourinho and to Inter Milan.

Leo was almost as inspired four days later at the Santiago Bernabéu in the second Clásico of the campaign, again terrorising the Real defence and creating the opening goal with a one-two with Xavi. Guardiola had, improbably, won his first four league Clásicos as coach. Two more League wins set Barça up for the Champions league semi with Inter Milan, where both José Mourinho and Samuel Eto'o were keen to prove points to their former club.

Pedro gave Barça an early lead at the San Siro, but they were under the cosh for long periods. Wesley Sneijder brought Inter level before the break and a rare goal from full-back Maicon, put the Italians in control. Diego Milito's hard-working performance was eventually rewarded with a third, as the reigning champions were put on the rack, the dream of hearing their club hymn played at full volume at the Santiago Bernabéu, venue for the final, put in serious jeopardy by Inter's deserved first-leg victory.

It was all or nothing a week later in Barcelona. Inter and Mourinho came to frustrate, and nothing went right for the hosts who were trying just that bit too hard. Then, with six minutes left, Gerard Piqué pirouetted in the area and brought the Catalans to within one goal of going through. In injury time, Bojan fired into the roof of the net but the officials ruled out the goal for a supposed handball from Yaya Touré in the build-up. That was it, the last chance to reach two successive finals had gone and the *Nerazzurri* were through. Mourinho didn't waste the opportunity to gloat. As soon as the final whistle sounded, he sprinted onto the pitch, circling wildly with his hands raised, a finger pointing skywards as though to say 'No.1'.

Victor Valdés was having none of it and chased Mourinho, attempting to get him to put his hands down. TV cameras would capture every last detail and 'The Special One' milked the moment for all that it was worth – a pretty classless display of one-upmanship and machismo he would top on a future trip to the city. The deflated Guardiola had further problems to contend with. The next game saw Villarreal torn to shreds 4-1 by a wounded Barcelona, but Zlatan was furious to be allowed only a cursory five minutes, and his outburst at the next training session effectively sealed his exit from the club. "He was staring at me and I lost it," Zlatan recalled. "I thought 'there is my enemy, scratching his bald head.' I yelled to him: 'You have no balls!' And probably worse things than that. I added 'you are shitting yourself because of Mourinho. You can go to hell.' I was completely mad and I threw a box full of training gear across the room. It crashed to the floor and Pep said nothing, just putting the stuff back in the box. I'm not violent, but if I were Guardiola, I would've been frightened."

Messi had scored twice in that game and added five more in Barça's final three games before joining Argentina for the World Cup. If the team had been under pressure to perform in 2006, it was nothing compared to 2010. The world's best player would be expected to lead *La Albiceleste* to glory, but it wasn't to be his greatest tournament...

10

El Clásico Overkill

The Wars of Attrition

"For me, the most awesome thing about Leo is his tireless capacity to decide every match he plays"

The 2010 World Cup tournament in South Africa was a milestone for many of Lionel Messi's club colleagues. It was Spain's first, and to date only, title triumph and had an FC Barcelona imprint all over it. That Andrés Iniesta would bookend the tournament with the winning goal against the Netherlands was somewhat poetic, but the Argentinian wouldn't share in the joy. Prior to *La Albiceleste*'s ill-fated meeting with Germany in the quarter-finals, Messi had failed to score in any of their previous four matches. Indeed, it was a hugely disappointing few weeks for someone who always seemed to come alive at the big tournaments. He had numerous chances to open his account in the 1-0 win in the opening Group B game against Nigeria, and a 4-1 thumping of South Korea, but failed to take them. Not that it concerned him, telling reporters after the victory over the Koreans: "It's not a problem, the important thing is that I had opportunities and although the ball didn't go in, eventually it will. The goals will come. I am happy that Gonzalo Higuaín scored a hat-trick against South Korea and I am delighted for the team. We took a step forward with respect to our opening game and hopefully we will take another one in our final game. We are in a good position. We have almost assured ourselves a place in the next round so everyone is calm and looking forward to our next game against Greece."

There were even suggestions that Argentina's coach, the prodigal son, Diego Maradona, should bench Messi for the final group game. "Lionel Messi always wants to play and I thought I should give him a break [in training], but if you have a player as good as Leo, who is the best player in the world, I think it would be a sin not to give Messi to the people, to the team, and leave out the player who can certainly make a difference in a match," Maradona remarked, when asked. "He goes out to play and help his team-mates. Leo helps define the match and creates things for the other players. If Messi is having a bad run then let him continue with that bad run, because I'm extremely pleased with Messi's performances."

Back home in Barcelona, Laporta's former friend and board member, Sandro Rosell succeeded him as president, winning 61 per cent of the 57,000 or so votes cast, a turnout he hailed as showing "the fans desire to play their part and show commitment to the club".

Cocooned away from Camp Nou politics, Messi continued to struggle in South Africa. He was still below his best when Argentina schooled Greece 2-0 to top their group, and the Round of 16 victory over Mexico is mostly remembered for the clearly offside goal headed-in by Carlos Tevez from a Messi pass after *El Tri* had more than held their own in the opening 25 minutes. "In a split second referees can spoil everything," Mexico coach, Javier Aguirre, said after the match. "Everyone is human but we lost concentration because of that decision, it hit us hard. The error for the second goal came because of that, and that was what changed the match dramatically." Higuaín then bagged a second and the game was effectively over as a contest. Another goal from Tevez in the second half made Javier Hernández's late goal nothing more than a consolation.

Any thoughts that Argentina's name was on the cup after that performance were dispelled by a brutally efficient German side in the quarter-finals. Maradona was close to tears at the final whistle, as the realisation finally dawned that his tactics just weren't good enough. Thomas Müller's third-minute opener was a warning shot, but in spite of being outplayed for much of the game *La Albiceleste* were still in it going into the latter stages. Messi put in a full shift, but was no more able than his team-mates to take the game by the scruff of the neck, and once Miroslav Klose added Germany's second with 22 minutes to play they were opened up as they chased the game. Arne Friedrich and Klose, again, rounded off the 4-0 scoreline which accurately reflected the balance of play. Messi had been kept goalless for the entire tournament, whilst the new contract initially offered to Maradona was later rescinded.

Back in Catalonia, FC Barcelona had signed Spain striker David Villa from Valencia and, just before the beginning of the season, added

Javier Mascherano, Messi's long-time team-mate at international level. Ibrahimović departed, with his ego, to Milan while Thierry Henry had gone to New York Red Bulls and Yaya Touré to Manchester City. Guardiola and Rosell had already clashed over Chyhrynskyi, the coach wanting to keep him while the new president wanted to recoup some of the cash used to buy him. "My opinion counts, but the needs of the club go above that and that's why he was sold, I would like to have kept him," Pep told a press conference before the season kicked-off in earnest.

Elsewhere, José Mourinho's treble-winning campaign with Inter had earned him the Real Madrid job, but the first Clásico was not until the end of November. The domestic season began with a second successive Spanish Super Cup victory, but it was hardly straightforward, with a Messi hat-trick in the second leg at Camp Nou needed to overturn Sevilla's 3-1 lead from the Ramón Sánchez Pizjuán. Then promoted Hércules took Barça's unbeaten home record dating back to May 2009, fully exploiting Pep's decision to name Sergio Busquets, Xavi, Carles Puyol and Pedro on the bench. By the time Xavi and Pedro were introduced after the break, Nelson Valdez already had the visitors ahead, and he doubled their lead on the hour. Victor Valdés's 89th-minute save from former Juventus striker, David Trezeguet, spared even greater embarassment but it was still the first time that the *Blaugranes* had been beaten by two clear goals since Pep had taken over. A seismic shock of a result, and *MARCA* were perhaps the politest with their 'Barça collide with Hércules' headline, going on to say that "Coach Esteban Vigo was the only one who trusted his team, and ended up shutting the mouths of all those who had accused him of dreaming".

Messi hadn't got going in common with most of his team-mates, and Pep blamed a lack of intensity for the defeat. "We couldn't find the spaces inside, and against such teams that keep things tight, it becomes difficult if you're not precise. They went ahead and we didn't know how to fix it. I see how we work every day and I don't have doubts about my team, but a difficult and hard year awaits us." If a kick up the backside was needed, it clearly worked. Barça would not lose again in the league until week 34, against Real Sociedad at their bogey ground, Anoeta.

Leo had scored in 10 consecutive matches, including the winner for Argentina against Brazil and a hat-trick in an 8-0 rout away at Almería, but his season might have already been over before it had really begun. In just the third league match of the season, away at Atlético Madrid, he was carried off on a stretcher, with serious damage feared, after a reckless challenge from Tomáš Ujfaluši. He'd put Barça ahead on 13 minutes, but Raúl García equalised in the 25th. Just after the half hour, Gerard Piqué restored Barça's lead, and a handful of half chances aside, there was no significant goalmouth action. Andrés Iniesta's World Cup heroics were recognised with an incredible standing ovation from the Vicente Calderón when he was subbed off, but all of the talk was about Leo, who held his head in his hands as he was carried off. Running at full speed, Ujfaluši simply steamed into him, coming down hard on his right ankle with no apparent attempt to play the ball whatsoever. His apology sounded a little hollow. "I wanted to apologise. It wasn't my intention to hurt Leo. I wanted to play the ball and had the misfortune to hit Leo when I came down on his leg. Yes it was scary to see his ankle bent, but it was not my intention to hurt him. Today I have sent a message through Agüero to apologise."

The initial prognosis from the club doctor's was that Leo could be out 'for weeks', but he was back in 10 days, playing 31 minutes against Rubin Kazan before setting off on a spectacular scoring run. Starting with a goal against Mallorca two weeks after his injury, he scored in every game but one before Real Madrid came to town on November 29. *Los Blancos* arrived unbeaten with Mourinho having made the best start of any Real coach in the club's history.

What followed was beyond the wildest dreams of most *culés*. It was as good a footballing masterclass as you're ever likely to see. Mourinho was glued to his seat for the most part, unable to stem the tide, just a few short months after lording it over 99,000 Barça fans. Long before Xavi had opened the scoring, thanks to a pinpoint Iniesta pass, the hosts were on top. Messi was the width of a post from scoring what would surely have been one of the most impudent goals ever seen. With no backlift he still managed to chip Casillas from the edge of the area, and with three defenders in close proximity. Soon after he would probe and prompt before feeding Iniesta to tee up Xavi. Although the finish was slightly fortuitous, no one could argue that it wasn't deserved. Marcelo's lack of awareness saw Pedro motor past him to add the second despite the Brazilian being three yards closer to the goal before the Canarian had started his run. It was a feisty affair with, just before half time, Cristiano Ronaldo incurring the wrath of the Camp Nou for pushing Pep Guardiola, and Messi was elbowed by Ricardo Carvalho which resulted in a yellow card for the Madrid player.

The second half began with Barça, and Messi in particular, really coming into their own. He supplied the assists for David Villa's two goals, both inside the space of two minutes, just before the hour. An eye-of-the-needle pass for Villa's second was one of those 'worth it for the admission money alone' moments. Holding the ball just inside the Real half, he was surrounded by three Madrid players, but in a split second rode a roughhouse challenge and zipped the ball in between centre-back Pepe and right-back Sergio Ramos. Villa didn't even have to break stride as he slid the ball under the advancing Casillas – that's how good the pass was. Substitute, Jeffrén, had time to add a fifth, prompting a huge celebration on the touchline from which Gerard Piqué emerged holding up five fingers (the '*manita*') for the cameras. *Los Blancos* were well and truly put to the sword in a 90-minute festival of football that is regarded by many as the best club performance ever seen.

Scoring that goal, Jeffrén explained to me in an interview:

"was one of the best moments I experienced in Barcelona. I went out to enjoy the few minutes that were left to finish the game, and I did! When the goal arrived it was a moment of great joy. I learned a lot with Pep Guardiola, on a daily basis. With him, above all, I learned how to read and analyse the matches better, and it was undoubtedly a good time. Being at the best Barcelona in history has to be respected."

As the game ticked into injury time, it was all too much for Sergio Ramos who hacked down Messi and then pushed both Carles Puyol and Xavi in the face. A red card was referee Iturralde González's only option, and it was a sour end to proceedings. The tenth league red for Ramos, as a Madrid player, came in just his 175th league game and equalled Fernando Hierro's record red card count but in 264 fewer matches. Ramos' petulance didn't, however, define the match. Even though he'd failed to score for the first time in 10 matches it was Messi's influence on proceedings that attracted the plaudits. A match billed, like so many Clásicos at the time, as the Messi v Ronaldo show had only one winner. Mourinho couldn't get down the tunnel quickly enough after his heaviest ever defeat as a coach. "One team played at the highest level and the other very badly," he told his press conference. "It's a defeat, not a humiliation. I have always said that Barça are the finished product and Madrid have a long way to go. You have to have character. When you win titles you can cry with joy, but when you let in five, you have to leave with the will to train, play and win."

The elation of the ceremonial stuffing of Real Madrid changed to disbelief two weeks later when, on December 10, came a bombshell to stick, not just in the memories, but in the craw of all *culés*. It may have been inevitable but it was no less palatable. President Sandro Rosell announced that for the first time in the club's history, they would have a commercial sponsor, and not just any sponsor either – The Qatar Foundation. The outcry was, unsurprisingly, fierce and immediate, but club director, Javier Faus quickly sought to justify the move. "It's the biggest in the history of football – and at a time of economic crisis, too. It would not have been signed if it were not for the debt which, as we have said before, is between €420m and €430m."

Faus was referring to the disputed state of Barça's finances when Rosell had taken over from Laporta, the new board stating on multiple occasions that Laporta had misled everyone regarding the shape he'd left the club in. "We are talking about a non-commercial organisation, a charity from a country that wants to make itself known through education and sport – one that, as you know, will host the 2022 World Cup." The deal was a whopping €150m over five years, dwarfing every other shirt sponsorship deal worldwide and was double Real Madrid's by way of example. It wouldn't be effective until the beginning of the following campaign but there was still the issue of where the UNICEF branding would go. "The marketing departments of the club and Nike are looking at a way of combining it with UNICEF," Faus said.

Needless to say, the uproar amongst the fan base was vehement and sustained. Antonio Giralt expressed his sense of betrayal:

"Seeing Qatar on our glorious outfit was one of the most disgusting experiences as a Barça fan. We went from heaven to hell, sponsoring a country which does not respect any human rights and that funds global terrorism. I will never forgive Sandro Rosell for that – although a different story is his disgraceful and unfair imprisonment, without bail, for two years which is a political exhibition of anti-Catalanism by the third-worldish Spanish Justice. The change to Rakuten in 2017 was a great relief and, to be honest, I don't even realise the name on the shirts these days."

January 12, 2011: Andrés Iniesta and Xavi join Leo to celebrate his second Ballon d'Or. It was the first time three players from the club made up the podium for the award. (© Shutterstock)

Craig McGeough of Penya Blaugrana London also shared his concerns:

> "I always predicted we would end up in a conventional agreement with a conglomerate of some sort on the shirt, but I couldn't have predicted it would have something to do with Qatar. I assumed we would go with Audi, who sponsored the club cars, Estrella Damm or something relatively innocuous like Toshiba, for example. My overriding feeling was, is, and will always be how on earth do you square the circle of *Més que un club* and Qatar? It's impossible. It's oxymoronic. It's almost the most offensive affiliation the club could have chosen whilst still remaining within the realms of legal commercial organisations. In its own right, the deal would've been horrendous. To follow the deal with UNICEF, a deal which 'screamed' *Més que un club* from the most graceful of high horses, with a junta like Qatar ... *Qué verguenza* ['Shame on you']."

As the uproar continued in Catalonia, the eyes of the football world were focussed on the 2010 FIFA Ballon d'Or ceremony, which was a triumph for Barça and for Guardiola's methods with an unprecedented single-club monopoly of the podium, and all *La Masia* products. Unfortunately, for all of Xavi and Iniesta's achievements, there was only ever going to be one winner – Messi.

Another downside of the shirt sponship furore was that it detracted somewhat from the incredible fare being served up on the pitch, with Pep doing a remarkable job of keeping everyone focussed on the job in hand. Only two games, a league game at Betis and a Champions League match at Arsenal, were lost between the New Year and mid-April. The Arsenal defeat was overturned at Camp Nou thanks to another Messi masterclass, which included two goals and prompted Arsene Wenger to declare Leo not only the best in the world at that time, but the best to have ever played the game.

Agreeing with Wenger's sentiments, Alex Delmas – author of *Messi Tactico* – said to me:

"If football would like to be represented by one player in its history, I think it would choose Lionel Messi without any doubt. He is the perfect mix for this sport. If players such as Pelé or Maradona represented football talent, Xavi, Cruyff, Guardiola, Pirlo, Iniesta, Zidane represented the part of the sport that's more cerebral. Messi has both things. For me, the most awesome thing about Leo is his tireless capacity to decide every match he plays. All football players have the capacity to have some perfect days and be important in a match, and a few can do this more often, but there's just one that can decide every situation. It's impossible to teach a player to be another Messi because, in general, it's impossible to teach a player in all aspects. The margin for teaching football is limited. You can teach technical concepts and also game concepts, positioning or tactical concepts, but there is always a point where the talent of the player himself must come out. Football is a sport where you have to make decisions constantly and the most intelligent players take advantage of their talent and build the best environment possible to bring out their potential.

I think Leo is the best player in history so it's very uncomfortable for me to talk about any weaknesses. Undoubtedly, he is better today [2019] than he was ten years ago for example. At the beginning of his career he didn't get involved in free-kicks and he's now the best striker of a dead ball. Ten years ago he didn't use his right leg and now he does fantastically well with it. Maybe the only weakness is penalties. It's obvious that he can improve from 12 yards, but I also think that it is unfair to use a negative aspect to influence people's views of the best player that has ever played the game. Over time he's learned to play with his surroundings, to associate with others, to use the passing lines more effectively and, above all, understand matches. Today, and for many years now, he's been the best reader of a game in the world. I sincerely believe that you can't compare two players from different times because the difficulties of each season are also different. For example, the players that Leo has played against for many years will have improved in their physical preparation or creativeness, compared to earlier generations.

Nor do I think you can take the numbers as a reference point to compare. So I think we should compare football arguments and sensations. I firmly believe that Messi is the best footballer in history for two basic reasons: Pelé, Cruyff, Maradona, Beckenbauer, Best, Ronaldo, Zidane, Ronaldinho, Xavi, Cristiano, Iniesta.... they are all among the best in history but none of them are or were as complete as Leo. They were great for a few years, but never gave their maximum performances for a sustained period and certainly didn't decide games three times a week. Deciding games three times a week – that is simply impossible to achieve, but Leo has managed it for more than 15 years! Nobody dominates like him. The continuity in his performance levels is unrivalled. He even created his own style. He started being an unstoppable dribbler, and over the years he acquired new skills. Soon he became the best in the world but didn't stop improving. Messi will finish his career by being the best passer, the best goalscorer, the best organiser, the best dribbler, the best free-kick taker, the best competitor, the most decisive player. That easily makes him the best player of all time. Leo Messi is pure football and his legacy is incomparable!"

Real Madrid had recovered from the debacle in November, losing only two more league games, while their progress in cup competitions led to four Clásicos in the space of 18 days: the second league clash on 16 April, followed by the Copa del Rey final at Mestalla on April 20, then the little matter of a two-legged Champions League semi-final. It was unprecedented and felt a little like overkill. Who'd come out on top in the Messi v Ronaldo battle this time? Well, both as it happened.

The league match is generally the least remembered, though it wasn't without its controversies. Both teams wanted to to put down markers for the knock-out games to come, and get into the heads of their opponent. It ended in a 1-1 draw, from two penalties – Messi floating his 53rd-minute kick agonisingly over the outstretched hand of Iker Casillas, then Ronaldo needing no second invitation when Dani Alves was contentiously ruled to have fouled fellow Brazilian Marcelo nine minutes from time.

Next, it was onto Mestalla for the first Copa del Rey Clásico final in 21 years (the previous one was, coincidentally, also at Mestalla), and Real's first in 18, the longest they'd ever gone between finals. Of the five previous finals between the teams, the *Blaugranes* had won three and *Los Blancos* the other two. A sell-out 52,600 crowd was in full voice with a war of attrition expected. Referee Undiano Mallenco gave three free-kicks in the opening six minutes amid the cacophony of noise and fervour, but lost control of the game early on, something that Messi as much as anyone else wasn't shy in letting him know. Álvaro Arbeloa went unpunished for a stamp on David Villa, but a final total of four yellow cards in the second half and two in the first was probably just about right on the balance of play.

Messi was among those booked, but also went closest to scoring before the end of normal time. Nothing of note occurred in extra-time until Ángel Di María's slick one-two with Marcelo set the Argentinian free. A pinpoint cross found Ronaldo rising at the far post and his towering header beat Pinto all ends up. At full-time, *Los Blancos* celebrated and Mourinho quite happily turned the screw in his post-match press conference. "I am thrilled to win the Copa del Rey – it is something special. It's a fantastic triumph against a great team like Barcelona – and we deserved it. I came here to do a job and change the mentality of the club. We have started to do that and it's satisfying – but it's just the start. We knew that whoever scored first would win it – and so it proved." His cocksure manner had got under the skin of Barça's players and staff once too often, and they were determined that the strutting 'Special One' was going to eat his words. Within a fortnight, the two Champions League semi-finals would be completed, but who would still be standing at the end of them?

If football is all about timing, Leo's magnificent performance at the Santiago Bernabéu the following week was as accurate as a Swiss timepiece. Mourinho hadn't been able resist another jibe at Pep in his pre-match press conference. "Up until now there was a very small group of coaches who didn't talk about referees and a very large group, in which I am included, who criticise referees. Now, with Pep's comments, we have started a new era with a third group, featuring only one person, a man who criticises the referee when he makes good decisions. This is completely new to me." Pep duly took the bait at Barça's final training session: "Señor Mourinho has permitted himself the luxury of calling me Pep, so I will call him José. Tomorrow at 8.45pm we face each other on the pitch. He has won the battle off the pitch. If he wants his own personal Champions League trophy away from the pitch, let him take it home and enjoy it. In this [press] room, he is the *puto jefe*, the *puto amo* – the fucking boss, the fucking master. And I don't want to compete with him for a moment. I know him and he knows me. If he prefers to value the views of the journalist friends who take their information in a drip feed from Florentino Pérez more than the relationship we had for four years then that's his choice. I try to learn from José on the pitch, but I prefer to learn as little as possible from him off the pitch."

It galvanised Barça's players to a man and by the time kick-off arrived the next day Messi was like a coiled spring, primed to unleash an electrifying performance. Although the first half was goalless, Barça had the upper hand and Leo had run Real Madrid ragged, getting bumped and bruised in the process. With so many players' nerves taut with tension, trouble was never far away, and it all came to a head as they walked off for half-time and tempers flared. As scuffles developed, warring players had to be separated by the officials. It wasn't really the best time for reserve 'keeper José Manuel Pinto to start throwing his weight about, and it left Wolfgang Stark with little alternative but to show the red card. If anything should now happen to Victor Valdés in the second half, Barça were in trouble.

Rather than calming the players down, the half-time break only served to heighten the tension between them and further red cards were shown in the second half. Fortunately for Barça, it was their opponents who incurred the displeasure of the referee. Just after the hour mark, Pepe went flying into a tackle on Dani Alves with his studs showing and caught him just below the knee. The Brazilian made a meal of it, no question, but it was still a sending off. Cue the usual histrionics from Mourinho, who was sent to the stands for his diatribe towards the fourth official. Now lacking a key defender and explicit instructions from their coach, Real had given Barça the upper hand, but their battle-hardened players were still more than a match for the *Blaugranes*.

At times it was hard to remember that the antics on the pitch were somehow supposed to be forming part of a plan to win a football match. Some of the tackles bordered on assault and would certainly have been more at home in a boxing or wrestling ring. The introduction of Ibrahim Afellay for Pedro with 20 minutes left proved pivotal as Real tired from the effects of their relentless physicality. Pep had identified that Marcelo in particular wasn't getting forward as much as he had earlier in the game, and so the switch was a sensible one it wasn't long before the young Dutchman's speed took him hurtling past the static Marcelo and his low cross found Messi who was sharper than the four defenders in the area. Only Sergio Ramos made an effort to stop him, but the Spaniard was on his heels and had no chance of getting to the ball ahead of Messi, who was in full flow by the time he connected: 0-1, advantage Barça.

Though the goal hadn't quite knocked the stuffing out of Madrid, it forced them to continue coming forward, leaving more space for the likes of Xavi to exploit. With three minutes left to play, Messi put the tie to bed. If a measure a player's true ability is the way they seize control and influence a game, this was Messi's Olympus, for FC Barcelona at least. It was surely one of the best individual goals ever seen at the Santiago Bernabéu, and effectively settled the tie.

Receiving the ball from a short Sergio Busquets free-kick inside the centre circle, there was little hint of the danger that would follow. As Lass Diarra came forward to block Messi, he returned the ball to Busquets who had moved into a pocket of space. Shielding the ball, he allowed Messi to take it off him as he did so, and the Argentinian was already well into his stride before beating Diarra for pace as he attempted to cover. Now at the mid-point between the centre circle and penalty area, Messi came face to face with both of *Los Blancos'* centre-backs, Sergio Ramos and Raúl Albiol. A drop of the shoulder and burst of acceleration took him past both and into the area, as Marcelo attempted to get across and make a last ditch challenge. Moving away from goal on a diagonal run, Messi darted in front of the Brazilian but now had Ramos back in close proximity and Iker Casillas coming out to narrow the angle. On his weaker right foot, the Argentinian simply rolled the ball into the opposite corner of the net, leaving Casillas no chance. Given the importance of the game and the standard of the opposition, it remains one of his best goals.

While there was still the second leg to come at Camp Nou, Real already knew they were beaten after a match that, Messi's majesty apart, was a poor advert for the best club fixture in the world. Real Madrid had dragged it into the gutter, and Mourinho made it worse afterwards, igniting another war of words. "One day, I would like Josep Guardiola to win this competition properly," he told reporters: "I can't say what I feel. If I say to UEFA what I think, my career ends today. I only leave one question. Why? Why? Øvrebø, Busacca, Frisk, Stark? [referees in UCL games that Barça won] Why to all these people? Each semi-final always brings the same. We're talking about a fantastic football team, so why do they need that? Why couldn't Chelsea go to the final? Last year it was a miracle that Inter got there playing with 10 men for so long. A miracle. Why weren't there four penalties against Chelsea? Why send off Van Persie? Where does their power come from? As a match strategy we were not going to lose. It could've been 0-0 tonight, but then suddenly we are down to 10 men and they have a free path to find solutions that they couldn't find before.

"We could've played for three hours and they wouldn't have scored," he continued. "But today we have seen that it is not difficult – it is impossible. I don't know if it's the advertising for UNICEF. I don't know if it's UEFA. Congratulations for a wonderful football team. It must be difficult to get this power. They have managed to get this power. No-one else has any chance really. Arsène Wenger. Today myself. I don't understand why. I hope one day I will find the answer. It's mission impossible. They have to reach the final and they will. That's it. Perhaps they could win on merit. This match was bound for a nil-nil result. Why did he do this? He won't answer because now he is going home. Last year was a miracle but this year absolutely nothing. Why don't they let other teams play against them? Yes we are out. We will go there with all the pride and respect for our world. Sometimes I feel disgusted living in this world and earning my living in this world. We have to do it with pride. Without Pepe. Without Sergio Ramos [suspended]. Without the coach. The result is practically impossible to revert. If we score in Barcelona they will kill us again. There is no chance for us. I know many Catalan friends and they will be happy and they're going to Wembley but to win this way cannot feel the same. I won two European titles and I won them on the pitch. I would've been embarrassed to win that title [2009] because it was won with the scandal of Stamford Bridge. This will be won with the scandal of the Bernabéu. I hope one day he [Guardiola] wins a Champions League title as it should be, perfect, spotless, without any scandal. I respect him as a person and as a manager. I didn't disrespect him before the game."

Even by his standards it was an extraordinary outburst, and a subsequent five-match ban from UEFA was well deserved. "More than words, the shocking images on television made the players realise this couldn't go on," Vicente Del Bosque, the Spain coach, told *The Coaches' Voice*. "The TV images were everywhere and they didn't benefit the players at all. They were not only players from Real Madrid and Barcelona, more importantly, they were an example for so many young people in Spain."

The second leg was a damp squib by comparison, a 1-1 draw with Marcelo equalising Pedro's goal for Barça. That the *Blaugranes* were on their way to the final at Wembley against Manchester United, at the expense of their biggest rivals, was all that mattered. Also, that they would travel with a third consecutive league title under their belts after clinching a 1-1 draw at Levante. A goalless draw at home to Deportivo La Coruña and a 3-1 win away at Málaga were incidental, but kept the team in good enough spirits for what was to follow.

11

Masterclass v Man Utd

The Maestro Wows Wembley

*"They thoroughly deserved beating us at Wembley, we were overcome
by brilliance really"*

Thousands of dancing, singing Barça fans had turned Trafalgar
Square into a corner of Catalonia on the afternoon of Saturday
May 28, 2011, but Manchester United expected to gain revenge for
what had happened two years earlier. As it turned out, the 2011
Champions League final would be worse for them. Much worse.

*May 28, 2011: FC Barcelona supporters take over Trafalgar Square ahead of the
Champions League Final at Wembley.*

By the time Pedro had scored the game's opening goal on 27 minutes, the *Blaugranes* were already well on top. Xavi, Iniesta and Busquets were bossing the game, and despite their best efforts, Ryan Giggs and Michael Carrick weren't able to get close enough to turn the tide United's way. Messi was keeping the Red Devils' defence quiet all on his own, and Rio Ferdinand would later describe the game, alongside the 2009 final, as "one of the most embarrassing moments of my life." During an interview on BT Sport's *The Clare Balding Show* in 2018 he commented; "the thing is with him [Messi], he doesn't even come anywhere near you. Me and Vidić stood on the halfway line at Wembley and looked at each other shaking our heads. We were losing and thinking we haven't even got close to anyone. If you're a defender in a game, you want to get near people, or at least get the ball. We didn't have the ball and I didn't get to put my hands on anyone – to rough them up or anything like that. The problem was that when we did get close to him, he was that small and quick that he was going underneath when we were throwing our arms out to get leverage. I was just thinking that this guy is a magician. He's the best player I've ever played against, he was just devastating. We all felt that if we played against that Barcelona team without Messi, we probably would've won."

Wayne Rooney scored a wonderful equaliser against the run of play which briefly gave United hope, and for a time they were the better side as Barça sought to regain their composure and control. Level at the break, the United fans who had acquired tickets for the Wembley showpiece in the Barça end were convinced that their time had come, but the second half would see an absolute masterclass, from Guardiola tactically and the players generally. If the first 45 was great, Barça were simply unstoppable after the break. With Park Ji-Sung running out of steam after having been run ragged for the first 50 minutes or so, Messi drove deep into the heart of United territory and unleashed a venomous low drive past Edwin van der Sar. His manic celebration famously included booting a TV boom mic into oblivion. David Villa's exquisite curling effort made it 3-1 on 69 minutes, allowing Pep to make three late changes, giving Seydou Keita, Carles Puyol and Ibrahim Afellay a very brief taste of the action.

What topped off the night for many was the trophy lift. Carles Puyol had lifted trophies before, and he handed the armband to Eric Abidal after the game. The Frenchman had battled back from cancer to play an integral part in Barça's success, and the image of the left-back holding the Champions League trophy aloft reduced many to tears. It remains the highlight of Puyol's Barça career. "The moment when Abidal lifted the Champions League trophy because of what it meant, because he fought while he was in the team, was amazing. It's very hard to explain. He deserved it the most," the shaggy-haired destroyer said years later during an interview.

Sir Alex Ferguson was gracious in defeat. "I expected us to do better, particularly after half-time, but it wasn't to be. Great teams do go in cycles and they're at the peak of the cycle they're in at the moment. They're the best in Europe, no question about that. In my time as a manager, I would say they're the best team we've faced. Everyone acknowledges that and I accept that. It's not easy when you've been well beaten like that to think another way. No one has given us a hiding like that. It's a great moment for them. They deserve it because they play the right way and enjoy their football. But how long it lasts ... whether they can replace that team at some point ... they certainly have the right philosophy, but it's always difficult to find players like Xavi, Iniesta and Messi all the time. But they're enjoying the moment that they have just now. We never controlled Lionel Messi, but many people have had to say that over the years."

Ferguson's assistant, Mike Phelan, agreed, as he explained to me:

"You always have a moment in the game where you feel as though you can hurt the opposition. That chance does always come and we had a moment where we believed enough in ourselves to get a draw. We always knew we would score against them, always. It was when they scored – how were we going to deal with that? That was always going to be the issue. Once they got a goal, they turned the screw, and it's something they'd done for many years as a club and a group of individuals. They managed their games really well, so even if they were losing 1-0, their belief was that they'd score at least two of their own. To be honest, with our league form in 2011 being as it was, we believed we'd do that as well. What we didn't quite grasp is how to manage that expectation. The longer the game stayed at 0-0, the better it was for us because when you go 1-0 up you know that there's going to be a reaction from Barcelona. They had that quality to be able to change things. If they went 1-0 up you knew it was going to be a possession game, or if they went 1-0 down they'd be good enough to get one back and then apply the pressure. It was like they'd say 'do you want

August 17, 2011: 'SuperMessi! Super Champions! Lamentable Mourinho' - Leo's goal three minutes from time handed Barça the Spanish Super Cup, but the match was marred by Jose Mourinho gauging Tito Vilanova in the eye. (© Sport)

to have another go at us?' That's something Barcelona always had at that time.

"They thoroughly deserved to beat us at Wembley, we were overcome by brilliance really. We caught them at their absolute pinnacle and they absorbed Wembley unbelievably well. They turned up and understood the magnitude of the game, the occasion ... I'm not saying we didn't because we contributed the best we could, but it was never going to be good enough. It was as simple as that. When I look back, I think 'what did we do wrong?' but there wasn't a lot, we were just beaten by a better team. That happens now and again and we had to hold our hands up and say well done. That's life. We were disappointed for a long while, but we had a group of players that were more than capable of handling the disappointment. It was only afterwards that you can reflect on the achievement of getting to the final. I got to three as a coach and you're blessed if you can get to one. So the players began to realise the journey they'd been on to get to that point. Getting to a European Cup final ... you're pinching yourself a little bit, and we had to express that back to the players. The fact that they'd got there meant they had something to offer, it's just getting over the line and sometimes you meet the right team, unfortunately we met the wrong team. Whoever is the best team in a final wins it. In Barcelona's case, once they got there, they produced. They understood it. They had the experience, the history. Man United teams in the past had always responded to adversity, and they'd always excelled when they'd won things because they wanted to do it again, so our challenges to the players were to do it all again, to go on another journey. That was important."

December 16, 2012: Leo wheels away in delight after scoring Barça's third goal in a 4-1 win at Camp Nou against Atlético Madrid. (© Shutterstock)

Barça touched down at El Prat Airport at 4pm but with an estimated one million *culés* lining the route it took more than two and a half hours to reach Camp Nou. Once there, the players were introduced, one by one. "Thanks so much to you all for making as all feel so happy," Pep said to them. "We appreciate everyone who came out to greet us and those who travelled with us to London. Your support through the year has been great and we hope to repeat these feats next year." Carles Puyol got one of the biggest roars of the afternoon when he said, "The trophies we have won this season took so much effort, so we want you to enjoy them." Messi, as usual, remained almost silent for the whole occasion, although his "Long live Barça and long live Catalonia" roused everyone and brought them to their feet. They recognised, once again, that he had been at the heart of a season in which only the Copa del Rey defeat denied them an unpredented second treble.

Another summer of football beckoned, with Argentina hosting the 2011 Copa América tournament. Before it began Messi enjoyed some downtime at home in Rosario, but the period of family relaxation was not without incident. After lunching at a local restaurant, he was set upon by a hooded young man who swung a punch at him. National papers would later claim the aggressor

March 31, 2012: Leo in action during a league game against Athletic Club Bilbao at Camp Nou. (© Shutterstock)

was a fan of Rosario Central, the arch rival of Messi's junior side, Newell's Old Boys. "We were taking photos and saw the guy raise his arm, but Messi dodged it," a witness identified as Carolina told reporters from the C5N news channel. "Messi didn't react badly, he just walked out and got in his car." Coverage of the incident, coming just six days before Leo was due to meet up with his national team colleagues, was extensive, though Messi himself tried to play it down. "I wasn't even touched. I didn't feel a thing and only found out after the kerfuffle, it was nothing," he told *Olé* in the aftermath of the incident. 'Nothing' or not, it was a distraction he and his family could've done without. So it might be argued, was the Copa in which Argentina scraped through the group stages with draws against Bolivia and Colombia, with Messi getting booed by his own supporters for the first time in the Colombia game. He managed to redress the balance somewhat with two assists in the 3-0 defeat of Costa Rica before Argentina crashed out of the tournament at the quarter-final stage, against Uruguay on penalties. Sergio Batista was sacked as coach and one of his successor, Alejandro Sabella's, first acts, surprising many, was installing Messi as one of the captains of the team, a role he would take over solo once Javier Mascherano retired.

January 25, 2012: FC Barcelona players line up before the Copa del Rey 2-2 draw against Real Madrid. (© Shutterstock)

An unexpected early exit at least allowed Leo a longer period of recovery before the start of the 2011-12 season, which opened with the two-legged Spanish Super Cup final against Real Madrid and the UEFA Super Cup against Porto.

The first leg against *Los Blancos*, at the Santiago Bernabéu in mid-August, certainly lived up to the pre-match hype. It was also the first appearance of the Qatar-sponsored Barça shirt, a design abomination with its uneven stripes and made ten times worse by the addition of 'Qatar Foundation'. Mesut Özil gave Real the lead early on, before a wonder goal from David Villa levelled things up before the break. Right on the stroke of half-time, Messi's persistence handed the visitors a second before a rare goal from Xabi Alonso saw the game end all-square and with everything to play for in Barcelona.

As so many times before, Leo rolled up his sleeves and made the difference. Real had most of the the opening quarter hour, but could do nothing about Messi's surgically precise pass for Andrés Iniesta to fire the hosts ahead on the night and on aggregate. Four minutes later, Cristiano Ronaldo's deflected equaliser silenced Camp Nou, but Messi had the final word of the half, clipping home after a fine back-heel assist from Piqué. With nine minutes left, a mix up in the Barça defence meant that Karim Benzema was able to poke home, and the teams were all square again at 4-4 on aggregate, and on away goals. Again Messi seized the moment, his late volley winning the cup for Barça, but he was squeezed out of the morning headlines by a squalid late drama on the touchlines.

Amid the scuffles which followed Marcelo's red card for a tackle on Fàbregas, José Mourinho strode into the melee and made contact with Barça's assistant manager, Tito Vilanova, poking him in the eye. As Vilanova recoiled, the Portuguese turned and smirked. It was unacceptable behaviour and a helpful distraction to his managerial shortcomings across the two matches. Mourinho could not be charged because the incident was not mentioned in the referee's report, but he tried to further enrage Catalans by saying he did not know who 'Pito' Vilanova was. Pito is slang for cock/penis and it brought a ferocious response from the club and its players. "It's not the players' fault," Gerard Piqué said later. "I have played against them [Real] before and this didn't happen. We even beat them 6-2 at their stadium and this didn't happen. I have played alongside them [in the national team] and they are brilliant people. I don't think they're the guilty parties. People accuse us, the Catalans, of being the guilty party but the guilty [man] is in Madrid. He is ruining Spanish football. They have to look at the video, analyse it and decide who is responsible. It's not the first time this has happened, it has happened many times, and something has to be done. It is always the same people. Measures are needed. Things can't always end up the same way." The defender wasn't the only one to express such anger, but it all detracted from a masterful Messi performance.

The Porto game was not the greatest final, with only 18,000 in attendance in Monaco, but brought Barça yet another trophy set up by a Messi goal, with Fàbregas making it 2-0 near the end.

A brace in Barça's opening league match against Villarreal meant Leo had scored in four successive games. He went scoreless in the next four but a hat-trick and two assists in an 8-0 home win over Osasuna set the pattern for a campaign of multiple hat-trick matches. There was another treble a week later against Atlético Madrid, and the season saw further triples against Mallorca, Plzen, Málaga (twice) and Granada, along with Switzerland and Brazil at international level.

If the hat-trick in the end-of-season 4-3 win over Brazil in New Jersey was special for being against Argentina's biggest rivals, and rounded off with a much-replayed classic goal, the earlier treble against Granada in March was more significant. Guardiola was annoyed to concede three goals at home in a 5-3 win, but Messi's goals took him past Cesár Rodríguez, whose Barça record of 232 goals had stood for over 60 years. Trust Leo to take the crown with not one, not two, but three goals. Yet neither match saw his greatest goal scoring performance of the season. He'd plundered four against Valencia on match day 24 and again in the last home game against Espanyol. His fourth, a penalty, produced a special moment.

A week before, Pep Guardiola had publicly announced his decision to quit as coach. The club had known for months, but had spent time unavailingly trying to change his mind. "The reason is simple: four years is enough," Guardiola said in a press conference that was attended by most of the players, but not Leo. "I'm drained and I need to fill up. The demand has been very high and a manager must be strong. At the beginning of December I announced to the chairman that I was seeing the end of my era at Barcelona. Time has taken its toll – I rise each day and don't feel the same. I am going with the understanding that I have done my duty. You can only recover by resting and getting away from everything. It would have been a bad idea to continue. Perhaps it would not have gone wrong but I have the perception that it would. It is my time to go. Now we are out of the two main competitions it is a good time to announce this. I did not want to continue with the confusion. I want to thank my players who are responsible for everything that has happened here. I don't want to manage at the moment."

As Messi tucked home his fourth against Barça's local rivals, he made a bee-line for his coach. Pep rose from his seat to shake hands and then embrace the player that, more than any other, had shaped FC Barcelona's success during his tenure. As Camp Nou cheered and applauded, Messi's team-mates joined in the huddle, knowing it was the last time they'd enjoy having Pep as their coach at their home stadium. It was, perhaps, a fitting way for Guardiola to sign off in front of the public who still idolised him. As for Messi's no show at his leaving announcement, the reason was simple. "Because of the emotions I feel I preferred not to be present at Pep's press conference and to stay away from the press because I know they will look for the pain on the players' faces," he said afterwards. "It's something I decided not to show."

Leo's high scoring season even included a five-goal haul, against Bayer Leverkusen at Camp Nou in the Champions League Round of 16. He scored 14 in the competition, but missed a penalty in the agonising semi-final defeat by Chelsea, who went on to beat Bayern on penalties in the final.

Despite the disappointments of La Liga and the Champions League, *culés* could still take plenty of positives from Guardioula's final season at the club. For a start, they'd pushed a very good Madrid side all the way in La Liga, and could at least still call themselves World Club champions after sweeping aside both Al-Sadd in the semi-final (4-0) and a Neymar-led Santos in the final (another 4-0). Needless to say, they were inspired by Messi who both opened and closed the scoring in the final in Japan. Although an individual honour, Messi's third successive Ballon d'Or award – taking almost half (47.88%) of the vote – was becoming a very welcome habit, even if Leo had said more than once that team awards meant much more to him than individual ones. The Copa del Rey final against Athletic Club at the Vicente Calderón, the team they'd beaten in Guardiola's opening campaign, closed out the season on a high.

Barça were two up in 20 minutes, thanks to a second-minute strike from Pedro and a right-footed finish by Messi, and at least three more presentable chances had been missed. The quality of their play was, again, on a different level and with 70 minutes still to play the question wasn't whether Athletic could make a game of it, but how many Barça would go on to score. Surprisingly, it would only be one more with Pedro netting again in the 24th minute. That definitely made it 'game over' and the 14th title secured in just four seasons. It eased the pain of being beaten in the league by Real Madrid, who amassed a record 121 goals and +89 goal difference, meaning that Pep's final campaign hadn't finished as he had hoped. Leo's goal in that final was, incredibly, his 73rd of the season for club and country, a player not regarded as a striker in the usual sense taking a European record from the great Gerd 'Der Bomber' Müller, widely regarded as the best penalty box predator in European football history. Even he had to bow to Messi's consistent and remarkable genius, later joking that Leo's "only defect is that he doesn't play for Bayern".

12

'La Pulga' Surpasses 'Der Bomber'

91 Goals in 2012

"He didn't pigeonhole himself into a specific role because his role was to be the difference, and that's what he did at Barcelona"

Pep's assistant, Tito Vilanova, was given the the reins for 2012-13. The appointment made a lot of sense given the continuity, and also that many saw Tito as the tactical brain of the Guardiola operation. He was hugely well respected by the squad too, so there was no risk of his not being accepted by the dressing room. He had taught Messi at La Masia, when he was 14, so implicit trust between the pair was a given. Vilanova signed a two-year deal on June 15, 2012, but was quick to distance himself from any comparisons to his former boss; "It's an honour the club chose me," he told reporters. "I'm excited and I feel strong enough to do the job. The normal thing is that you're offered the Barça job when things aren't going well. I accept this challenge because I know how football is understood here and, furthermore, I feel that I've been part of the successes of these past four years. Repeating them will be very difficult. Very difficult. Many circumstances need to fall into place. We won't give up on any match or titles, we'll try to win them all. We're very aware of how hard that is. I'm ok with how most of the things have been done to this point. Therefore, many of the methodologies will be similar; in training, press conferences and when we play away from home. It would be silly to try and change all of that now.

"However, I lose in any comparisons [with Pep], and I didn't come here to compete with anyone. I'll try to do a good job, I'll dedicate as many hours to the job as I have in the past. I talked with my doctors and they all told me to go forward with it. I'm very eager to get started, the challenge is very big but having the memory of what recently happened to me, I doubt that it will be more difficult." Vilanova was referring, of course, to the parotid gland cancer that he was first diagnosed with on November 22, 2011. "I'm convinced that if we win, everyone will help us a lot. If not, we won't get as much help. We're all very well accustomed and we want to continue watching the team play the way they have been up until now. I'm not asking for patience. Pep's my friend, almost like a brother. My relationship with him is perfect. If he had signed for another club I wouldn't be here right now. I'm here because the club offered me the job and I have the drive to do it. I worked very closely with Pep, and in the last five years, we have never ended on a sour note. We worked well with each other. Now I need someone by my side that knows how to do my old job without having to teach someone new. Jordi [Roura], who was already part of the technical staff, is the ideal person. Despite the fact that we're good friends, if he wasn't qualified for the job, he wouldn't be by my side."

It turned out to be another master stroke by the club, even if the away goals loss to Real Madrid in the Spanish Super Cup (4-4 on aggregate) was a disappointing way to begin the campaign. Messi still managed to get on the score sheet in the 3-2 first leg win, and would continue to score at an astonishing rate in a dazzling opening half of the season. The 2012-13 vintage achieved the club's best-ever start, unbeaten in La Liga until the winter break with a record 55 points. Messi had scored at least twice in 12 of those league matches, helping fire the *Blaugranes* well ahead of their rivals.

The solitary defeat in the first four months of the campaign came away at Celtic in the Champions League. Leo's 90th minute penalty was nothing more than a consolation in a game which had two main talking points. The first was what turned out to be the winning goal, from Tony Watt. An uncharacteristic error from Xavi allowed the 18-year-old a free run on goal, and as Javier Mascherano came back to cover, Watt made no mistake, slotting past Victor Valdés. Celtic Park can rarely have been so loud as at the point when the ball hit the back of the net. A sea of green and white and a mass of heaving bodies greeted Watt as he ran to the corner. Barça had done everything they possibly could, bar score, something that the Celtic striker acknowledged when I spoke to him:

"They were 11 players who were miles ahead of us, and we had to look to stifle every single one. We had to make sure that they didn't play like they usually do. Everything came together, it was just perseverance on our part, not giving up and I know it's easy to say, just giving our best. Something like that doesn't happen every year, more like once every 20-30 years, but we had the luck. Barcelona were amazing, you could see that, just everything went our way on the night.

I was happy to get on the pitch. We'd hoped for a positive result, maybe a draw or to nick a goal, but we certainly didn't go into the game thinking we were going to win it. Neil [Lennon] told me I would get on at some point because we had a lot of injuries. I didn't really know when that would be because you can never really know what will happen during a game and things sometimes occur that you don't expect, but obviously I did play and I think I did quite well. The goal was one of my best moments, but making my debut was probably better. I don't really remember too much about the goal because of how long ago it was, and even at the time, everything happened so quickly that it was all a bit of a blur. Playing Barça was great because of the players we had in front of us who we knew were capable of getting a couple of goals at any time. As for Messi ... for me, he's the best ever. I think everyone appreciates greatness. A lot of people speak about Ronaldo, but Messi is much more natural. A genius."

Xavi's 166 passes, the same as the entire Celtic team across the 90 minutes and whom Kris Commons led the way with 22, spoke volumes of Barça's dominance. In total, Barça completed 955 passes and restricted their hosts to just 16.4% possession. The key statistical comparision, though, was that Celtic scored twice from three shots on target, while Barça had only Messi's penalty to show for their eight. It was only the *Blaugranes* second defeat in 21 Champions League games. No wonder Celtic manager, Neil Lennon, was overjoyed. "This is up there with anything I have done in my life," he beamed after the match. "As a player I won things, I had a special 10 years under Martin O'Neill and played in some great teams, beating Manchester United and getting to the last 16 of the Champions League. As a manager, I don't know if I will top this. I hope I do because I'm still young and am still learning, but this is up there with anything I have achieved, not just in my football career but in my life. This was one of the greatest nights in the club's recent history. It was very poignant, firstly to be playing Barcelona at this point but also to beat them given the way our squad had been decimated. The players are heroes to me, I cannot speak highly enough of our performance."

Five days before the game Leo's wife, Antonella, had given birth to the couple's first child, who was named Thiago. Aware of the incessant press interest in the event, Leo took to *Facebook* and announced: "Today I am the happiest man in the world, my son has been born, thanks to God for this gift! Thanks to my family for their support. Love to you all!" Life was never going to be quite the same for the Messi family again, but it at least gave Leo a new perspective. "It makes me think of things in a different way," he told *El Pais*. "I can no longer just think about myself, I think about him, and how I hope he doesn't have any problems."

In the game following the Celtic defeat, a 4-2 away win at Mallorca, Messi grabbed another brace to begin a scoring record unlikely to ever be surpassed. The Celtic blip aside, Barça were regularly scoring three, four or five goals and although Vilanova might not have wanted to be compared to Pep, Barça's immaculate play made it inevitable. He was more than matching his predecessor at this stage, with Leo once again the driving force behind the team's successes. He was again listed as one of the final three for the Ballon d'Or award, alongside team-mate, Andrés Iniesta, and nemesis, Cristiano Ronaldo, but was odds-on favourite to win – for the fourth consecutive year – an award nobody had ever won more than three times across their whole career.

Barça signed off 2012 with with a stunning 4-1 demolition of Atlético Madrid at Camp Nou and a 3-1 win at Valladolid. Leo scored in both to take another of Gerd Müller's records, most goals scored in a calendar year. He had bagged a seemingly impossible total of 91 goals for club and country in 2012, and the least he could do was send a shirt signed with a respectful message to the former Bayern man.

In between those two matches Vilanova had announced that his cancer had returned. Tests during a routine check-up confirmed the worst. Surgery was scheduled within a day of the announcement, and Jordi Roura took over first team duties until Tito felt well enough to return. While more chemo and radiotherapy lay ahead for their manager, not once did the club intimate that he intended to stand down. This was, for all intents and purposes, just another bump in the road. "Tito is very strong," president, Sandro Rosell, said after the announcement, that sent shockwaves through the club. "He has shown that before and we hope that he will be back with us very soon. We will wait for him."

The players had to digest the news and deal with it as they sought to continue the good form they'd shown to that point of the campaign. While the pressure was immediately focussed on stand-in Jordi Roura, with Leo spearheading the charge he had little to worry about. The day before the Catalan derby against Espanyol, Leo and an FC Barcelona delegation that included shortlisted team-mate Iniesta, headed to the Ballon d'Or awards. Messi took the crown, and with 41.60% of the vote it was almost as clear cut as in 2011, as Cristiano Ronaldo once again found himself in second place. Leo celebrated by scoring one and assisting another in the 4-0 demolition of Espanyol. He simply couldn't stop scoring.

From the Mallorca game on November 11, 2012, until the match against Celta Vigo on March 30, 2013, he scored in 21 consecutive league matches against all 19 La Liga opponents. One came in an El Clásico defeat earlier in March, only five days after they'd been knocked out of the Copa del Rey by Real, dashing hopes of another final. With a 2-0 first leg defeat by AC Milan in the Champions League Round of 16, it seemed that in spite of Messi's goals, the wheels were starting to fall off, but then Milan came to Camp Nou for the return.

No team had ever overturned a two-goal first leg deficit in the Champions League but Leo wasn't hanging about. Two goals in the opening 40 minutes, his 52nd and 53rd of another outrageous season, had the hosts level at half-time. David Villa put them into the lead in the tie thanks to a sumptuous Xavi pass, before Jordi Alba completed a famous *remuntada* ('comeback' in Catalan) with a late fourth. The 90 minutes showcased the best that Barça and Leo had to offer.

In the very next game, on March 17, when Rayo Vallecano were the visitors to Camp Nou, Leo wore the captain's armband for the first time. This had been predicted for some time but a good proportion of journalists had suggested that he wasn't 'captain material' in any event. Though he may not have seemed so in the traditional sense, in the way that Puyol would marshal and talk to his players throughout, Leo always led by example and when the day eventually arrived, it seemed a completely natural step for the club. Any fears that the responsibility might take its toll on his influence were emphatically answered as he was involved in all three goals, an assist for David

Villa to open the scoring on 26 minutes followed by a brace either side of half-time.

After a brief interlude for two World Cup qualifiers with Argentina there was the fillip of Vilanova's return from two months of treatment in New York. The club website announced: "Jordi Roura has been in charge of the team over the last couple of months and has been in permanent contact with Vilanova to agree on important decisions, but Vilanova's place on the bench has always been kept for him and this week the team will welcome their boss back. Welcome home Tito."

While his return was an emotionaly positive experience, Vilanova made known his disappoinment towards his old friend Guardiola, saying later in the year that: "We didn't see each other after my treatment and my operation. It wasn't my fault. He's my friend and I needed him [Pep]. The person who was alone was me, the person going through a rough time was me, the person who needed help was me. I saw Pep when I was on a two-day trip to New York. Then I was there for two months, when I underwent my operation and they gave me the treatment. He must have thought it was better for us not to see each other. I would have acted differently to the way Pep did. You know that I've always tried to avoid personal matters and only talk about football, but I heard what Pep said and I don't think it was right. He surprised me. I don't think anyone on the board of directors has used me to attack him. They've helped me in every way possible."

By the time Tito returned, the league title race was over. Well, in truth, it'd probably been over since the start of 2013. Barça ended the season as they had begun, with their imperious domestic form resulting in a record 15-point lead over defending champions Real Madrid, thus equalling *Los Blancos*' record 100 points tally from the previous season and beating the club record for goals scored in a season – Tito's 115 was one better than Pep's the year before – and having scored in every league game they'd played in 2012-13.

Ray Hudson has since admitted that Leo's goal in Bilbao on 27 April was his favourite Messi moment, of many.

"His goal at the old San Mamés against Athletic Club was the pure essence of Leo. Confronted by half a dozen players ahead of him, the first three in an area the size of the telephone box ... the confines were ridiculous. The defenders were wrestling with a ghost after he'd evaporated them, but he still had to slingshot his pass into the goal from the edge of the box. The multiple hesitations he displayed in nano-seconds, as he shifted his balance to elude defenders was stupendously magnificent, and it's a goal that should be hung up in the Louvre as the example of pure footballing art."

In spite of a horror show in the Champions League semi-final, routed 7-0 on aggregate by Bayern, and the loss of the Copa del Rey, it was very much a job well done and there was a genuine belief that the team, post-Guardiola, would now go on to bigger and better things. When Eric Abidal, another former cancer survivor, played his final home game, the 4-1 win over Málaga on 5 May, Carles Puyol was able to hand another trophy to the Frenchman and also to his coach, for them to lift to an adoring Camp Nou, a moment which disappointed only Alex Song, who mistakenly believed that he was being called forward to take the acclaim.

A goal haul of 46 league goals gave Leo yet another trophy, his third European Golden Shoe in four seasons, and the second in a row. He and Cristiano Ronaldo were regularly posting numbers that seemed unattainable years before. Mario Jardel's 42 for Sporting in 2001-02 had been the previous highest, but because the Portuguese league wasn't one of the 'big five', it was never given the same value as, for instance, Ronaldo Nazario's 34 in La Liga in 1996-97 campaign. Over the 2011-12 and 2012-13 seasons, Leo had scored a staggering 96 league goals.

On May 24, Santos announced they'd received two bids for Neymar, who a day later confirmed he would sign for Barça. The transfer fee was a matter of much debate, but regardless of financial minutiae, the Brazilian wunderkind was presented to a record 56,500 supporters at the Camp Nou on June 3. Securing another world-class talent looked a positive step for a team regularly accused of Messi-dependence. Leo's reward for his continued excellence had been another contract, his seventh since breaking into the first team but the first for three and a half years. Taking him up to June 30, 2018, the new contract delighted him, his family, his team-mates and the supporters. His salary also increased to €13M per year. "I can't imagine what Messi will be like in 2018," Jordi Alba said at the time. "But it's great news for Barça fans that he's staying. He is the best player in the world and as long as nothing happens, he'll be the best ever. We'll try to make him feel as comfortable here as we can."

It was a tonic for Leo after injuries curtailed some of the latter half of the season. A hamstring pull in the first leg of the Champions League quarter-final against Paris Saint-Germain meant he played only a bit part in the return, but still engineered the goal the goal that took the *Blaugranes* through to their ill-fated meeting with Bayern Munich. David Beckham, then playing for the French side, was in awe. "Messi came on when we were 1-0 up and they scored. A player like him, 100% fit or not, will always make the difference. Messi is the best player in the world, simple as that. The only player who can even get near him is Ronaldo." Hampered by injury in the first leg of the Bayern match, he missed the second leg completely.

Then, on July 19, 2013, came the shattering announcement that Vilanova had suffered another relapse with his throat cancer and was standing down from his coaching duties. Leo, Carles Puyol and others, attended a press conference given by Sandro Rosell and sporting director, Andoni Zubizarreta. "Following routine tests, it was decided that he [Vilanova] would follow a course of treatment to control his illness that is incompatible with fulfilling his role as coach of the first team," the president told a shocked audience. "We will present the new coach in the next few days, hopefully by early next week."

Within three days Gerardo 'Tata' Martino, little known in Europe but a great success in Argentina with Newell's Old Boys, Leo's first club, was confirmed in the role. Before he'd had the chance to oversee a game, there was a fresh outcry amongst *culés* as Qatar Foundation gave way on the club shirts to Qatar Airways. The party line had always been that the Qatar Foundation was a charitable organisation rather than a commercial organisation, but there was no doubt about the airline. "We will be able to work with global company, Qatar Airways, with whom we share many things such as the search for excellence," said president Rosell. "This sponsorship deal will bring great advantages, not just for the club, but also for our city and our country." However it was dressed up, the outcry was entirely predictable, but the club at least managed to get a large majority back on side when they revealed the new, yellow and red striped, away shirt that resembled the Catalan flag. Inflammatory? Yes. A stroke of marketing genius? Undoubtedly.

Leo, true to form scored the first goal of the new season after 12 minutes, adding another plus an assist in the 7-0 demolition of Levante. Then came the two-legged Spanish Super Cup final against

March 16, 2014: 'Historic hat-trick' - Leo's three goals in the 7-0 thumping of Osasuna took his Barça total to 371, beating the 369 scored by Paulinho Alcántara whose club record had stood for 80 years. (© Sport)

Atlético Madrid. Playing away first, Neymar's header equalised the first-half volley by David Villa who had joined Atléti that summer. Neymar's goal ultimately won Barça their only trophy of the campaign after a 0-0 draw at Camp Nou saw the *Blaugranes* win on the away *gole* rule. Winning a solitary trophy was an outcome nobody would have anticipated as Martino set a club record by going unbeaten in his first 16 fixtures. He'd had to make do without Leo for a couple of games too, after another hamstring injury at Almería in late September.

Back after 19 days out, Barça had clearly rushed their talisman back too soon and his fifth injury of the calendar year came just over three weeks later. A far more serious tear ruled him out for 56 days and nine matches, bad news for his team and hardly ideal in a World Cup year. Cesc Fàbregas' comments appeared to offer a warning shot to his employers: "Leo needs to take as much time as he needs in order to recover and get back to his level. We need him at his best. I had something similar at Arsenal. You think you're OK and you're not. I had this injury and I wasn't right for up to a year and a half. It's a really frustrating injury, and you need to take whatever time you need because if you don't, it won't heal properly."

Within three weeks of his injury, Barça fell to their first loss under Martino, a 2-1 defeat by Ajax in Amsterdam, and their first league defeat, away to Athletic Club. The cry of Messi-dependence went up again, a concept I discussed with Mike Phelan, who said:

"He was always given the freedom of expression to be able to decision make. I think that's why he was so successful at Barcelona, he made more correct decisions than anyone on a football field. He didn't pigeon hole himself into a specific role because his role was to be the difference, and that's what he did at Barcelona. I think he would've been exactly the same anywhere else, and perhaps his freedom of expression would've been greater because you'd give him greater responsibility in that role. I don't think you should stifle that type of talent."

Phelan's professional insight reinforced the views of many. Yes, FC Barcelona did rely on him an awful lot, but it's the role he wanted to play within the team dynamic, the role the technical staff wanted him to fulfil and, moreover, he was hugely successful at it. So why change anything?

To call his return a relief was was an understatement. Two goals in a 27 minute Copa del Rey appearance against Getafe in early January 2014 helped Barça to a 4-0 home win. A few days later, Leo would lose out to Ronaldo in that year's Ballon d'Or, with all three finalists – Franck Ribéry being the other – separated by just 4% of the votes. There was controversy over FIFA's extension of the voting period the previous November, citing "a response of less than 50%

from eligible voters before the original deadline." During the two-week extension Ronaldo had bagged a stunning hat-trick for Portugal against Sweden which sent his country to the following summer's World Cup finals. It seemed possible this one performance tipped the scales in Ronaldo's favour, and conspiracy theorists would have you believe that Messi was ahead when the original voting period closed.

Towards the end of the month, Leo's three assists in a 4-1 away win at Levante, were resoundingly overshadowed the following day when Rosell resigned as president. Club member, Jordi Cases, had filed a lawsuit earlier in the week, accepted by a Spanish court judge, alleging that the amount paid for Neymar the previous summer was more than the reported fee and Rosell had misappropriated funds. Rosell had maintained his innocence but felt compelled when the court accepted the suit to resign, handing power to his vice president, Josep Maria Bartomeu. "For some time, my family and I have suffered threats and attacks in silence," Rosell told a news conference. "These threats and attacks have made me wonder if being president means having to jeopardise my family. From the beginning, I have said that the signing of Neymar has been correct and his signing has caused despair and envy from some of our adversaries. These unfair attacks could negatively affect the management and image of the club. It's been an honour to serve the Barcelonistas and it's been a privilege to be the president of FC Barcelona."

Such upheaval could have affected the team, but Leo at least was already back in the groove, scoring in nine of the next 12 games and setting further records with back-to-back hat-tricks in March. His three, when Osasuna were put to the sword 7-0 at the Camp Nou on March 16, took him past Paulinho Alcántara longstanding club record of 369 goals in all matches, including friendlies, a mark from a bygone era thought to be untouchable in the modern game. His three at the Santiago Bernabéu in a 4-3 win over Real Madrid in the next game edged him ahead of the legendary Alfredo Di Stéfano as El Clásico's all-time top scorer.

The good run of form soon came to a halt as the wheels came off the campaign in the space of 16 days in April. Barça were knocked out of the Champions League by a dogged Atlético Madrid, lost at Granada in La Liga to hand the advantage to the *Rojiblancos* (the red and whites), and were again beaten in the Copa del Rey final by Real Madrid, this time thanks to an epic, late, lung-bursting run and finish from Gareth Bale. All of this hurt, but paled alongside the blow which fell on April

25, 2014, when Tito Vilanova died aged just 45. It hit everybody hard. The club erected a 'space for condolence' in the main Camp Nou stand, and the players and staff connected with the first team were the first to pay their respects. All were extremely emotional, particularly those with a bond with Tito from their youth team days. "FC Barcelona is in immense mourning," a club statement began. "Tito Vilanova has died at the age of 45. May he rest in peace. The club wishes to express its most heartfelt sympathy to his family, who are being joined in these moments of mourning by FC Barcelona members and fans all around the world, as well as the rest of the footballing and sporting world. The Vilanova family has asked for respect for their desire for the strictest intimacy in the moments after his death."

Two days later, the team had to compose themselves for the fixture against Villarreal at El Madrigal. With Atléti still in the box seat for the title it was a 'must win' game, but with a minute's silence for Vilanova almost reducing the visitors to tears, it was clearly going to take a monumental effort. The 'Yellow Submarine' took a 2-0 lead early in the second half, but gave Barça, who had not played badly in the circumstances, unlikely assistance with own goals from Gabriel Paulista and Mateo Musacchio. With just seven minutes left Leo fired home the winner.

The following day, a service for Tito saw everyone attend Barcelona Cathedral. What should really have been a private ocassion was broadcast to the world, and the needless intrusion which saw grieving players in tears felt totally inappropriate. "The death of Tito has really affected us," Iniesta had said the day before. "We knew him for a very long time. With him we won the league with a haul of 100 points, but what we'll remember about him is what he gave us on a personal level."

With three league games left, Barça knew that if Atléti won against Levante or Málaga they would be champions before their final match brought them at the Camp Nou, whatever Barça did in their matches. As it turned out, both teams got the jitters. Barça could only draw 2-2 against Getafe and 0-0 against Elche, whilst Diego Simeone's side lost 2-0 against Levante and could only draw 1-1 at home to Málaga. It meant that Atléti, who also faced an all-Madrid Champions League final six days later, needed just a point in the final game to lift their first title since 1996, while Barça simply had to win.

Atléti lost big-game players Diego Costa and Arda Turan to early injuries, and fell behind to Alexis Sánchez acute-angled rocket from an assist by Leo, but a soaring second-half header from Diego Godín and referee Mateu Lahoz's failure to give a penalty for a blatant late foul on Gerard Piqué handed the title to the visitors. A first season in five years without a major trophy certainly wasn't what anyone connected with Barça had expected.

The following day Messi signed yet another contract extension, increasing his salary to a remarkable €36m before tax (€20m post-tax), the highest in the world. It tied him to the club for a further year, until 2019, and was seen as an essential counter-measure to a one-year transfer ban imposed on the club for violations of the rules on signing minors. Tata Martino also resigned which meant another new coach for Leo to get used to, but he'd worry about that another day. He had the World Cup to look forward to.

13

The Double Treble

Job Done in Berlin

"It's even more of a special moment when it comes from a player who shouldn't be allowed to play by FIFA until it's proven that he's actually human!"

The World Cup in Brazil at least offered Messi hope of ending 2013-14 on a high. If he could come through the tournament unscathed Argentina would be there or thereabouts at the business end, and he was off to a fine start with a wonderful solo effort to win Argentina's opener against Bosnia and Herzegovina. His contribution in the next game against Iran was even more timely. Beyond 90 minutes with

June 21, 2014: Messi wheels away after scoring a 91st-minute winner against Iran for Argentina in the 2014 World Cup. (© Shutterstock)

time almost up, Messi dropped his left shoulder and bent a beautiful 25 yarder into the opposite corner to send his side into the knockout stages.

"As soon as I got the ball at the end, we were all in attack because we wanted to put Argentina through with a win," Messi acknowledged post-match. "Obviously I was very happy with the strike and then I heard people screaming and saw them smiling. Iran were able to close us down at the back and it was very difficult to find space. It was very hot too ... Now we're qualified for the next round and that was our objective today." Iran's coach, Carlos Queiroz, said some years later that he considered it a beautiful moment. He told FIFA.com: "I've always said that Messi is an extraordinary player. He's out of this world. If he were human, he wouldn't have had that magical moment in that match. I don't usually like losing, but I didn't come away from that defeat with a negative feeling. It's when something magical like that happens that you know that football is alive and kicking, and that's why it's one of the best sports in the world to watch. And it's even more of a special moment when it comes from a player who shouldn't be allowed to play by FIFA until it's proven that he's actually human!"

Two goals in a 3-2 win over Nigeria seemed almost incidental, but then came three games where he failed to score in normal time. Switzerland proved much tougher opponents than expected and Argentina only progressed thanks to Ángel Di María's 118th-minute strike, courtesy of Messi's run and perfectly timed pass. There was still time for Switzerland to hit the post too, when it looked easier to score, and maybe football watchers began to believe that Argentina's name was finally on the trophy again. A 1-0 win over Belgium did nothing to dispel that feeling, Gonzalo Higuaín slamming home an eighth-minute volley. A fantastic 0-0 – if there is such a thing – came in the semi-final against the Netherlands, which went all the way to an agonising set of penalties. Ron Vlaar missed the first for the Dutch, with Messi handing his team the advantage immediately. It was his first contribution for a while, and even pundits such as former Barça player, Gary Lineker, a true Messista, said that he'd been disappointed with him during the tournament.

Wesley Sneijder's miss, or more accurately, Sergio Romero's brilliant flying save from the Netherlands' third spot-kick put Argentina on the brink of the World Cup final, and their passage was secured once Maxi Rodríguez smashed one past Jasper Cillessen.

July 9, 2014: Leo converted his spot-kick in the 2014 World Cup semi-finals game against the Netherlands at Arena Corinthians and Argentina won the penalty shoot out 4-2. (© Shutterstock)

Germany's stunning 7-1 demolition of the hosts Brazil in the other semi-final, ensured a repeat of the 1986 and 1990 finals. Here was the chance for Leo to finally match Diego Maradona, and where better to do it than in the backyard of their fiercest international rivals, and at the Estadio Maracanã, once Brazil's greatest stadium. Sadly it wasn't to be. Leo had another quiet game by his standards, with Higuaín missing his team's best chance. Both teams had 10 shots, but where Germany had half of theirs on target, Argentina had none. Controlling two-thirds of possession, Joachim Löw's side seized the trophy thanks to an opportune finish by Mario Götze seven minutes from the end of extra time. Leo's award for best player at the end of the final meant absolutely nothing to him, his evident disappointment beamed to watching millions around the world.

As captain, he had shouldered the responsibility of a nation and played well, but failed to give them what they wanted. The stats-based website WhoScored.com reported that he had completed more dribbles and created more chances than any other player at the tournament, but it wasn't enough.

Barça had delayed their transfer ban by appealing the sanction, allowing them to sign Luis Suárez, while Jérémy Mathieu, Thomas

Vermaelen, Ivan Rakitić, Douglas and, unusually, two goalkeepers in Claudio Bravo and Marc-André ter Stegen, also joined to bulk up the squad. The signing of Suárez caused the most consternation at the time, since he had been banned from 'all football related activity' until late October after biting Italy's Giorgio Chiellini during Uruguay's World Cup group game against Italy. The pictures were damning, with bite marks clearly seen on the Italian's shoulder. It's largely unknown what the Barça squad felt about their new team-mate but even if his morals were questionable, his footballing talent was not, and president Bartomeu refused to include a 'biting clause' in his contract.

Suárez had been approached before the World Cup and his camp feared Barça might pull out following his transgression, with the weight of public opinion firmly against such a deal. A striker who took a chunk out of opponents seemed at odds with the ethos of a club that prided itself on the way it conducted its business, but Suárez need not have worried. "We knew from years ago that he liked our club and our city," Bartomeu noted. "And we had the advantage because his agent is Pep Guardiola's brother. He has Barça in his heart, so everything was perfect, and we know that he had better offers than ours. We didn't rethink the decision and we told Luis that after the bite. He knows he did wrong but he apologised. That's very important for us. That means he knows that he didn't do things properly ... What we know is that we accept this responsibility and we also want this responsibility of bringing Luis Suárez to the family of football."

Rakitić even took time out of his own presentation to mention the Uruguayan's character. "The fact that he has had the character and the strength to go in front of everyone and say sorry says a lot about him as a person. Not everyone has that strength to admit they've done something stupid. I rarely say that I'm wrong so this says a lot about him. He has shown character and strength so he should be commended for that. His quality is unquestionable and he has the necessary attributes to play for Barça."

Both the Croatian and the Uruguayan would be playing for a new coach. While underwhelmed by Tata Martino's evident failure, supporters weren't exactly thrilled by his successor, their former player, Luis Enrique Martínez, also known as Lucho or Luis Enrique. He'd done well at Barça B a few years previously, but had not impressed at Roma and had completed an ordinary season with Celta

August 18, 2014: The FC Barcelona team are presented to the culés at Camp Nou before the traditional season opening Joan Gamper Trophy match. Barça beat Club Leon 6-0. (© Shutterstock)

Vigo. Most felt he lacked the experience needed to take the helm at the Camp Nou. That his hard-line manner upset a few of the players during the initial stages of his tenure also played into the narrative that, perhaps, the job was too big for him. His forceful message during his first press conference, that he was the "leader of this team", got a few backs up immediately.

That tension soon came to a head despite the team starting the season well with nine wins a draw and single loss from 11 games in all competitions. Eibar, the smallest team to ever compete in La Liga, with a ground, Ipurua, that held just 5,500 supporters, arrived at Camp Nou for the first time for a real 'David v Goliath' encounter. The entire population of the Basque town would fit inside the Camp Nou, and still leave space for 60,000 Barça supporters! A home win was always on the cards, and when Leo had made the game safe at 3-0 in the 74th minute, his coach motioned for him to come off. Yes, Leo Messi, the one player that was never substituted was being told to leave the pitch. Given he'd barely rested since the World Cup, Enrique was within his rights to want to keep Leo fresh, but all he got from the player was a thumbs up. If not quite a downright refusal to come off, it was certainly a red rag to the coach, who put his hands out in front of him in a 'what are you playing at?' gesture. Messi just kept his thumb in the air and carried on playing.

In the end, Neymar was hauled off for Munir El Haddadi but the mounting tension behind the scenes between Messi and Enrique was laid bare for everyone to see. There had been press rumours for a while but this was the first public spat.

The coach's cause wasn't helped a week later by a first defeat of the league season at, of all places, the Santiago Bernabéu. Much pre-game narrative centred around Luis Enrique's penchant for consistently changing his line-ups and tactics, and more leaks about unhappy players appeared in the Spanish press. This Clásico was also Suárez's official debut for the club, and the Uruguayan was soon in the thick of the action. He set up Neymar for the opening goal after just four minutes then, with another cross, found Messi who inexplicably fired wide from close range.

It proved an expensive miss. Ronaldo soon equalised from the penalty spot and Pepe rose unmarked in the second half to power Real into the lead from a corner. On 61 minutes, a mix up between Mascherano and Iniesta as *Los Blancos* counter-attacked, enabled Karim Benzema to kill the game off, the win bringing Real to within a point of Barça at the top of the league table. Worse was to follow. Barça lost their next fixture, at home to Enrique's former employers, Celta Vigo, in spite of hitting the woodwork four times. Joaquín Larrivey's 55th-minute finish gave Celta their first win at Camp Nou and their first in Barcelona since October 1941, when Barça were still playing at the Les Corts stadium. It put a real dampener on what was supposed to be a special night for Leo. He was within a couple of goals of setting the new all-time record for goals scored in La Liga, but he'd have to wait to surpass Telmo Zarra's 59-year-old mark of 251. In the dressing room afterwards, Messi took his frustrations out on Luis Enrique, moaning about the team selection and his coach's tactics.

It took the visit of Sevilla, Leo's favourite opponents, three weeks later, to see off the record. Enrique had made another six changes from the previous match, but rumblings of discontent soon subsided when Leo won a free-kick just outside the area. His 'postage stamp' finish was worthy of equalling Zarra's record, a monkey off his back after a month of lost opportunities. Sevilla 'keeper, Beto, screamed at his wall, but there was little point in blaming them, given the quality of the finish. Having equalled the record in just 289 league appearances, the only question was how long he would take to claim it as his own.

With 19 minutes left to play, Leo picked the ball up just inside Sevilla's half and motored towards the area. As both centre-backs closed in, he found Neymar to his left, and with Beto narrowing the angle the Brazilian returned the favour setting up Leo to slide the ball into an unguarded net. As he hugged Neymar and Suárez, Camp Nou, even including the presidential box, erupted. 'Supera Zarra' with a picture of Leo's face adorned the scoreboard. Hoisted above his team-mates' shoulders, he was 'bumped', with the entire team uniting in his joy. Once the celebrations subsided Leo got back to work. He wasn't finished with Sevilla. A typical finish, dribbling right to left across the area, the ball stuck to his left foot before unleashing a low drive, completed yet another hat-trick. The papers couldn't get enough of it. Even Real Madrid-leaning *MARCA* went with a '*Rey Gol*' (King of Goals) strapline on its front page. '*No te vayas nunca, Leo!*' (Never leave, Leo) screamed the headline in *Sport*, whilst *Mundo Deportivo* went for 'King Messi' and *L'Esportiu* noted simply, '*Esta tot dit*' (It's all said).

Leo followed up his record-breaking achievement with a Champions League hat-trick against APOEL in Cyprus three days later, and another, his third in four games, in a 5-1 pummelling of Espanyol. The goal-spree ended a fortnight before Christmas when lowly Getafe held the *Blaugranes* to a dull goalless draw. Leo would hit the crossbar, but only two of Barça's 23 shots were on target. It left Luis Enrique raging, again, and much more significant bad news followed on December 30, when the Court of Arbitration for Sport (CAS) rejected their appeal against the transfer ban, giving Messi-dependence a whole new meaning.

Enrique's anger at the Getafe game was evident when he chose the team to play Real Sociedad at Anoeta, Barça's bogey ground. A win for the *Blaugranes* would put them two points clear at the top of La Liga, but Messi, Neymar and Dani Alves were benched, supposedly because they had had club dispensation to return late from their Christmas holidays. Gerard Piqué was also dropped and his replacement, Jérémy Mathieu, had a stinker. TV shots of a dejected and furious Leo sat on the bench conveyed the mood perfectly.

Barça were dire in the first 45 minutes, improving only marginally when Messi and Neymar were brought on at half-time in the eventual

1-0 defeat. The almighty post-match row between between the coach and his best player was downplayed at the time, but confirmed years later by Enrique, who revealed: "Until the issue was resolved there was a period of tension, which I was not looking for in any way, but which happened and needed to be managed," he noted.

Messi missed the following morning's open training session, a rare occasion when supporters have half a chance of getting close to the players. The official line was that he had gastroenteritis, but nobody believed a word of it.

Nor was this the only tension at Camp Nou. Sporting director, Zubizaretta, made effectively redundant by the the CAS ruling, was sacked, his assistant, former captain, Carles Puyol, chose to resign, and president, Josep Maria Bartomeu called early club elections. "The principle motive to call elections is to relieve tension that the club is experiencing, a tension that is out of proportion. This noise, this tension that is out of proportion inevitably affects the team, of course ... I ask that there is fair play among all the candidates and we all concentrate on what is best for the club ... We will seek re-election. We started in 2010 and we want to keep going."

Another Ballon d'Or win for Ronaldo, much expected because of Messi's injury-hit 2014, barely raised a ripple at Barça, but the ceremony did provide some amusement for Barça's players, who were initially unsure what to make of Ronaldo's 'SIIIIIUUUU' shout at the end of his speech.

The much-needed 'clearing of the air' wanted by Enrique had a galvanising effect on the pitch. Barça won their next 10 games with Leo scoring in nine of them and, after a surprise 1-0 home loss to Málaga, reeled off another nine wins. A draw at Sevilla was the only other time they dropped points in the second half of the season. For all the misgivings about Luis Enrique, his record began to speak for itself. A 5-1 aggregate win over Paris Saint-Germain took the *Blaugranes* to another Champions League semi-final appearance, the second leg giving Luis Enrique his 42nd win in just 50 games in charge, even better than Pep had managed.

In the six games prior to the Champions League semi-final against Bayern Munich, Barça had scored 23 goals and were were favourites. Bayern, though, had a coach who knew almost every detail of their play, not to mention possessing experienced players of high quality like Xabi Alonso and Bastian Schweinsteiger. The embrace before the first leg at Camp Nou between the two coaches, former Barça team-

May 6, 2015: 'Mr Messi' - A brace from Leo and one from Neymar see Barça beat Bayern Munich 3-0 in the first leg of the Champions League semi-final. (© Mundo Deportivo)

mates, was genuine and warm, but once the whistle blew they were enemies for the next 90 minutes.

Barça dominated from the start, but took 77 minutes to score, as Leo fired a low drive past Manuel Neuer. It was his 76th Champions League goal, drawing him level with Ronaldo again, and also his first in the knockout stages. His second goal (or goal 77) arrived three minutes later and was one of the greatest goals the competition has seen. Receiving the ball from Ivan Rakitić in the right channel, he was placed in a one-on-one with Jérôme Boateng. As Messi twisted and turned, the big German had no idea what to do and completely lost his balance. Like a tree being felled by a skilled lumberjack, Boateng hit the turf in a split second as Leo glided by. Neuer advanced towards the edge of the six yard box but Leo dinked it over him with his right foot. There was nothing simple about the finish, it was truly world class. As the visitors piled forward in the hope of an away goal, a breakaway saw Leo play Neymar in to finish the tie as a contest, and gain some revenge for their hammering at the same stage of the competition some two years previously.

Guardiola who had feared that nothing and no one could stop Leo, was proved right on the night. He'd help create the little magician who had continued to mesmerise opponents Europe-wide and after the game, he had little complaint. Yet again Messi had risen to tbe big-game occasion. Luis Enrique, by now on good terms with Leo, described him as a player from another dimension. In the reverse fixture Neymar's brace before the half-hour in Bayern's 3-2 home win sealed Barça's place in the final against Juventus in Berlin.

Off the pitch, incumbent president Josep Maria Bartomeu was being challenged by former president, Joan Laporta, Agustí Benedito

The four candidates who contested the FC Barcelona presidential election in 2015, L-R: Toni Freixa (3.7%), Joan Laporta (15.6%), Josep Maria Bartomeu (54.6%) and Agustí Benedito (7.1%). (© Roderic Alves)

and Toni Freixa in an election including live television debates. Laporta was making no secret of his relationship with Leo, and while the player never publicly backed any one candidate, he didn't have the best relationship with the board in 2015 and is believed to have preferred Laporta.

Real Madrid pushed hard in the league and only lost out to the *Blaugranes* by two points in a tight run-in. There was also drama on the final day. Barça were cruising to victory at home to Deportivo La Coruña thanks to Messi's brace. The Galicians were all but relegated to the Segunda División, until goals in the 67th and 76th minutes (and results elsewhere going their way) saw them stay up on goal difference, and head to head records, against the other teams on 35 points – Eibar and Granada.

Once the disquiet over the result, and the way in which the team had capitulated, had died down, Barça's season ended once again with two finals – the Copa del Rey against Athletic Club and the Champions League against Juve. Following Real Madrid's refusal to host the game, the Copa del Rey was held at Camp Nou, despite the *Blaugranes* being one of the finalists. Athletic had no objection since it meant more of their supporters would be able to see the final, and the pressure would be all on the 'home' team.

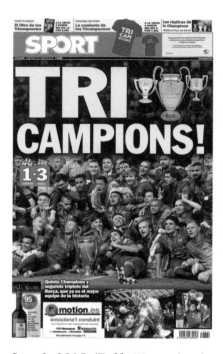

June 6, 2015: 'Treble Winners' - The entire FC Barcelona squad celebrate on Berlin's Olimpiastadion pitch after beating Juventus 3-1 in the 2015 Champions League Final. The victory meant Barça had won the treble for the second time in its history. (© Sport)

Barça, who had created a stir by wearing their suposedly away 'Senyera' (Catalan flag) kit for the first time at Camp Nou for Athletic's visit in the league the previous September, citing the 300th anniversary of the fall of Barcelona at the hands of Philip V's troops and the French in 1714, were warned by the Spanish Football Federation that they wouldn't tolerate political banners or symbols being brought to the final by the club's supporters, nor did they expect the Spanish national anthem to be abused, as it had been at the 2009 final. There was little chance of Basque or Catalan fans deferring to the Spanish monarchy and the whistles, boos and verbal abuse aimed in the direction of the King only heightened the already mind-blowing atmosphere.

Just as in 2009, Barça started off like Usain Bolt out of the blocks. With Messi clearly well up for the game, the ruling out for offside of Neymar's 10th-minute volley merely postponed the inevitable. Ten minutes later, Leo received the ball six yards into Athletic's half and about two yards in from the touchline. With a defender in close proximity, there was absolutely no danger at all. Turning into the middle of the pitch, Leo swiftly changed direction, leaving his marker for dead and opening up the right-hand channel. He couldn't, could he? Off he scampered on another of his exhilarating expeditions. 'Catch me if you can' seemed be an apt metaphor as, without straying far from the sideline, he made it midway into Athletic's half unchallenged.

With not one, not two, but three defenders all within six feet of him, Messi, somehow, managed to evade any tackles and bore down diagonally on the area. Turning Aymeric Laporte inside out, he buried the ball in the bottom corner for what was one of the greatest Copa del Rey final goals ever scored. Gareth Bale's was good, but was more about pace and out-running the defence. This slaloming effort took skill, pace and technique as well as a sniper's vision to ensure a successful outcome, and his team-mates' reaction showed how special it was. A tap-in late in the second half sandwiched a lovely team goal finished off by Neymar, to earn the *Blaugranes* a thoroughly deserved second title of the season. Leo's man-of-the-match award was probably the easiest ever to judge.

Barça were acutely aware of the challenge facing them in seeking a second treble. Juventus, who had also won their domestic double, had knocked out holders Real Madrid in the semi-finals, and with players like Morata, Pogba and Vidal were a class outfit.

Any sense of foreboding in the Barça sections of the spectacular Olympiastadion were eased by Ivan Rakitić's fourth minute goal, and even though Morata equalised, the match became a further triumph for Messi. Constantly involved, he registered an assist to top the list for that season's tournament and was joined as leading scorer on 10 by both Neymar and Suárez when they claimed their second-half goals. The victory, which gave Xavi Hernández a fitting finish to his magnificent Barça career, completed another journey for the club from turbulent beginnings to a triumphant conclusion, with Messi at the heart of everything.

14

Adios Argentina?

Retirement on the Cards

"I've appreciated trying to stop him performing, it's been fantastic to be around someone like that, albeit from afar. He has to be appreciated."

Within a week of completing his second Barça treble Leo was thrust headlong into another Copa América tournament, this time in Chile. Argentina, now coached by Tata Martino, were amongst the favourites to take the crown, particularly with Messi in such fine form in European football. Again they, and he, disappointed. A penalty in the opening game, a 2-2 draw with Paraguay, was his only normal time goal in the tournament and even though wins over Uruguay and Jamaica saw them through as group winners, the turn in the narrative showed the bind Leo was in with his home public and media. The search for a 'new Diego' was ever more desperate. Leo's level was often well above that of his colleagues, and he was arguably responsible for getting his country to the latter stages of tournaments, but then their collective failure somehow also became his responsibility. There was no middle ground, and he had millions of Argentines on his case because the team couldn't get over the line when it mattered. Every match for Argentina brought pressures akin to asking an orchestra conductor to also lead the string section, the woodwind section and percussion, then moan when you leave the theatre that it 'wasn't that good'. FC Barcelona may have been accused of being Messi-dependent, but the Argentina team took that Messi-dependence to the very limit.

Eventually he would crack, but not this year. He took and converted the first penalty as Colombia were eliminated 5-4 in the shoot-out after a goalless draw, then contributed three assists in the semi as Argentina at last clicked into gear, hammering Paraguay 6-1. That performance made them hot favourites in the final against Chile, but Leo struggled to get into a rough, highly physical contest and being the only Argentinian to score when they lost the penalty shoot-out 4-1 was no consolation at all.

Once again he took the blame. Never one to resist an opportunity to get himself in the limelight, Diego Maradona went in hard. "It's logical that he's come in for flak," he would tell *Ole*. "It's easy to explain. We've got the best player in the world, who goes and scores four goals against Real Socieded, and then he comes here and doesn't touch the ball. You're left saying to yourself, 'Dammit, are you Argentinian or Swedish?' People have got to stop droning on about Messi needing to be pampered. Messi should be treated just like any other player who pulls on the national team shirt. Like the best in the world, for better or worse. Still, it's not like Messi killed or raped someone; we mustn't make a drama out of this. We musn't be extremist, but we mustn't get used to always finishing second either."

Much less predictably, Messi's own grandfather, Antonio Cuccittini, weighed in, causing family issues behind the scenes. "Some of him was there and triumphs are the greatest things there are, but the last three games he was bad, he was lazy," Cuccittini told Radio Casilda. His comments echoed many others, but weren't fair. His performances would have been more than acceptable from any other player, but the issues were precisely because he was Lionel Messi – the 'best player in the world'. A man who was supposed to be a world-beater every single week, even if his own team-mates were well below their own level. Named Most Valuable Player (MVP) for the tournament – at least his efforts were recognised by those in power – he refused to take the award, knowing it would only fan the flames further.

In the FC Barcelona presidential election Joan Laporta challenged hard, lacerating incumbent Bartomeu's way of running the club when he gave me a one-on-one interview in the early hours at his campaign headquarters:

> "Well it's a different model. One of my opponents is changing our model and this is the reason why I am running in the elections. We think that the best model is a model that has La Masia, our academy, as a system to make the club sustainable. Not just sportingly, economically as well. In my opinion these opponents decided to extinguish La Masia. For them it was easier to go to the market than

August 11, 2015: The FC Barcelona squad celebrate after winning the UEFA Super Cup at the Dinamo Arena in Tbilisi, Georgia. (© Shutterstock)

work very hard in order to create players like Valdés, Piqué, Puyol, Xavi, Iniesta, Busi, Pedro and of course Messi. This takes time. It takes a big effort to develop this system and it's a long process. I think that it is much better for the club to have La Masia as a pillar of the model of managing the club than to have another system that continues to go to the market. Bartomeu, Rosell and these kind of people – they are being processed for corruption, tax evasion, and for fraud. And specifically because of their positions, FC Barcelona is processed as well for corruption and tax evasion. It's another reason why I think that he [Bartomeu] is not the right person to proceed in FC Barcelona."

He also planned to return UNICEF back to what he considered its rightful place, on the front of the shirt.

"He [Bartomeu] prefers Qatar, they prefer to sell practically most of our assets to Qatar because it's not only the sponsorship of our shirt, under that contract, there are more assets. If you go to the club you will see that Qatar is everywhere. We are proposing to recover UNICEF on our shirt because to me UNICEF has been the best non-sporting decision that we have taken. It was in my time as a president that I took that decision and I think that the project with FC Barcelona ... we were pioneers in social corporate responsibility of football clubs. We were launching a message to the less fortunate that they are not alone, there is a football club, the name is FC Barcelona, a club that was born in Barcelona, in Catalonia, and that we have a special sensibility in order to take care of the less fortunate, especially vulnerable boys and girls. It's not difficult. And can I say that this statement *'Més que un club'* [more than a club] - we have to demonstrate it."

Unseating an incumbent who had overseen a triumphant treble, along with the signing of Arda Turan from Atlético Madrid less than a fortnight before the election, was a tough ask, and Bartomeu was returned to the presidency.

Barça started the following – 2015-16 – season with mixed fortunes in the two Super Cups. A 115th-minute goal from Pedro, one of his last before joining Chelsea, clinched a 5-4 win over Sevilla in an epic European Super Cup in Tbilisi. Much earlier, Leo had scored two direct free-kicks in the first 16 minutes as Barça built what looked like, before a remarkable Sevilla fightback, an unassailable 4-1 lead. The Spanish Super Cup was a different story and there was no comeback from a 4-0 first leg thumping by Athletic Club at San Mamés as the Basques claimed their first trophy in 30 years.

After Leo had gone scoreless in Barça's first two league games, while scoring in both matches for Argentina during the international break, fans went into meltdown when it was announced that he was missing training the day before they played Atlético Madrid.

Rumours of an injury spread before a club announcement that it was for 'family reasons' brought reassurance that there was instead something to celebrate. Antonella had given birth to a healthy baby brother for Thiago, to be named Mateo. Amid the outpouring of love and well wishes that followed on social media, there was evident surprise that the club still expected Leo to play the following day in Madrid. Not only did he play, but his first league goal of the season, followed by an apt thumb-sucking celebration for the cameras, was the winner at the Vicente Calderón.

By the end of the month, Leo was able to spend a lot more time with his family than he'd anticipated. Just three minutes into the game against Las Palmas, he was injured by a challenge from Pedro Bigas. Though he initially tried to play on, after eight minutes his game was over. Subsequent tests revealed a torn lateral collateral ligament in his left knee, ruling him out for 51 days and nine matches. He returned for the season's first Clásico, but hardly had to exert himself as his team-mates inflicted a 4-0 drubbing which, although he lasted another six weeks, effectively ended Rafa Benítez tenure at the Bernabéu.

The injury was soon forgotten as Barça went unbeaten until the second tussle against *Los Blancos* in early April. Messi scored in all but eight of those intervening 19 La Liga matches, and once more had every supporter in the palms of his hands. Hardened professional he may have been, but Mike Phelan could identify with that emotion:

"As a fan of Messi I always enjoyed him as a guy that could get bums off seats. He excited people. One on ones, beating people – that type of thing. That was never me as a player by the way [laughs]. I've always loved players that can dribble and run with the ball, they're two different things, and Messi's got that in abundance. It's him and the ball. He's that type of player ... the master. That's always impressed me with any player, but with Messi ... you know yourself when you've watched him ... when I've seen him live or even on the TV, he has this movement with the ball ... it's as if you end up being stood right behind him mimicking him because you want to be that guy, and before you know it you're stood on your feet because you're urging him to go on and on and on. That is Messi to me.

Unpredictability, excitement, delivery ... it's all in that one flowing movement that he seems to be able to do easier than anyone else. He definitely stands as one of the most outstanding footballers to have ever played football. The reason for that is his longevity, he never seemed to get injured and he played almost all the time. He always seemed to train and that's a quality in itself that not everyone has got. He always delivered, so from the point of view of being a student of the game, he probably had everything that you can't find from one player – all the time. He was the only one that constantly delivered and he did it with such force that everyone went 'wow!' He probably couldn't explain it himself if you asked him. He gave everyone such joy and that's what puts him up there for me as definitely in the world's best during my time. I've appreciated watching him, I've appreciated trying to stop him performing, it's been fantastic to be around someone like that, albeit from afar. He has to be appreciated."

The 19-match winning run saw Barça reclaim the Club World Cup in Japan, Suárez the hero on this occasion with a hat-trick in the semi-final against Guangzhou Evergrande, and two more, to add to Messi's solitary goal in the final against River Plate. It sat nicely alongside the 2015 Ballon d'Or, Messi's fifth, with Cristiano Ronaldo in a distant second place.

Defeat in the second Clásico, though, was followed by further setbacks. Losing to Real Sociedad at Anoeta – no surprise there – meant Real Madrid were breathing down their necks in the league, while Atléti knocked them out of the Champions League Round of 16. Messi's goal against Valencia in the next match was also in vain as *Los Che* walked away from Camp Nou with a 2-1 win. Barça were in full-on crisis mode now, with no margin left for error as Real were only a point behind.

Real won every game from the beginning of March, but came up short because Luis Enrique managed to steady the ship with his team not conceding a goal in their final five games. At the other end Barça banged in 24. They ended the season against the same opponent as they started, Sevilla, in the Copa del Rey final with another domestic double at stake. Luis Enrique was keen to talk up Leo's contribution: "I don't know what the future holds for us. We all think that Messi will be at Barça in the next few years and that is what all the *culés* want. The thought of having a team without Messi is not even something we contemplate." But it was something worth contemplating, of course. Every team has a talisman. During his tenure at Real Madrid, Cristiano Ronaldo was their go-to hero. No teams would do as well without their star name. Those who bang the Messi-dependence drum miss the point that every big club is the same, except that nobody else has a player that can do all of the things that Messi can, or as well as he can.

Assists for Jordi Alba and Neymar helped Barça win the Copa del Rey and while Iniesta was named man of the match, the papers were fulsome in their praise of the Argentinian. "The extraordinary talent of Leo Messi served up the double for Barça," said one, and it was a common theme. The contrast between the Spanish and Argentinian media was striking, however, and would be tested again in the third Copa América in as many summers, the *Centenario*. This surely had to be third time lucky for Leo & Co. There simply was no more margin for error as far as anyone in Argentina was concerned.

Just imagine having to play under that sort of pressure. Forget that the opponents might be your equal, or that some of your own team-mates are not really up to the required standard. The fate of a nation rests squarely upon your shoulders because you happen to be the best of a generation, probably the best ever, and are therefore an appointed standard bearer for the masses. You're not allowed to be human, can't ever make a mistake, and woe betide you if you do. Why would anyone want to go to work on that basis?

Nor did he start very happily, a back injury in the warm-up match against Honduras keeping him out of the opener against Chile, a game won 2-1 in his absence. Argentina led 1-0 when he came off the bench an hour into the second game against Panama. Cue the fireworks! Messi doubled the lead within seven minutes and had a hat-trick within 19 minutes of his introduction, grabbing the match by the scruff of the neck as if to say to his detractors 'stick that in your pipe and smoke it'. Aguero added a late fifth.

Easy victories over Bolivia (3-0), Venezuela (4-1) and the USA (4-0), in which Messi scored once and assisted twice, set them up for another final ... against Chile. It was time for revenge and to take out the frustrations of the last year. This had to be it, the game where Leo would finally elevate himself to stand shoulder to shoulder alongside Maradona. During normal time Leo did everything but apply the finishing touches, and found the Chilean 'keeper, Claudio Bravo, in inspired form. No goals in either normal or extra time meant the dreaded penalties again. The law of averages would surely fall the way of *La Albiceleste* this time wouldn't it?

Stepping forward after his future club-mate Arturo Vidal had failed with Chile's first penalty, Leo blazed his shot over the bar. Inevitably, and somewhat cruelly, that was the precursor to another gut-wrenching defeat – Lucas Biglia's miss and Francisco Silva's goal handing a second successive title to the Chileans. That was it, Leo had had enough. The day after the final, he announced his retirement from international football. "For me, the national team is over. I've done all I can. It hurts not to be a champion. It was the thing I wanted the most, but I couldn't get it, so I think it's over. I think this is the best for everyone – first of all for me, then for everyone. I think there's a lot of people who want this, who obviously are not satisfied, as we are not satisfied reaching a final and not winning it. It's very hard, but the decision is taken. Now I will not try more and there will be no going back."

15

Bernabéu Brilliance

500 Goals for Barça

"What surprised me is how much he knows about football, because he knows everything about his team-mates, his technical team, about football. He's aware of everything"

Leo's announcement sent shockwaves through Argentina, the realisation that the country would be bereft of their best player quickly hit home. Hashtags such as #NoTeVayasMessi (Don't go Messi), #ComeBackMessi and #StayMessi did the rounds on social media, and a campaign to get him to reverse his decision soon gained traction, but received no response from the Messi camp.

In any case, he had other worries. Before the season began he and Jorge were convicted by a Spanish court of tax fraud. Occasional shouts of "thief" greeted Leo as he made his way to the courthouse, but these were drowned out by adoring Barça fans who just wanted to see their hero. The Spanish government had alleged that over $5 million in taxes owing for image rights relating to Adidas, PepsiCo, Procter & Gamble and a number of other companies had not been paid, but hidden in offshore companies in Belize and Uruguay. Both were sentenced to 21 months in prison, suspended as they were first time offenders. "I never asked my dad about these things. The truth is that as my dad explained before, I trusted him and the lawyers. I didn't know anything about it, I just played football," was Leo's explanation, and an appeal was lodged.

The international retirement proved short-lived. Just before the domestic campaign started with the first leg of the Spanish Super Cup final against Seville, Messi told the Argentinian media "A lot of things went through my mind on the night of the final and I gave serious thought to quitting, but my love for my country and this shirt

Blondes have more fun. The change to Leo's appearance at the start of the 2016/17 season set tongues wagging. (© Shutterstock)

is too great. We need to fix many things in Argentinian football, but I prefer to do this from inside and not criticise from outside."

The new Argentina national coach, Edgardo Bauza, had travelled to Barcelona to appeal to Messi to play in the World Cup qualifiers against Uruguay and Venezuela. "First we asked him if he would receive us," Bauza told *Sport* newspaper. "When he accepted, I knew that there would be no problem with him because it was going to be a chat about football. I didn't go to convince Messi, I was convinced that in the chat a possibility would arise. He received me with Javier Mascherano at the Ciutat Esportiva, and after the chat there was nothing more to say other than: 'Boys, you're called up for the next game.' What surprised me is how much he knows about football, because he knows everything about his team-mates, his technical team, about football. He's aware of everything."

The truth of that quip about needing to "fix many things" would be shown when Argentina were beaten 3-0 by Brazil in mid-November. Messi scored in the second leg of the 5-0 aggregate Super Cup defeat of Sevilla, twice in a 6-2 romp against Betis and on his international return against Uruguay, but did not appear to be firing on all cylinders until he claimed a hat-trick and an assist in 7-0 Champions League win over Celtic.

A month later Pep Guardiola returned to Camp Nou having now left Bayern for Manchester City. Before the game he was grilled about alleged approaches to Messi and other Barça players: "If I ever called a player playing in any other club it would be in a special situation of him not playing, and it would be my right to. It's okay, I could've phoned someone if he wasn't playing, but I never called Leo Messi. In his case, I really want him to play there [FC Barcelona] and finish his career there. But maybe he will think, 'OK, I want to go and play somewhere else' because maybe he wants his kids to speak English or enjoy a different experience, like what has happened to many of us. Maybe it could happen, but if he decides to go and it happens, there would be a list of seven or eight clubs that would want to sign him, and it would be down to him. Messi will decide where to go. If you are talking about this summer, I never called Messi, Neymar, Luis Suárez, Busquets, Iniesta ... I didn't call anybody."

He did admit, though, to approaching Marc-André ter Stegen, who decided to stay at Barça, and Claudio Bravo who did take up City's offer. Both Guardiola and City defender, Pablo Zabaleta, Messi's international team-mate, acknowledged the challenge they faced and were proved right when Leo scored a hat-trick (his 37th for Barça) on a night when City were shown how much further they needed to progress to regularly challenge for the Champions League and join Europe's elite. Leo's goal in the return leg was his 54th in the UCL group stages, overtaking the previous record holder, Raúl.

Leo's international career was also back on track, albeit not on the pitch. While Argentina's 3-0 loss to Brazil might once have brought the media down on his head, when the disarray behind the scenes – and Messi's part solution to it – phoning his father and arranging for payment for the workers who had fallen victim to the Argentinian FA's current financial problems – there was a much more conciliatory tone.

The Argentinian Football Association (AFA) were in such a mess, believed to be bankrupt and unable to pay their staff, that an external FIFA committee were overseeing their work. Journalist Juan Pablo Varsky told *Sport*: "Messi was in his room waiting for the game against Brazil in Belo Horizonte, when there was a knock at the door. Two or three people appeared, all from the security team that look after the players, and they said 'Leo we have to talk with you. For five or six months they [AFA] have not paid us. The situation is complicated, you are the captain of the team, you know us, we are asking for your help.' When Messi finds out that I've said about this situation he will be furious, but it doesn't matter. There are a lot of actions that he doesn't want people to know about but I thought it pertinent to tell this story because there is no reason not to, save for his anger."

It helped switch the narrative surrounding Leo's commitment to his country, with the Argentine public now more aware and sympathetic to Messi's on-field and off-field efforts for their national team. His highly critical social media messages about the AFA now made more sense. One posted on Instagram read 'Once again waiting in an airplane to take off ... what a disaster the AFA is, for God's sake!' It was also speculated that his exasperation with the AFA was partly behind his decision to quit the national team after the Copa defeat. Fortunately, he had no further international commitments until March 2017, leaving him to focus on FC Barcelona.

During that period Barça would lose just three competitive matches, Cristiano Ronaldo reclaimed the Ballon d'Or and Messi received the Golden Boot for his 51 goals in 2016. The first defeat, a surprise 2-1 Copa del Rey Round of 16 first leg loss to Athletic Club, was overturned in the second leg, while three draws and eight wins out of the next 11 matches, with goals in both legs of the Copa del Rey semi-final defeat of Atlético Madrid, brought him and Barça to a St. Valentine's Day date with Paris Saint-Germain at the Parc des Princes.

There was certainly no love for the Catalans in Paris that night as Luis Enrique's side were torn to shreds. Messi's Argentina team-mate, Ángel Di María, started the 4-0 rout with a wonderful direct free-kick that Leo himself would've been proud of. Di María's second, PSG's third, was another world class finish, with Julian Draxler (after a Messi error) and Edinson Cavani, on his 30th birthday, grabbing two more which appeared to put the *Blaugrana* out of the Champions League for another season.

Returning to league action, Leo scored six goals in the following four games, Barça winning all four with a collective aggregate of 14-2, but the 6-1 win over Sporting Gijón was tinged with sadness. "I won't be at Barcelona next season," Luis Enrique announced in his post-match press conference. "I need to rest. I would like to thank the club for the confidence they have shown in me. It's been three unforgettable years. It's a very difficult decision for me, one I've thought about a lot, but I think I need to be true to myself and fair to my way of thinking. In the pre-season I had a meeting with Albert Soler and Robert Fernández where I mooted the possibility that I might not renew my contract. They told me that there was no rush to take the decision. That moment has arrived. I'm announcing it ... I'm not forgetting there are still three incredible months to go."

When Celta Vigo were hammered 5-0, three days before PSG were due at Camp Nou, talk began of a *remuntada* (comeback). Quite why there was even the slightest thought of an upset is beyond comprehension. This was in spite of none of the previous 213 Champions League or European Cup first legs ending 4-0, dating back to the start of the competition in 1955, having been reversed in the second leg. Luis Enrique did nothing to dispel the optimism in his pre-game press conference. "We are only halfway through the tie, there are 95 minutes left and lots of things can happen. I go into the game with a positive mood. We have to do everything really well, both in defence and in attack because PSG are a really good side. Of course, lots of things have happened since the first leg. We have improved and have put in some good performances. We are optimistic by nature and convinced of what we can do. We will try to make the most of the favourable circumstances because if a team can score four against us, we can score six against them. We've seen that before this season and we have nothing to lose."

Few journalists took him seriously. The most PSG had conceded that season was three, they had gone through the Coupe de France without letting in a single goal and were unbeaten in the Champions League. Most took the view that while Barça were certainly capable of winning the second leg, it was impossible for them to be in the draw for the quarter-finals.

The *culés* packed into Camp Nou and got right behind the team from the very first whistle, perhaps feeling Enrique's resignation had set the wheels in motion for one last hurrah. After only two and a half minutes, Luis Suárez's scrambled opener set the place alight and Barça dominated most of the first half with PSG looking increasingly rattled. In the 39th minute a comedy of errors in the visitors' defence saw Layvin Kurzawa put through his own net. Luis Enrique's fist-pumping celebration on the touchline was mirrored all around the stadium and up in the press box. The comeback was on!

Five minutes after the break Leo slammed home a penalty after Neymar was upended, but the dream looked to be over after Cavani netted just after the hour. The score stayed at 3-1 right up until three minutes from the end of normal time. Yet almost nobody had left the stadium, and their support galvanised the XI on the field in those final few minutes. Neymar's tracer bullet of a free-kick got Barça within touching distance (4-1) then Suárez was felled in the box with 30 seconds of normal time to play. A successful penalty would put Barça within one more goal of the most improbable result in the competition's history. Neymar was probably the coolest person in the stadium when he tucked the ball home (5-1), and five minutes of injury-time felt like five hours.

There was an 'attack v defence' feel about the match, as PSG retreated into themselves and allowed the *Blaugranes* to come forward at every opportunity. This was the expression 'throwing the kitchen sink at it,' played out on a football pitch. With 22 seconds left to play, Neymar floated a ball into the area, and as six PSG players attempted to play the offside trap just one more time, it was sprung by Sergi Roberto who launched himself towards the ball. The *culés* in Camp Nou held its breath in disbelief as Roberto stretched his right foot to meet the flight of the ball and, in the same movement, keep it under control as he diverted it past the flailing PSG 'keeper, Kevin Trapp. The contrast in emotions as the ball nestled in the back of the net was stark. While PSG coach Unai Emery sat crestfallen, knowing his tenure with the French club was over, Luis Enrique, following a sprint onto the pitch and a sliding celebration, joined players and staff partying on the sidelines. Roberto himself was buried beneath a sea of bodies, but Leo was not among them.

He'd rushed behind the goal to stand on the advertising hoardings, furiously beating his chest and waving his fist at the crowd. Commentators screamed superlatives into their microphones, even the journalists in the press box – much like when Rivaldo had scored a last-minute bicycle kick against Valencia in the UCL some years before – had taken temporary leave of their senses and were up on their feet cheering. A minute later, it was all over and the celebrations began again in earnest. *Cant del Barça*, the club's anthem was sung as never before, with every player and member of staff dancing joyfully on the pitch in front of a Camp Nou awash with flags as 90,000 Catalans attempted to make sense of what they had just witnessed. Their club's exhilarating *remuntada* ('comeback' in Catalan) quickly became global news, hit the headlines as *La Remontada* (the Spanish for 'The Comeback'), and the term is now part of football's global dictionary.

Yet much of the sports news the following day tended to focus on the refereeing of Deniz Aytekin. The 'UEFAlona' tag that had become a bit of a buzzword over the years reared its ugly head again and, bizarrely, there was even a petition to get the game replayed which garnered thousands of signatures. A Real Madrid supporter called Luis Melendo Olmedo started the petition on change.org citing 'incidents that seriously damaged PSG as a result of the German referee Deniz Aytekin, who gave Barcelona an advantage with his refereeing decisions.' At the core of Olmedo's 'complaint,' were the two penalties Aytekin handed the Catalans, and the one he failed to give to PSG. By the time the petition had closed, more than 100,000 people had signed it!

The comedown from such a high was always likely to be swift. Defeats by Deportivo La Coruña the following weekend and at Málaga three games later hit Barça's league hopes, and they were outplayed by Juventus at Camp Nou in the first leg of the Champions League quarter-final, going down 3-0, and eliminated following a goalless draw in Italy. In just over five weeks, the *Blaugranes* had gone from being the toast of Europe to also rans. Luis Enrique knew anything other than a win in the Clásico at Real Madrid would more or less end the title race.

An expectant crowd were treated to a fantastic 90 minutes of football, which ultimately gave the pocket of Barça supporters high up in the gods cause for celebration. Leo received treatment for blood pouring from a blow to the mouth from Marcelo, but chose to play on, and Real took an early lead through Casemiro.

A static Real defence stood and watched as Ivan Rakitić played a square ball for Messi to dart in between three defenders and fire beyond a helpless Keylor Navas. It was his his 499th goal for the club in all competitions, and should soon have been followed by his 500th, but he missed a sitter when Navas misjudged a simple cross. As if in imitation, Cristiano Ronaldo, quiet for the most part, missed Real's best chance of the game from six yards out with the goal at his mercy. They were made to pay when, with 17 minutes left to play, Rakitić hammered home a stunning shot. Ramos' red card for going in on Messi with his studs up was deserved, and compounded by his gestures at Gerard Piqué, who'd given pre-match interviews suggesting that some league referees were in the pocket of *Los Blancos*. The inference from Ramos was crystal clear.

April 23, 2017: Leo raises his No.10 shirt to the Santiago Bernabéu faithful in one of his most iconic celebrations. It came after scoring his 500th Barça goal in the last minute of El Clásico which won the match for the Catalans, 3-2, and kept their league title hopes alive. (© Mundo Deportivo)

Yet Real hit back. With five minutes left, the out-of-favour James Rodríguez was allowed to waltz right through the entire Barça defensive line before hooking a Marcelo cross into the roof of the net. Instead of saving the game, Rodríguez goal instead proved to be the cue for Messi's 500th.

Barça were hemmed deep in their own territory with 30 seconds of injury time left when Sergio Busquets' simple five-yard ball to

Sergi Roberto set it in motion. Roberto took off and both Luka Modrić attempted tackle, and Marcelo's excuse for one, left him with acres of space to run into. Much further infield than he had been, Roberto entered Real's half unchallenged before releasing André Gomes in the left-wing position. Receiving the ball, Gomes instinctively knew that Jordi Alba was overlapping and the precise timing of his pass meant the left-back didn't have to check his run. Alba's first-time pass found Messi, who had checked his run until he knew the ball was coming. Only then did Leo motor into position and with a swing of the left foot, found the only part of the goal that Navas was unable to reach.

Messi stripped off his shirt and, after being mobbed by his team-mates, lifted it up with the shirt number facing the crowd, holding it aloft for all to see. With 14 seconds left, he'd scored his 500th goal, secured a win that drew Barça level at the top with Real, and instigated probably the most iconic image of his career. 'Here I am,' it screamed. His usual celebration of crossing himself before pointing to the sky followed, as did a yellow card from referee Alejandro Hernández Hernández, but Leo was too busy fist-pumping at the travelling support to worry about such minor indiscretions. Zidane's players were prone on the floor or, in the case of Ronaldo, gesticulating wildly.

The goal was the very epitome of Barça, in every facet of play from the very beginning of the build up to the eventual killer blow. It reignited the argument that Messi could only score such goals because his colleagues always played to his strengths, knowing that more often than not he would always deliver, and that he would not enjoy such success anywhere else. Rob Palmer, who commentated on the match in the UK for Sky Sports, disagreed, telling me:

"It's a tame argument. A player of his ability is always going to rise to the top. It's like a great singer. The band is the accompanying music. Without music the voice would still be beautiful, with accompaniment the voice is elevated. The better the band, the better the complete product. Put Sinatra with a symphony orchestra and it can't be beaten. But stick him with a pianist and it is still special. The records are just a log of what he's achieved. There are many times when he's passed the ball when he could have scored yet he still averages a goal per game. They are only relevant in measuring the effect he's had in the period. In this day and age there is too

March 8, 2012: 'A spectacular Messi scores five' proclaims the Catalan press. (© L'Esportiu de Catalunya)

much statistical analysis. The goals to games ratio and goals in major games sums him up in numbers. Some argue that he hasn't achieved with Argentina either. In truth it is a pretty poor period for Argentinian football and he's almost single handedly taken the team to Copa América finals. He's lacked the backing band there that Barça have, and one or two of the players accompanying him are buskers in comparison."

With five league games remaining, Barça had to win them all and hope Real, who had a game in hand, slipped up. Keeping to the script, the *Blaugranes* won all their games, most memorably in a 7-1 thrashing of Osasuna which saw Javier Mascherano score his only goal for the club – a penalty at 5-1 with 15 minutes left, at which the entire bench erupted and then collapsed in fits of giggles.

But Real won their six matches for their first title since 2011-12, leaving Barça second with a more than respectable 90 points. Consolation came in the Copa del Rey final at the Vicente Calderón against surprise package Alavés. Leo's opener on the half-hour, his 54th goal of the season, was cancelled out by a blockbuster direct free-kick from Theo Hernández, on loan to Alavés from Atlético Madrid and shortly to sign for Real, but Barça led 3-1 by the break. Neymar scored the second before Paco Alcácer claimed the third in first-half injury time thanks to Messi's run and perfectly timed pass, and the cup was retained for Luis Enrique's ninth title in three seasons. Leo could, for once, enjoy a relatively relaxing summer, and would need all the rest he could get ahead of the 2017-18 campaign.

16

More Than a Club

The Day Camp Nou Fell Silent

"I went to the Celtic game at the Nou Camp and spent the night just observing Leo. For large parts he just rested on the halfway line spectating. Strolling around. Then he became a human bluebottle."

Two days after the final, Ernesto Valverde was confirmed as Luis Enrique's successor, on a two-year deal with an option for a third. It was not a universally popular choice. Valverde had rarely figured near the top of media polls of fans and *culés* feared, rightly as it turned out, that the Basque coach would be much more pragmatic than his predecessors and his style of football wouldn't be at all brave or exciting. Compared to Jorge Sampaoli, heavily tipped at one stage, it was chalk and cheese. However, the board saw him as a 'safe pair of hands' – non-controversial, always courteous to the media, unlike Lucho who routinely fell out with journalists who irked him, and with the experience needed to manage a changing room full of world stars.

Valverde said he was particularly looking forward to working with Leo, who he reiterated was "the best player in the world". Spanish football expert and sports journalist, Andy West, writing on the BBC website, took a sceptical view: "Valverde will receive little more than a lukewarm welcome from many fans, who are sceptical of his abilities to master the internal politics inherent at such a huge club. There are fears that his understated personality will see him become a 'yes man' to an increasingly unpopular board of directors, lacking the strength of character to reinvigorate a team who have been treading water for too long." The summer media coverage was full of transfer rumours and reporting of the Spanish Supreme Court's decision to uphold Messi's tax conviction.

Stories of Neymar being courted by Paris Saint-Germain were largely ignored by FC Barcelona's board. After all, he was one of the best players in the world, lining up alongside two more world class exponents in Suárez and Messi. There was little, save for extra cash, that any other club could offer to match what he had in Barcelona. However, the rumours just wouldn't go away, and followed Barça on to their tour of the USA.

Gerard Piqué's social media image ahead of the first Clásico to be played in the USA, on July 29, 2017, and its caption '*Se queda*' ('he stays') was seen by many as the end of the matter. Yet the match in Miami, where he provided two assists and Messi scored, was Neymar's last for Barcelona.

A few days later, the bomb dropped, sending shockwaves through football. Neymar signed for PSG, who were paying his full buyout clause of €222m (£200m) – more than double the previous record of £89m Manchester United had paid Juventus for Paul Pogba a year earlier. Not even Barça were immune to the vast financial wealth provided to PSG by their Qatari backers. They reported PSG to UEFA for a breach of Financial Fair Play, and La Liga backed them by refusing to take payment at the league offices, forcing Neymar's representatives to pay the fee at the club offices.

Bartomeu and the board faced a sustained and vehement backlash, but there was little anyone could do to prevent a sale to a club willing to pay the buyout clause. In hindsight, setting Neymar's at €222m was far too low, but no one really believed that such figures would ever be reached. Neymar wanted to go and Barça had to move on – quickly.

The two-legged Spanish Super Cup final against Real Madrid brought little cheer, as Barça went down 5-1 across the two legs. Camp Nou spectators enjoyed seeing Ronaldo get a yellow card for taking off his shirt, then another two minutes later for diving (and derided his attempt to mimic Messi's goalscoring celebration) but little else – least of all the goal which gave Ronaldo his excuse and a Piqué own goal – in a 3-1 home defeat.

The 2-0 loss in the return at the Santiago Bernabéu led many supporters to believe that they were in for a very long and hard season. Instead, bar one or two results, it would be among the club's better recent seasons. Within days of the Super Cup defeat they'd spent a large chunk of the Neymar money on Dortmund's Ousmane Dembélé, a young Frenchman who'd gone on strike in order to push through his move to Camp Nou for a reported €105m plus add-ons, the second highest transfer fee of all time, but he injured his hamstring in his second match against Getafe and was out for four months – cue fresh abuse of the board for buying a 'crock'. Yet Barça were still unbeaten at Christmas and Leo was also undefeated in five matches for Argentina. He'd also gone on one of his runs, a run of braces, netting at least twice in the five consecutive matches in which he scored.

The last of the five, against Las Palmas, was to take on extra and unwanted significance. It took place on October 1, 2017, the day of the independence referendum called by the Catalan government, but with its legitimacy contested by the Spanish Constitutional Court and the central government in Madrid. Gerard Piqué was seen among the 43% of the electorate who voted, while more than 800 injuries were reported as voters across Catalonia were attacked by the Guardia Civil, a semi-paramilitary force sent in by the Spanish authorities to disrupt the vote.

The game against Las Palmas was scheduled for 4.15pm but, with the backing of some players and Catalan institutions, the club considered postponing the game to protect the public. The Catalan police, known as the Mossos d'Esquadra (or Mossos for short) said it was safe to go ahead, but president Bartomeu called off the traditional directors' lunch and moved to suspend the match. La Liga chief Javier Tebas warned him that if he did, FC Barcelona would be docked six points. Bartomeu was prepared to take the punishment and found support in the dressing room from Piqué, who thought the game should not be played under any circumstances, and Sergi Roberto. Other players, including Messi, were more concerned by the loss of points.

After further discussions it was decided to play, but to register their protest by doing so behind closed doors. Fans gathering for the game learnt of this just 30 minutes before the scheduled kick-off. The club's statement read: "FC Barcelona condemns the events which have taken place in many parts of Catalonia today in order to prevent its citizens exercising their democratic right to free expression. Given the exceptional nature of events, the board of directors have decided that the FC Barcelona first-team game against Las Palmas will be played behind closed doors following the Professional Football League's refusal to postpone the game." The tension rose inside the empty Camp Nou before the match as the Barça players warmed up in the *Senyera* (Catalan flag) shirt, whilst Las Palmas showed where their loyalties lay by sewing a Spanish flag onto their match shirts.

A 3-0 victory in the eeriest of atmospheres seemed of little consequence given the violence and civil disorder going on across Barcelona, but at least it maintained Barça's unbeaten run. Fans could be heard jeering and booing outside the stadium but the crowd eventually dissipated. The mental toll it had taken on some players was clear after the game. Piqué approached the microphones in the mixed zone and broke down in tears. "It's been the worst experience of my life. The pictures speak for themselves, everyone has seen them and there has to be consequences. We've spent years peacefully demonstrating and today the Police and the Civil Guard have come to act as they have done. I believe that there are a lot of people in Spain that are very against what has happened. I'm more proud than ever of a country that despite the violence has been more peaceful than ever." A watching world struggled to reconcile Spain's claims to be a progressive European state with the barbaric acts of its national police force which were more akin to the actions of authoritarian regimes.

Despite the unbeaten run, and 19 wins in the first 23 matches in all competitions following the Super Cup defeat, *culés*, whose expectations were conditioned by the Guardiola era, were unhappy. There was a feeling that whatever Valverde did, it was never going to be good enough and it would take an El Clásico victory to prove him as the real deal.

He duly got that win in the final match before Christmas. Goalless at the break, Luis Suárez opened the floodgates and the result was never in doubt. A penalty from Messi – which sparked another wonderfully antagonistic goal celebration – as well as a late third from sub, Aleix Vidal, handed Barça an unprecedented third straight league win at the Bernabéu and opened up a 14 point gap at the top of the table, effectively settling the title before Christmas. Valverde, however, still struggled to win over the *culés* and the media.

His demeanour didn't help. Valverde was indifferent to how he was perceived outside the club. He knew he was well liked by the players and staff and fully understood he was paid for the results he'd been delivering since joining the club, and so had the full support of the board. Unlike his predecessor, Valverde would never 'bite' on press questions designed to provoke him. He had no interest in playing the journalists' games, preferring to point to his record in his

February 20, 2018: Andrés Iniesta and Lionel Messi celebrate the Argentinian's equaliser during the first leg of the UEFA Champions League Round of 16 match against Chelsea FC at Stamford Bridge. (© Shutterstock)

deadpan style. He was a master of saying just enough to be polite, but never satisfying editors whose sole interest was controversey and sensationalism.

Messi netted in six of the first seven games of the New Year but was then scoreless in the next five, although that didn't impact on the growing strength of the team. As the season progressed, the more formidable Barça looked, and the possibility of a third coach grabbing a treble in his debut season started to loom. While it's fair to note that not many matches were swashbuckling, high scoring affairs, the *Blaugranes* rarely looked troubled. They'd again qualified for the Copa final back in early February after seeing off Valencia, had secured the league title before the winter break, and were also performing well in the Champions League.

Their victory at Stamford Bridge on February 20 typified this period. The atmosphere was oddly flat for what was arguably Chelsea's biggest game of the campaign at that point. The Blues were probably the better side in terms of intensity and on another night their shots against the woodwork would have gone in, but Willian's well worked opener was cancelled out by Messi's shot 15 minutes from time. Barça played as they had done all season – nothing spectacular, and riding their luck at times, but still so difficult to beat and, above all, getting the results they needed. That away goal would be crucial.

Before the return leg, Leo and Antonella had happy news to share. "Welcome Ciro!" Messi posted on Instagram to announce the birth of his third son. "Thank God everything went perfect. Mum and he are very well. We are super happy." Not quite as happy was Pancho Schroder, Barça's financial and strategy director, who told a Finance in Sport event: "We set up a clause which we think is enough to have Messi retire at FC Barcelona, but having said that, we thought a year ago that the clause for Neymar was also good enough to retain the player, and that proved last summer not to be the case. Looking at the future, I think, is difficult, but I don't have a crystal ball and these days things are getting a little bit crazy."

Two goals from Leo either side of an assist for Dembélé duly ejected Chelsea from the Champions League at Camp Nou, and encouraged Rob Palmer to analyse the player's evolution:

"It has been an evolution, because initially he fitted into the team. The likes of Ronaldinho and Xavi would dictate his play. Messi was given a role or position to play. As we reached the Guardiola era, Pep worked on tactics to maximise the talents of Messi. I remember analysing one performance with the great Michael Laudrup. He pointed out that Messi's starting position was often just in front of the right back position. His team-mates would clear the stage, giving him a clear 10 yards to work in. Each would offer an outlet if needed for a quick one two but keep a respectable distance away to allow him to dribble past the opponent. Over the years he has learnt to conserve energy. Wasn't there a game when the goalkeeper covered more yards in 90 minutes than Messi, who scored a couple of goals? I went to the Celtic game at the Nou Camp and spent the night just observing Leo. For large parts he just rested on the half way line spectating – strolling around. Then he became a human bluebottle. At a speed the human eye could hardly focus on, he'd touch the ball on the right hand side by the half way line, and after blinking he'd be playing a one-two at the edge of the penalty area. Within a breath he was smacking the ball into the goal from an Iniesta delivery."

Roma, less threatening on paper than several alternatives, came out of the hat for the quarter-final, with the first leg in Catalonia. Perhaps mistakenly, speculation about semi-final opponents began. An adductor injury for Messi dampened some optimism, but he came off the bench on his return at Sevilla to inspire the improbable revival, scoring the second of two last minute goals, which preserved Barça's unbeaten league record. A 4-1 first-leg win over Roma looked conclusive in spite of Edin Džeko's 80th minute 'consolation' away goal.

It would, however, prove much more than a consolation. Six minutes into the return, Džeko scored again and Barça were immediately on the ropes. In spite of controlling long periods, they never really got going against a Roma team who were 21 points off the Serie A lead at the time, and never looked like scoring. Everything changed just before the hour when Daniele De Rossi, who'd scored an own goal in the first leg, netted a penalty at the right end to give the locals some belief. Eight minutes from time, terrible marking at a corner allowed Kostas Manolas to head home a third which put Roma level on aggregate and ahead on away goals at 4-4.

Iniesta could have played until the weekend without scoring, and the Stadio Olimpico erupted at full-time to celebrate Roma's victory. Andrés Iniestia trudged off in tears, his last chance of a Champions League title with Barça gone. Messi had a face like thunder. *MARCA* called it 'The fall of Barça's Empire' whilst *Sport* went with 'Another Ridicule.' Most supporter and media ire was directed at Valverde's failure to introduce any subs until the 80th minute. Leo wasn't at his best, or anywhere close to it, and *Diario GOL* noted that Piqué had called out his captain post-match, suggesting that he'd "coasted" through the 90 minutes. Barça, as a team, lacked intensity and Mike Phelan has pointed to one way in which Messi could contribute to such problems:

> "Possibly, if anything, depending on what system he plays in and which country he plays in, maybe his weakness would be tracking back. He probably isn't the greatest defender, but does he have to defend because that isn't what he's paid to do? His capabilities to defend are more sitting in space rather than getting up against anybody, but it's horses for courses because different leagues demand different things. In Spain he's exceptional."

Valverde accepted responsibility. "We had no response. Everything went for them and we struggled to build our play. I am responsible, absolutely. I am the visible head of the team and it was down to me. With their pressure it forced us to knock balls long, we became disjointed and we were not able to win the second ball. When you lose and the opposition are better, then the analysis is often extreme. They were strong, physical and we had a lot of problems." Instead of earning him credit, this served to perpetuate the narrative that he didn't have what it took and the uproar threatened to destabilise the club ahead of the 2018 Copa del Rey final against Sevilla.

17

One Goal From Invincibility

The Perfect League Season, Almost

"He scored almost every time I saw him, and he always did something magic, no matter what it was: dribbling, assisting, scoring... But that goal, THAT GOAL, was beyond anything Messi had done previously."

Barça and Sevilla fans will not forget Saturday, April 21, 2018, in a hurry. It was a day on which their fans flocked into Madrid for the Copa del Rey final at Atléti's spectacular new Wanda Metropolitano stadium and mixed amicably with local fans and police in the city's cafes and bars. It was fun for all, at least until kick-off, when Sevilla rapidly lost their previous sense of enjoyment.

As early as the fifth minute, the signs were ominous for the Andalusians, and they were behind from the 13th when Barça 'keeper Jasper Cillessen realised that every Sevilla player was in his half and launched a long pass from his six-yard box. It wasn't touched until Philippe Coutinho picked it up, unmarked and level with Sevilla's penalty spot. Three touches later, he fed the unmarked Luis Suárez, who finished from close range. A quickfire sequence 15 minutes later – surgical, clinical, beautiful – was worthy of a cup final: from Messi to Iniesta to Alba to Iniesta to Alba, then a backheel to Messi who smashed the ball into the roof of the net. Alba, Messi and Iniesta combined again to create a third for Suárez before the break, yet the best moment of the match had still to arrive. Six minutes after the break, Iniesta, playing in his last ever final for the club before moving to Japan, was again at the heart of the move, playing a one-two with Leo before running unchecked into the area, rounding the 'keeper and sliding the ball into an empty net. The loudest cheers of the day echoed for one of the greatest midfielders ever to have graced the game. "Inieeeesta, Inieeeesta, Inieeeesta" sang the Barça faithful.

Coutinho made it five from a penalty and Samuel Umtiti could easily have added to what was already the biggest winning margin in a Copa del Rey final.

Despite their obvious disappointment, Sevilla's supporters showed their class when Iniesta was substituted with three minutes to go, rising with their Barça counterparts to acclaim him as he strode off of the pitch in tears. The outpouring of his emotions whilst on the bench remain one of the enduring images of the night, along with the trophy lift in which his team-mates allowed Iniesta to ascend the stairs by himself to enjoy the limelight in solitude.

The unprecented unbeaten league season remained as the final challenge facing the *Blaugranes*. Leo claimed a hat-trick at Riazor against Deportivo La Coruña the following week, then came a draw with Real Madrid and a 5-1 thumping of Villarreal. Just two more, very winnable, league games, away to Levante and at home to Real Sociedad, and the record was theirs.

The day after the Yellow Submarine had been sent home with their tails between their legs, a friendly against South African side, Mamelodi Sundowns, was officially confirmed. It had been known about for some time, but given that it would be being played, unusually, before the end of the league season, it wasn't 100% confirmed until May 10, 2018. An understanding that all of the big stars would play meant that the announcement caused uproar with supporters. The general consensus was that no amount of money was worth sabotaging league games for, particularly as the Catalans had arrived at this point still to lose a La Liga match. The only people who seemed delighted about the match were the organisers themselves. Sundowns boss, Patrice Motsepe, told reporters that he was never in any doubt that the game would take place: "We had no doubt, but we had to allow the internal processes within Barcelona to take place. We were told in good faith to make the announcement. What we did not recognise is that it is the World Cup year. The main concern was that players have to avoid fatigue. Today [Thursday] is the right time to announce it. We would like to express our deep gratitude as Motsepe Foundation and Mamelodi Sundowns."

No great concern was felt over Messi and Piqué absence at Levante. Even without them, Barça expected a relatively comfortable 90 minutes. It proved anything but. Piqué was replaced by Yerry Mina, a towering Colombian signed in the January window, who made two errors in the first half-hour, both leading to goals for Levante.

Philippe Coutinho's 38th-minute response was nothing more than a temporary reprieve as within three minutes of the re-start, Emmanuel Boateng had completed his hat-trick and Enis Bardhi had scored the first of his two goals. His second, Levante's fifth, arrived in the 56th minute – the first time Barça had conceded five goals in 15 years.

The *culés* watched on as the team fought back to 5-4 with 19 minutes to go, Coutinho completing a hat-trick of his own and Luis Suárez scoring a penalty, but the equaliser eluded them and the unbeaten season was gone. Official club statements argued that it didn't really matter, and the league title more than compensated. That's true of course, but PR spin wasn't cutting it for many. 'Barcelona's second fiasco of the season,' and 'An evening to forget for Yerry Mina' were two of the more polite headlines in the following day's sports papers. Social media users again roasted Valverde, going to town on the coach who had 'got it wrong again just as he had against Roma'. Anyone trying to present a more positive outlook on radio phone in shows was shot down in flames – 'How could Barça not have an answer against Levante?' It 'had to be Valverde's fault'.

Yet the Basque had won the league at a canter in his first season and hadn't relinquished the top spot in the table after week three. He'd won the Copa del Rey with arguably the best performance seen in a Spanish cup final in decades, and was two games away from mirroring Pep and Lucho's treble-winning first seasons at the helm. The support of his tactics, managerial style and general demeanour from Messi and his colleagues spoke volumes too. The final game of the league campaign wasn't quite the walkover expected, but 1-0 win meant that Barça had missed out on their unbeaten league season by a solitary goal. Coming so late in the season, though, it left a feeling of disappointment that detracted from the record 14-point margin over Atlético Madrid in second place or the 17 points by which Real Madrid trailed.

Another World Cup loomed, although it was generally accepted that Messi would have to show himself to be a true miracle worker to drag Argentina to victory in Russia. Messi, who was injured, was for once absolved from blame in March when *La Albiceleste* capitulated against Spain in Madrid, losing 6-1, but the implication of the result was clear, and a 4-0 warm-up win over Haiti in which he scored a hat-trick wasn't fooling anyone. The AFA excelled themselves as disorganisers by failing to arrange another fixture before the tournament started, in their wisdom organising a game against Israel in Jerusalem before pulling out because of political tensions.

There was little to cheer in their first match against World Cup debutants Iceland. Sergio Agüero's opener was soon cancelled out by Alfred Finnbogason, and Leo missed a penalty which would have won them the game. "It would've changed the script. It was the advantage," he told reporters. "Obviously it hurts me to miss the penalty as they would've opened up a little more and we could've found more spaces. We have the bitterness of not being able to take the three points that we deserved. To start with winning is always important, now we have to think about Croatia. We will try to pass this quickly."

The cracks exposed against Iceland, where they were often disorganised at the back, inviting their opponents on to them during the middle portion of the game, were brutally exposed by a Croatia side that included Leo's club mate, Ivan Rakitić, and Real's Luka Modrić. Both scored in a one-sided 3-0 victory. Goalkeeper Willy Caballero's howler for the opening goal, by Ante Rebić, got him replaced by Franco Armani for the final win-or-go-home group game against Nigeria, before which coach Sampaoli made the remarkable admission that his team was handicapping Messi: "I think that because of the reality of the Argentine squad, it sort of clouds Leo's brilliance. Leo is limited because the team doesn't gel ideally with him as it should. As coaches we need to realise these things and try to deal with them. I'm the one that needs to accept it."

That brilliance was to be showcased in Messi's first goal of the tournament. A wonderfully flighted cross-field ball from Éver Banega dropped over the head of Kenneth Omeruo. In one jaw-dropping movement, Leo collected the ball on his left thigh, allowed it to drop onto his left foot, with one motion pushed away from Omeruo and then delivered the coup-de-grâce with a right foot finish. No wonder he celebrated wildly, arms outstretched as he raced to the corner before sinking on his knees, arms aloft in the pose we know so well. He'd then hit the post with a free-kick, the closest his side came to a second before Victor Moses equalised with a second-half penalty. The tension was unbearable, and the more Argentina pressed for the winner they so desperately needed, the more susceptible they looked at the back.

With four minutes to play, Gabriel Mercado's perfect cross from the right was begging for the right connection. It came from centre-back Marcos Rojo, pushed forward in Sampaoli's last roll of the dice, who volleyed into the bottom corner with a finish that Messi himself would've been proud of. The captain hitched a piggy-back ride on the goalscorer, joined by the entire team and subs. Diego Maradona, watching on from a private box, could barely contain himself. TV footage picking up a conversation between Messi and Sampoali which appeared to lead to Sergio Agüero's introduction as a sub against Nigeria was rapidly exaggerated into suggestions that the captain rather than the coach was picking the team and organising the tactics. But as Sampaoli pointed out: "We looked at different options in an important game and had to make a decision. I was simply communicating this, saying we were going to use a strategy we had rehearsed to use more attacking players. It was a simple exchange I had with one of my players, that is all."

The less said about the game against eventual World Cup winners, France, the better. Argentinians had little to cheer other than Ángel Di María's blockbuster to equalise Antoine Griezmann's opener from the spot. The 4-3 scoreline was misleading, for Argentina were well beaten with Kylian Mbappé looking every inch the teenage world beater, and perhaps, longer term, the rightful heir to Messi's throne. Another tournament, another disappointment for Leo. Another where he'd failed to score in the knockout stages. Another disappointment for the country that would blame their captain and No.10 for all of their ills – different tournament, same theme. As rumours of another retirement circulated, he found an unlikely ally in Maradona: "Messi shouldn't rejoin the national team again," El Diego told *Clarin* newspaper. "If the U15 side loses, it's Messi's fault. He is always at fault and I'd tell him not to play anymore. I would have liked for him to have sent everyone to hell, because it's not his fault they're not world champions ... today the national team doesn't awaken absolutely anything. Not even the people. We've lost that passion. We're throwing all of the prestige that we won in the toilet."

While they gave the dimmer sections of the Argentinian media a stick to beat him with, pictures of Leo and his family on a yacht in the Balearic Islands, showed him as happy, relaxed and calm as he'd been for many a year. Laughing and joking with Antonella, his boys and the wider family, Leo didn't appear to have a care in the world, happily focussed on what was most important to him.

Carlos Tevez, speaking to ESPN, backed him resolutely: "I think Leo has to think about himself now. If there's not a project that makes him happy and in which he feels comfortable, it's very difficult to take the responsibility of leading Argentina to become champions by himself. We are wasting a lot of time not having him happy and not being able to give him a hand to achieve that target. I think we are wrong in not being able to help him feel comfortable. As a player and as an Argentine I tell him that we need him, that he should try to rest and that he keeps a cool head. We need him because he is the soul of Argentina and, as long as he continues playing football, it has to be that way because he is Argentina's biggest idol."

Iniesta's departure made Messi the senior club captain and he started with a bold prediction at the Gamper Trophy: "This year we have built an exciting squad," he said, his voice booming out of Camp Nou's sound system, lending it a depth not previously heard. "The new signings will help us to improve a lot. Last season was very good – winning the cup and La Liga – but it's true that we all got a bit frustrated in the Champions League, especially because of the way we got knocked out. So today we promise you all that we will do our best to bring that beautiful and longed-for cup here to Camp Nou." Those words would return to haunt him.

If anyone felt haunted as the season started it was Sevilla, facing Messi once more in the Spanish Super Cup final, played on this

September 15, 2018: Leo preparing to take a free kick against Real Sociedad, a match that Barça won 2-1 thanks to goals from Luis Suárez and Ousmane Dembélé. It was only the Catalans' second win in 11 years at Anoeta. (© Shutterstock)

occasion in Morocco. He didn't score, but two assists added further to his record against the Andalusians. Then, when the Champions League campaign began, he scored his 42nd Barça hat-trick against PSV Eindhoven in the opener, before heading to Wembley to face Tottenham, still awaiting the completion of their new White Hart Lane stadium.

Spurs simply could not live with him. Only the woodwork stopped his two goals becoming four as Barça won 4-2. Ivan Rakitić incredible airborne volley was named goal of the round and the way the team, and in particular Messi, were playing made his bullish words at the Gamper look more than mere rhetoric.

Just over a fortnight later, however, disaster struck against Sevilla. Already 2-0 up – Messi had set up Coutinho's opener, then scored himself – he fell awkwardly and didn't get straight back up. More than 80,000 people went quiet in an instant. Clearly, something was wrong, and before long he was replaced. Without him Barça toiled to a 4-2 win.

The initial medical prognosis wasn't good, and it became known he had fractured his arm. Returning within 19 days seemed impossibly quick but he still missed five important matches including the Clásico that was Julen Lopetegui's first, and last, as Real Madrid coach. The

September 18 2018: Luis Suárez congratulates goalscorer Lionel Messi during Barça's Champions League match against PSV Eindhoven. (© Shutterstock)

October 3, 2018: Leo celebrates one of his two goals at Wembley Stadium as his man-of-the-match performance helped Barça beat Tottenham Hotspur 4-2 in the Champions League group stage. (© Shutterstock)

camera kept panning to Messi's grinning face as goal after goal went in. Five, to be precise, including a Suárez hat-trick. *Los Blancos* were awful, and Lopetegui was soon gone, yet culés still booed every mention of Ernesto Valverde's name.

As Messi returned from his injury, so did the regular scoring blitzes, although his brace at home to Betis could not prevent a 4-3 defeat by the visitors who richly merited both the win and the plaudits they were earning for their play. There were also three goals and two assists in a 5-0 win at Levante and another hat-trick, including two 'goal of the season' contenders, against Sevilla, but the highlight came in the return at Betis on March 17, 2019. His hat-trick was noteworthy in itself, but it was his third goal and the reaction to it which filled column inches for days afterwards.

Heading towards the left edge of the box he received a short pass from Ivan Rakitić before, without even breaking stride or looking up, he chipped – like a golfer caressing a ball onto the green with a soft effortless swing – the 'keeper, who was stood no more than two yards off of his line. The ball glanced off the underside of the bar before bouncing over the line. It remains one of the best goals he has ever

December 11, 2018: Leo in action during the 1-1 Champions League group game against Tottenham Hotspur at Camp Nou. (© Shutterstock)

scored. Stuck in silence for a moment, the Benito Villamarín broke into spontaneous applause from all sides. Then a familiar refrain rose up from the heart of the stadium. "Messi, Messi, Messi," they roared, bowing as they did so. Words heard many times before, but this time from Betis supporters. They were on their feet in their thousands. No matter that their team were being well beaten by this point, Messi's level of greatness had taken them beyond team rivalry. This was football as art, with Messi as Michaelangelo. Even the Betis players were shaking their heads at each other as if to say "what on earth was that?!"

Carlos Urbano, a journalist and also a *Bético*, was in the stands that night.

"I've seen Lionel Messi play live around ten times; all of them at Benito Villamarín. He gets better every time he comes to face Real Betis, even though Barcelona didn't always win. He scored almost every time I saw him, and he always did something magic, no matter what it was: dribbling, assisting, scoring ... but that goal, THAT GOAL, was beyond anything Messi had done previously. Some people stood up from their seats when Leo raised the ball above Pau López. Nobody expected that. In fact, nobody really knew what he was going to do, but he did something extraordinary. The ball barely hit the crossbar before crossing the line. The referee blew his whistle ... and people started clapping! It wasn't new. Béticos love beautiful football and tend to let players know, even though they're rivals. I must admit I kept silent, shocked, watching the scene. I had goose bumps. In the end, that is what football is about – 50.000 people felt they had just seen a serious candidate to be the best goal of the season. Another one from Messi; another one from the best football player ever. A wonder to remember. It wasn't time to boo him or to get angry, but to pay tribute to a legend."

The acclaim didn't last long, mind. Five days later Argentina lost at home, 1-3 to Venezuela in a friendly, and if Leo thought that was a low point, there was worse yet to come.

18

One Night in Liverpool

European Nightmare at Anfield

"Liverpool were too good to let Messi or Barcelona dominate the ball or the game, but the free-kick was just one of those moments, and it left me thinking 'oh my god'."

Premier League opposition in the quarter and semi-finals of the Champions League brought with it the usual entitled and pompous coverage from the English media. Ahead of the quarter-final against Manchester United, the media ignored Messi's erasure of Lyon in the previous round and followed the hackneyed, "But can he do it on a wet Wednesday in Stoke?" narrative. Leo showed himself more than capable of doing it in Manchester, with a hand in the winner at Old Trafford followed by two goals in a 3-0 win in the return.

Next up were Liverpool, and the direct free-kick Leo fizzed past Alisson Becker in the Liverpool goal was the highlight of Barça's 3-0 first leg win. It was his 600th goal for the *Blaugranes* and made him the tournament's top scorer. It was also named as the goal of the tournament. I asked Sky Sports pundit and Liverpool stalwart Jamie Carragher, if the wall or the 'keeper could have done anything more to stop it:

"I don't think so. Listen, in my job we analyse so many goals and we're always looking where someone can do better, but sometimes you've just gotta say 'wow'. The game didn't see a typical 'Messi performance' as such because I think Liverpool were too good to let Messi or Barcelona dominate the ball or the game, but the free-kick was just one of those moments, and it left me thinking 'Oh my God'."

The final scoreline flattered the hosts a little, because for long periods between the first and second goals Barça were second best, but, at the death, Ousmane Dembélé – from a pass by Messi – missed the most glorious chance to make it four. Even at 3-0 and lacking an away goal, most thought that the tie was still one Liverpool could win. Jürgen Klopp, said it was difficult but not impossible, and Liverpool legend, Sir Kenny Dalglish told me he agreed with the manager's assessment:

> "The result wasn't a fair reflection on the game, but it never is impossible. Whatever way round you want to put it, the result didn't reflect the performance – of either team. I didn't think Barcelona were that good to be perfectly honest, although they scored three goals. And Messi had had a quiet game. I wouldn't say he'd played brilliantly. He was pretty quiet and then scored two goals."

Carragher also thought Barça were fortunate on the night:

> "To be honest, I was looking at the match and thinking that I'd been to the Nou Camp as a player and we'd played there, I think, three times. We won one and drew two, so we'd never lost at the Nou Camp. And then I was watching this Liverpool team losing 3-0, and it was the best performance I'd seen from us at that stadium. It was better than any performance we'd ever given there, that's what I was thinking. And to be honest, I wasn't even angry. I almost felt sorry for the team because it seemed ... not that the season was over, because it was still neck and neck for the league, but I just don't think they deserved that. I thought Barcelona were very fortunate if I'm being honest, and even after that game their players would've thought 'that was a good team, that'.

> Liverpool looked so much more full of running and energy and I think that Barcelona were hanging on for dear life. Hanging on to try and win the last Champions League before it sort of fell apart. Liverpool just kept winning the ball back and recycled it, and kept playing, having chances ... They were out quickly getting the ball back off of Barcelona and were brilliant, but what really struck me was we were still watching possibly the greatest player of all time basically take the game away from Liverpool on his own – and he wasn't even at his best! I don't mind admitting that whenever Liverpool don't win the Champions League, I always want Barcelona to win it – for Messi.

I actually think he should've had a lot more than what he's won and really Barcelona have probably let themselves down a lot in the Champions League when it's been there for them. I think of the Roma game, that Inter Milan semi- final with Pep Guardiola's team ... they were the best team in Europe but I find that they haven't achieved enough, and they could've achieved a lot more really. I was disappointed after the first leg but I remember thinking 'at least it means Messi is gonna win another one.' That was the only saving grace watching it in the stadium."

Despite the 3-0 lead, many *culés* had a sneaking suspicion that the miss by Dembélé would have consequences. If Liverpool were to get an early goal at Anfield, and Barça's defensive frailties, when pressed, continued, three goals to take the tie to extra-time and penalties wasn't beyond them. Four would have made the likelihood of the Reds coming back very slim indeed. Sir Kenny Dalglish knew the miss was crucial too:

"Right at the last minute they went through about three on one ... breaking away from a set play we had. Dembélé had a side-footer into the net and miskicked it. I said there and then 'we'll get through now'. It makes it a lot more difficult [having to score 5], that's what I thought, but four isn't far away if you get one is it? Getting five was a wee bit different. So, I thought that was a huge point of interest for everybody at the time, and I think it made the task coming back to Anfield more feasible for us, that we could do it."

But when the return kicked off Carragher had given up on the miracle following the pre-match warm-up:

"I remember that I was at the side of the pitch in the warm up and I was at the Barcelona end so I was by their fans. I was watching and just hoping to see signs of 'they think it's won' or something like that. And there was something that unnerved me just before the players went in and that was when Messi got them all in a huddle. Liverpool had Salah and Firmino out as well so it wasn't a great team out really, and when Messi did that, it made my heart sink a little bit. The only chance we realistically had was by catching them in the first 15/20 minutes and getting a goal, and then seeing what happens, seeing if things could change. But when Messi gave that speech to the players,

I was a bit like 'oh no, they've had the experience against Roma before, and these are really on it, they know how important this is'."

Sir Kenny evidently felt more confident:

"Barça were coming to a place that's notorious for the atmosphere. The help that you get from the fans when you're on the pitch, for European nights, especially when it's a club with the standing of Barcelona coming, and the position that we were in ... Liverpool knew their backs were against the wall, but that's when everybody really gets together and gets behind the team."

Liverpool, as expected, came charging out of the blocks and took the lead on six minutes when Divock Origi slotted home after Jordan Henderson had taken advantage of Jordi Alba's misplaced header. The noise from three and a half sides of the ground was deafening, but in the away end it was total silence. Messi forced a save from Alisson on 13 minutes but the visitors were being well contained. Anfield, led by the Kop was playing its part perfectly, willing the team forward at every opportunity. If they were going to go down, the locals wanted to see them go down fighting.

Still, Barça had chances on the break. Leo handed Philippe Coutinho one on a plate four minutes later, but the Brazilian's shot – against his former side – was weak. Another pass in first-half injury time found Alba in the area, but Alisson was out quickly to deny the left-back, as Carragher recalled:

"Liverpool didn't absolutely blitz Barcelona because it was still 1-0 at half-time. So they had almost weathered the storm, had a couple of half chances and Alisson made a couple of decent saves. But going towards the Kop they just couldn't seem to handle it and just stopped."

The pendulum swung after half-time, even as Messi continued to do all in his power to take Barça forward. After 53 minutes Gini Wijnaldum stormed into the area to drive home Trent Alexander-Arnold's low, driven cross and Anfield erupted, believing another Champions League final was within their grasp. The crowd was still buzzing when, two minutes later, the Dutch midfielder headed Liverpool level on aggregate. At that point, Barça were beaten. If

May 7, 2019: 'Historic Failure'.
(© MARCA)

the tie went to extra-time and penalties, everyone except the most fervent *culés* knew it before wasn't going to be their night. Messi forced another quality stop from Alisson, but that would be the visitors' final chance of note. With 12 minutes left to play, Trent Alexander-Arnold's inventiveness decided the game. A corner in front of the Kop saw just two Liverpool players in the area, faced by nine Barça players including 'keeper, Marc-André ter Stegen. Despite being so heavily outnumbered, Origi reacted fastest to the quickly-taken corner and some Barça players were still talking amongst themselves as he stroked home the winner. Cue utter delirium on the Liverpool bench and around Anfield.

Personal experience enabled Carragher to put the second half into perspective.

> "When you're attacking the Kop it feels like you're going downhill, and it's uphill for the others to get out. They can get penned back in at the Kop end and they can't seem to move. It felt like the game was basically played in one half of the pitch – there was just nowhere for Barcelona to go. Messi is quick but a lot of their players want ball to feet, and there wasn't anyone [other than Leo] that Liverpool were absolutely terrified of because of their blistering pace. Coutinho is another one who was always looking for it to come to feet, and it made it really easy for Liverpool to hem Barcelona in. When you look at that second leg performance from Barcelona, and the performance from Liverpool, it was chalk and cheese in terms of the intensity. I still thought Messi was Barcelona's best player, and when I saw the game back he was the one that was creating the chances that Barcelona had. It must've been a massive frustration for him.

> Maybe the 'Premier League intensity' is at its best when a team has got the quality that Liverpool and Man City had. I think it's very

difficult for foreign teams to cope with it. I always felt that was the case when English teams were dominating Europe in the mid to late 2000s – Chelsea, ourselves, Man Utd and even Arsenal. The pace we were playing at every week in the Premier League ... if you took that into the Champions League the other teams couldn't cope with that. I think Barcelona were one of the few that could, AC Milan also at that time, but everyone else was just knocked out of the way. I mean, we beat Real Madrid 5-0 on aggregate. Barcelona just couldn't cope on that night."

Sir Kenny happily recalled earlier epic Liverpool European nights, knowing that there was now a modern example to sit alongside them.

"Liverpool have had a few nights like that. They talk about St. Etienne when David Fairclough went through and scored the winning goal ... they had a great night against Olympiacos when Steven Gerrard grabbed one from 20 odd yards, and this'll be up there alongside those games. Another one was beating Chelsea when there was the dispute of whether the ball had crossed the line or not, to get us through, when García scored. So there's been a few nights when Anfield has really been rocking and it's been really helpful to the players. This was one of those nights, the fans were unbelievable, the players responded to it, and whether the players wind the fans up or whether the fans lift the players up is debatable, but if they both help each other there's no debate that there's going to be a fantastic, fantastic atmosphere. Getting a goal in the first half was helpful. Was it the best European night? I don't know how you define best. I mean you've got to have been there to define the best haven't you. Me, I wasn't at the St. Etienne game, I wasn't at the Olympiacos game. I was at the Chelsea game and that was only 1-0 and the place was jumping. It's like ... do you like steak or fish? Everybody's got a different taste haven't they. So, everybody will have a different preference but there's certainly one thing ... it must've been some night if it beat the Barça game."

It was Roma all over again, a three-goal first leg lead lost in almost identical circumstances after an early goal which questioned that air of invincibility. Carragher was clear, both that Liverpool had taken belief from the first leg and the second leg performance was the best ever seen at Anfield:

"I think what would've given them huge hope is the first game. No one goes there and plays like that against Barcelona. Some teams may win as we did in 2007, but we didn't dominate Barcelona in that game. This Liverpool did that, they were much the better side in the Nou Camp and that very rarely happens.

The very interesting thing was, I was by the bench before the final whistle [in the first leg] and I think the goalkeeper went up for a set piece for Liverpool, and they put all their players in the box. I remember thinking ... not that 3-0 is doable, but you're hanging on in there. At 4-0 it's finished. And I was just a bit like 'oooh putting the 'keeper up for a set piece and there's no one back. Don't do that, don't do that.' But that was Jürgen Klopp's instruction onto the pitch and they were lucky, Liverpool, that they got away with that. On European nights you always think there's half a chance with an early goal and different things, but 4-0 is too big a mountain to climb. It was just interesting that Klopp almost felt he had to get the away goal and even risk being totally knocked out of the tie. We talk a lot about luck in football and it was lucky that the chance at the end never went in because I think that would've been curtains. I think the Liverpool players would've believed it would've been over too. At 3-0, I'm sure they thought there was still half a chance.

The second leg was Liverpool's best ever moment and game at Anfield, there's no doubt about that. You have a lot of finals, they're obviously on neutral ground, but unless Liverpool had an Agüero moment and won the league with the last kick of the game, I don't see how that game can ever be beaten. The reason why is obviously the comeback ... and it's against Messi. He's the player of our times, he's the player of this generation, that's what it was. It wasn't Pep's Barcelona team, but it was a very good Barcelona team who were winning the league almost every year, and it was Messi and the way he'd performed in the first leg. For Liverpool to come back and to win like that considering that they never had two of their biggest stars ... it just made it special. There's been the Barcelona v PSG comeback and some others... but I think you do need a special club to produce things like that, big moments ... almost like a togetherness with the crowd, the players on the pitch – a connection. I think special clubs do special things, and I don't think there's too many that can. Barcelona and Liverpool are both those types of teams, but for Messi now, to have gone so long without a Champions League ... it doesn't look like he's that close to getting another one, unless the club rebuild the team. I do hope he gets one more crack at it or certainly lifts it.

Liverpool fans, including some old enough to remember the glory days of the 1970s and '80s under Shankly, Paisley, Fagan and Dalglish, said it was the best the best atmosphere they'd ever witnessed. Some reckoned that Luis Suárez's first-leg celebration in the first leg had pumped up the Reds too, and Carragher agreed:

"I think Suárez is someone the Liverpool fans adored, and still do really, but, it was the fact that he was so ... he was basically Luis Suárez as he was in a Liverpool shirt every week, but he was doing it for Barcelona – against Liverpool. We all felt we might get a Suárez at 90%, not in terms of him trying to score but his antics off of the ball and what he'd get up to. He could do that in a Liverpool shirt and Liverpool fans loved him for it ... but not for Barcelona. It was a bit of cheating if you like, you know, trying to get someone booked, going down, never stopping, in someone's face, putting his finger in Robertson's face and trying to get the referee to book someone. I felt, as I'm sure others did, that 'hang on a minute, you're doing that to your own family.' But then that's Luis Suárez, it's win at all costs, it doesn't matter who he's up against. I think it really riled the Liverpool supporters, and I think at the start of the second leg there was a challenge by Fabinho on him and it seemed to lift the crowd. The Liverpool players that hadn't played with him at the club were wound up by his antics and it didn't matter whether he'd played for Liverpool or not. Everyone was out to get him then."

Another notable incident had seen Andy Robertson push Messi in the head whilst he was on the ground. While the Scot later said he'd regretted it, the fans were roused. Carragher said:

"I think, in the heat of the battle, even as a supporter, you think 'oh brilliant, Robertson,' but I can understand where he's coming from. It's Messi and I think there's players that you have that certain level of respect for. Looking back, if I was Andy Robertson, I'd probably say the same. It's like rubbing someone's face in it isn't it. Did it put Messi off of his game? I don't know. I imagine Andy Robertson looks up to Messi and probably still couldn't believe he was on the pitch with him."

While the *culés* in the Barça end had the grace to applaud Liverpool at the end, there was little class from the English media, who mostly took the easy path of writing how Messi was unable to inspire Barcelona. He'd not been at his best, but he'd been involved in just about every chance his team-mates had during the game.

Catalan criticism homed in on the coach. #ValverdeOut trended on Twitter for some time, while supporters asked why he had reverted to type, starting players like the woefully out of form Coutinho yet leaving the fast and incisive Malcom on the bench. As in Rome, he had played it safe again, with the same catastrophic result.

If the outcome had been disappointing, visiting Liverpool compensated through the education of hearing people who had played at the top for years analyse Messi. Carragher said:

> "Well there's always this debate about Ronaldo and Messi and what annoys me is that it seems like we judge the best player in the world by how many goals they've got. 'Ronaldo got two, Messi got three' ... whereas years ago when I was a kid growing up, the goalscorer was never the best player in the world. If I think of Liverpool, and you speak to Liverpool fans, they'd say that Kenny Dalglish was the best player, not Ian Rush. And Ian Rush scored double the amount of goals.
>
> What I would say on that debate is I always put Messi above Ronaldo. You could make an argument to say that Ronaldo is possibly the greatest goalscorer of all time. How he's changed his role, he's gone to centre-forward, come in from the left wing, the different types of goals he scored ... headers, acrobatics, free-kicks, penalties ... he scores every type of goal and he probably will break all the numbers for goals, but, for me, the best player in the world is always a No.10, who does things that take your breath away. And what I see with Ronaldo is he'll do things and you'll go 'wow, what a goal,' but we've seen great goals scored before. We see goals every single game, and it's true, he's like a machine, he's very ruthless. Messi though, he does things that no one else can do. What I mean by that is the dribbling in tight areas ... there's not many dribblers in football now,

very few. Every team might have a player who thinks he can dribble, but compared to Messi? Pfff!

He's the one player when you give him the ball, he can have two or three men around him but he can still do something that actually just takes your breath away. That's why I'd always put Messi above Ronaldo. He had a performance at Tottenham ... [2018-19] where he played in centre-midfield and he ran the game. Ronaldo couldn't do that, really he couldn't. I think Messi can dictate a game, the pace of a game, everything. The games are not just about the stats and the goals and the assists. Sometimes it's about sitting back and watching a game and it making you smile. Making you think 'wow', and I think that Messi has had more of those moments.

If he doesn't win the World Cup, unfortunately, people will argue against him being the best, but in reality the World Cup is six games. It's every four years and it's about your team coming together in that month. You need that little bit of luck. You know, if Higuaín scores against Germany, does that define if Messi is better than Maradona? If Higuaín misses a chance in the first half in the World Cup final when he goes through on goal ... [or] scores that and the game finishes 1-0, does that mean that Messi is better than Pelé or Maradona when he had nothing to do with whether Higuaín finished or not. That's how ridiculous that argument is. I mean, when you look at Pelé winning three World Cups that's just unbelievable – off the scale. Maradona – it was just ... it was different then because you didn't see those players week-in and week-out so they were almost like Gods you only saw them in World Cups, whereas now you can see Messi every week. I think it will be something that will be held against him, maybe more so in Argentina where 'he never took us to this trophy,' but, I look at it a different way.

Pelé only stayed in Brazil, at Santos. Maradona, when he was at Napoli, was amazing, but Maradona played for Barcelona and didn't do anything close to what Messi did, so I've always got around the hype by saying that Messi's the best club footballer of all time, and in some ways that then takes the debate away. People always throw Pelé and Maradona into the best-ever argument, but I think what Messi has done year in and year out in the Champions League trumps that. Unfortunately, people will always say things like 'he never did this, won that.' It's the same for Liverpool in some seasons. Whatever we achieved, we got opposition fans saying 'well, you didn't win the league.' The reality is that it can be to do with the manager at the time, the squad of players, the opposition, whatever ... Messi could even legitimately argue that he wasn't even playing in the best international team in the world. They did well getting to a final, in which he was player of the tournament. What more can he do?!

Ronaldo's quite clever. I think a lot of his moves have been on the back of 'what can I do that's different?' He can say he's won the league in all these countries, been the top scorer in all these countries and these are more strings to his bow. He probably does the opposite to what Messi does to try and paint himself as being slightly different and better. But listen, I don't think of Franco Baresi and Paolo Maldini being any less of a defender because they never left AC Milan. So that's not going to change my opinion with Lionel Messi not leaving Barcelona. I mean, why would you leave Barcelona?! That also gets thrown at Pep Guardiola as a manager. 'Oh he only takes the big jobs, what would he be like with a team at the bottom or a team in the middle?' But why the hell would he do that?

It's like saying to Messi 'go and sign for Southampton.' It's just stupid, absolutely daft. He's at the top club, he's the best player there, he's the best player in Europe and has been for more than a decade. The best show up against the best on the biggest occasions and that's what he does so I don't really listen ... I think you've got to give credit to Ronaldo for doing it in different leagues and different cultures, under different managers, but I don't think it should be a stick to beat Messi with. Leo sits alongside Maradona and Pelé. I think he supercedes your Cruyff's, your Zidane's, Di Stéfano's ... players like that. He sits alongside the top two, who've always been seen as such, with probably about 10 to 20 players behind them. Messi makes that a top three, though lots of different people would argue and say he's No.1, others would say No.2 and some will say he's No.3. He's in that bracket with the other two for sure, and that will be his legacy. His legacy for Barcelona will be amazing in that there's almost a before Messi and after Messi.

I think when you look at the actual trophies that Barcelona had won before Messi arrived, compared to what they had when he finished

... Barcelona have always been one of the great teams, they always will be and will always attract the best players in the world. But they hadn't necessarily always won the biggest trophies, and they hadn't really won a lot of leagues either before Messi came. So what he's actually done for Barcelona is made them the biggest Spanish club in his time. Maybe in Spain, Real Madrid are still seen as the biggest team, but I think outside of Spain it's no longer the Catalans fighting against the country and the government's team in Madrid. Barcelona are now seen as the best, and that's because of Messi.

When I think back to when we played against him in 2007 and he was a very young boy on the right wing trying to come in on his left foot ... he just smelt where the danger was. I watched him at stadiums where he actually just walked about a lot. He knew when he needed to be on it, saving himself ... just walking, then bang! He knew what was going to happen. Whether he was going to get the ball between the lines, whether he was going to run onto something, wherever he was with the ball he could always associate with players being on the move and difficult to mark. He saved himself for those moments. I don't know if that's something he did to prolong his career, and I did actually wonder at one point if maybe his legs had gone a bit! But he was still getting the same amount of goals and assists, and his understanding was on a different level to everyone else on the pitch. There was no weakness to his game I can assure you."

Carragher was refreshing in his delight at being able to share Messi's great football career with FC Barcelona and Argentina. Sir Kenny clearly felt much the same:

"I think he's brave you know. You can't play at his level with the tackles that he's had, then stood up and gone back for more unless you've got huge courage. And he's done it. I mean, Maradona was the same – Pelé ... all the greats ... Ronaldo ... you get kicked, you get up, you go again. Some people might've tried to flush him out when he was younger, have a kick and see how he reacts to it, and he always reacted very positively. If you kick him, he'll go back, and then you're under pressure because if you do it again, you're off. For me, that was very important, and I think also ... his demeanour. Some people might have expected a man of his quality on the pitch to be arrogant, and I don't know the guy – I've never met him – but he appears to me to be just a guy that's very well liked in and around the place, and somebody that they can relate to.

He never undermined anybody, he never had a strop if he didn't get the pass exactly how he wanted it, and I think he had a lot of respect from the people he played with because of that. I don't know ... but that's just me looking in from the outside. In and around the dressing room, it's important that the players playing with him feel part of it as well. I think he's always, always enjoyed any success he's had and shared it with everybody else. I'm not going to be someone that's going to pick somewhere where he should've played, or he shouldn't have played. The only thing I would say ... is it's a privilege to be able to watch him. You've been able to watch him play and enjoy watching him play. His stats don't lie, the number of goals he's scored, the success he's had at Barça, it doesn't lie. Certainly, he needs other people, everybody needs somebody to play with, that's why it's a team game. He respects that, he respects people that can do the job that he didn't do [but] I don't think any have been better than Lionel Messi. The question goes up about him and Ronaldo ... and by the way shouldn't we just say that we're very, very fortunate to be able to watch both at the same time ... and what would've been interesting maybe, is if the two of them were on the same team at any time ... but you'd need to have some good runners running about mind you!"

19

The Joy of Six

Another Golden Shoe

"You can fit Pelé's best moments into a one-hour video, or you can make a two-hour video for the best of Maradona. With Messi's best... it's a one-day long video."

Their pursuit of the treble derailed at Anfield, Barça ended up falling short of the domestic double. The league title was safely secured but Valencia thwarted hopes of a record fifth consecutive Copa del Rey, richly deserving their first final win since 2007-08. The pressure on Valverde increased but the support of senior players like Messi, Busquets and Piqué helped to convince the board that he was still the right man for the job.

"The planning for next season is already underway and has been for some time," president Josep Maria Bartomeu said before the Copa final. "Ernesto told you the other day that he has my support and that of the board. He's the coach we want. We're halfway through a large project. He has a contract and we are very happy with him. Now it's about how the players recover from an enormous setback. It's been a magnificent season, we've won the league with games to spare. We all want more."

While the Copa América loomed that summer, expectations were minimal. Not a single pundit or bookmaker rated Argentina a serious contender, so there was little surprise, or outcry, when hosts Brazil beat *La Albiceleste* in the semi-final.

Leo had done what he could but it was never going to be enough for Lionel Scaloni's side. The third-place play-off against Chile wasn't without incident either. Leo had already set up the opener for Agüero with some quick thinking from a free-kick, and Paulo Dybala had doubled their lead on 22 minutes, but with eight minutes left to play before half-time, an unsavoury incident occurred between Messi and Gary Medel. Certainly Leo's part in it might be described as 'handbags' – giving the Chilean a little shove as the ball was shepherded out of play. Medel's response, as befits a player nicknamed The Pitbull, was to headbut Messi. The Argentinian stood his ground, but holding his hands aloft was hardly the act of an aggressor. As Medal continued pushing into Leo with his chest, looking to knock him over as he did so, referee Mario Díaz de Vivar was far too quick to brandish red cards for both players. Medel could hardly complain but Messi did, vehemently and in a manner sure to lead to further sanctions: "We don't have to be part of this corruption," he told reporters after the game. "They have showed us a lack of respect throughout this tournament. Sadly, the corruption, the referees, they don't allow people to enjoy football, they ruined it a bit. The cup was fixed for Brazil." CONMEBOL, the South American Football Confederation, were swift in fining him $50,000 (£41,121) and issuing him with a three-month international ban.

A month later he was back at the microphone seeking to inspire the *culés*, who had already booed Valverde at the Gamper Trophy, when he said: "The truth is that it's difficult to tell you something after last season, but I don't regret anything. I'll repeat the same thing I said then. I trust in this team and in the coaching staff, and I have no doubt that we are going to fight again for everything. Last season I ended up being a bit bitter about everything, but I think we have to give value to the league we won, the eighth in 11 years. It's very important and we give it the value it deserves and we know how difficult it is. But this club always fights for everything and this year isn't going to be any different."

Too bad that he promptly damaged his calf in training and missed six weeks of the season, during which Barça lost at Athletic Club, drew away to Osasuna but at least kept home crowds happy with two 5-2 wins, over Betis and Valencia.

When he finally did get to play, Barça lost 2-0 at Granada and any pleasure at picking up FIFA's 'The Best' player award was lost the following night when he suffered an adductor injury against Villareal.

Fortunately, Leo missed only one match, against Getafe, before returning for a crucial Champions League encounter against unbeaten Inter. This was prefaced by an incident forcing him to call on his diplomatic skills as Piqué went way beyond even his usual level of outspokenness to directly accuse Barça's board of leaking. "We know the club, we know who the newspapers are and who writes each article, even if it doesn't have their byline," was just a small part of it. As captain, Messi was forced to respond, and managed to defuse the immediate issue in an interview with the Catalan radio station RAC1.

Inter were ahead from the second minute, and should have been out of sight before half-time, but were thwarted by a mixture of poor finishing and bad luck. Luis Suárez's double gave Barça a scarcely deserved win, the second – thanks to a typical Messi run and assist. Next up were Sevilla who also took the game to the *Blaugranes*, but suffered their usual fate when facing Leo – his spectacular free-kick completing a 4-0 rout.

Events off the field during October compelled attention as, 10 days into the month, Cirque de Soleil premiered their 'Messi 10' touring show – 'an inspiring story about greatness' – in Barcelona. Leo was joined at the event by team-mates, the Barça board, and entertainment stars like: singers Carlos Vives, Dani Martín, Paulo Londra and Nicky Jam; actors Santi Millán and Paz Vega; comedians Carlos Latre and Manel Fuentes; sportsperson Gemma Mengual; and cook Carme Ruscalleda. Leo looked comfortable in the limelight, in spite of his dislike of being likened to any kind of God.

A few days later, on October 14, the Monday of the second international break of the season, news broke that Catalan politicians and activists involved in the 2017 independence vote had been jailed after a trial in Madrid. An FC Barcelona statement, headed 'Prison is not the solution,' spelt out their protest: "FC Barcelona, as one of the leading entities in Catalonia, and in accordance with its historical record, for the defence of freedom of expression and the right to decide, today, after the condemnatory ruling issued by the Supreme Court in relation to the open process against the Catalan civic and political leaders, states that: In the same way that the preventive prison sentence didn't help to resolve the conflict, neither will the prison sentence given today, because prison is not the solution. The resolution of the conflict in Catalonia must come exclusively from political dialogue. Therefore, now more than ever, the club asks all political leaders to lead a process of dialogue and negotiation to resolve this conflict, which should also allow for the release of convicted civic and political leaders. FC Barcelona also expresses all its support and solidarity to the families of those who are deprived of their freedom."

With the mood in Barcelona tense and El Prat airport blockaded on more than one occasion, the Spanish Football Federation (RFEF) decided, on October 18, to postpone the Clásico scheduled for eight days later. Neither club had asked for a postponement, or was very keen on the eventual replay date of December 18.

There was happier news in the shape of a sixth Golden Shoe, Messi's third in a row, taking him two ahead of Ronaldo and four in front of anyone else – not bad for an attacking midfielder! It was presented to him in the Estrella Damm brewery by his young sons, Thiago and Mateo.

With Barça rather treading water, losing in the league at Levante and drawing in the Champions League against Slavia Prague, an international break was something of a respite for Messi. The performance in a friendly against Brazil, *La Albiceleste*'s best in some time, merited a bigger margin of victory than Messi's penalty. Hopes that Argentina might at last have found a team of serious contenders rose again. The highly respected Argentinian journalist Jorge Barraza, former chief editor of *Magazine CONMEBOL* and contributor to numerous prestigious outlets including *El Gráfico*, explained his view of Messi's contentious relationship with his homeland:

October 29, 2019: Leo preparing to take a corner during the La Liga match against Valladolid at Camp Nou. He scored twice in a 5-1 victory. (© Shutterstock)

"He doesn't disappoint me or a lot of people. I hope he plays for many more years for Argentina, even if we win nothing. I'm not desperate for a title, I love watching him play because never has a football player been at such a brilliant level for so many consecutive years. No one has ever achieved that regularity. Messi failed to play in the First Division in Argentina and that obviously plays against him because Maradona not only played there, but also did it at Boca, the most popular club. And Boca fans are reluctant to compare Maradona with any other. Much less say that Messi is better. Besides, Maradona won a World Cup and that weighs heavily on people's opinions. Many people in Argentina believe that the only thing that exists in football is a World Cup, hence it tends to undervalue those who failed. But it's not so. Di Stéfano, Cruyff, Puskás, Kubala, Zico, Van Basten, George Best, Platini, Eusébio and so many others didn't win a World Cup and were football geniuses. Messi's advantage is he's number one without having won a World Cup [at this point].

The thing to remember is that Messi has not had the good fortune to coincide with great leaders, coaches or players in the Argentinian national team. He hasn't got to play with a Maradona, a Bochini, a Kempes, a Batistuta, a Houseman, a Caniggia, even a Burruchaga. Not even with a defender like Passarella or a player like Fillol. Nor has he been coached by Menotti or a coach of that caliber. It's very simple: when the ideal Argentina XI of all time is made, none of the chosen ones has played with Messi. Even so, he reached the final of a World Cup, three Copa América finals, was world youth champion, Olympic champion. His time in the national team, in my opinion, has been excellent. In almost every game he's played for them he's been the main man on the pitch, and he is the all-time top scorer for the team. There's really no argument as to his place in the pantheon of greatness. Let me put it like this. You can fit Pelé's best moments into a one hour video, or you can make a two-hour video for the best of Maradona. With Messi's best ... it's a one-day long video."

Messi returned to Barça for a lacklustre victory, away to bottom club Leganés, before a must-win Champions League clash with Borussia Dortmund. Fortunately, the German side weren't in great form either and Barça seized control with two goals, Messi and Suárez assisting each other, in four first half minutes.

Antoine Griezmann's 67th-minute third, again from a Messi assist, made it the first time 'MSG' (Messi, Suárez, Griezmann) had all scored in the same match. From being in some jeopardy, Barça were through to the Round of 16 as group winners, and with a game to spare.

In the league, Barça went to play Atlético Madrid at the Wanda Metropolitano, knowing a win would take them to the top on goal difference. Only ter Stegen's brilliance kept Barça in contention in torrential rain, making yet another late winner possible. With five minutes left Messi drove home a featherlight assist from Suaréz, the fourth time he'd scored the only goal in a win over Atléti. TV cameras picked up combative Atléti coach Diego Simeone clapping the goal and shrugging his shoulders as if to say 'how do you stop him?'

The following day, Leo received his sixth Ballon d'Or. Ronaldo, reluctant to attend awards ceremonies where he knew he wasn't going to win, stayed away and Messi was announced in first place ahead of Virgil Van Dijk, whose 'was he a rival then?' joke at Ronaldo's expense set the Portuguese's sister Katia Aveiro off on a venomous social media diatribe at his expense.

Barça remained unbeaten before the winter break and, in the final group stage match at Inter, Ansu Fati – aged 17 years and 40 days – became the Champions League's youngest goalscorer. The postponed Clásico was dull and, for the first time in 17 years, scoreless, and there was a welcome point at Real Sociedad. Barça looked in good shape, but it would not take long for that to unravel.

Their troubles began with Wu Lei's late equaliser for Espanyol in the Barcelona derby, costing two points, and mounted at the Spanish Super Cup, which the RFEF in their wisdom had shifted from its traditional pre-season slot into a four-team competition – Valencia, Barça, Atléti and Real Madrid – played in Jeddah, Saudi Arabia.

Barça were on top against Atléti, and on course for a final against Real, before a late collapse saw them beaten 3-2. There seemed no great cause for concern, but news quickly spread that coach Valverde's job was in jeopardy. Sporting director, Eric Abidal's meeting with Xavi was plastered all over the back pages, but the former midfielder threw a spanner in the works by saying he wouldn't take the job.

Within four days Abidal and the board had settled on Quique Setién, a former Betis man who was well respected in the game and the Barça dressing room. A slender 1-0 win against Granada on his debut at least gave Setién a winning start, but needing a 90th minute winner from Griezmann to beat third-tier Ibiza in the Copa del Rey,

December, 2020: A special cover celebrates Messi's then record six Ballon d'Or awards. (© MARCA)

hinted at the problems ahead. A 2-0 loss to Valencia followed in which Messi looked off of the pace and wasn't running smoothly. Matters came to a head in early February when Abidal, in an interview with *Sport*, accused players of deliberately not trying hard enough under Valverde. "Many players weren't satisfied or working hard and there was also an internal communication problem. The relationship between the coach and the dressing room has always been good but there are things, as an ex-player, that I could smell. I told the club what I thought and we reached a decision [on Valverde]."

A line had been crossed and Messi, famed for the scarcity, blandness and 'party line' of his interviews was stung into retaliation. A vehement and strongly-worded denial came, unusually, straight back from Messi via his official Instagram page: "Sincerely, I don't like to do these things but I think that people have to be responsible for their jobs and own their decisions. The players [are responsible] for what happens on the pitch and we are the first to admit when we haven't been good. The heads of the sports department have to take their responsibilities too and above all own the decisions they make. Finally, I think that when players are talked about, names should be given because, if not, we are all being dirtied and it feeds comments that are made and are not true."

A low-key transfer window, with no replacements for the players who'd left, made Barça vulnerable to injuries and by the time of their Copa del Rey quarter-final on February 6, Setién had just 16 fit first-teamers.

Speaking to beIN Sports' Ray Hudson, at that time, He admitted that it was becoming more and more difficult to come up with new ways to describe 'The G.O.A.T.'

> "It's immensely challenging. Like describing an explosion or candle light, or the bubbles in a glass of champagne! If I was writing about him post-game it would be far easier in many regards, as it would give me time to contemplate and design my words accordingly. Or if I was a painter, I'd be able to change the image, but verbally capturing and describing Messi's genius instantaneously, in moments of pure magic, requires stretching and expanding the descriptives in an attempt, as futile as it may be, to frame such footballing beauty. It often calls for a sense of the ridiculous, a sentence of emotional madness laced with my natural emotion. Sometimes, just like the fans at home or in the stadium, I want to roar in euphoria – and sometimes I have! But then I have to immediately select the words, phrases, analogies ... Often with Leo, it's like looking directly into the sun and being called to describe it!"

It was clear from Ray's enthusiastic in-game calls that he considered Messi was a class apart, but it was still interesting and intriguing to hear Leo being called the best of all time from someone who did get to play professionally against and with the likes of Pelé and George Best, to name just two.

> "It's the promise of magic, fulfilled. His ability to make the insane become predictable. Where the impossible became the expected. He matches or beats every other player that's ever played. Besides

the endless individual skill that sets him apart, plus his astonishing consistency over his entire career, for me, no player has ever held such a rapturous operatic high-note for so very long. Remember, during his career, Spain were the pre-eminent force in football, domestically and internationally. Spain produced dominant club sides along with World Cup and European Championship successes. Amidst all of that, Leo towered over every individual in La Liga during that golden era, the best football league in the world at the time. His challenge was to be the best, amongst the best ... Q.E.D."

Of course, a footballer's career is short in comparison to many others, and many supporters of the game won't have ever had the pleasure of seeing Leo live. Watching endless *YouTube* videos isn't quite the same. Trying to describe the feeling of seeing Leo just a few feet away to anyone not familiar with his exploits was almost impossible, but Ray had a go:

"I'd have told them to keep their eyes closed when the match kicked off and only open them when they heard something 'different' in the crowd noise. When they opened them, Messi would have the ball. Then they'll have seen a player who analysed every option available in an instant. Depending on the situation, he exploited it to the maximum. Whether it was simply keeping possession or inventing passing lanes for his team-mates to create danger, or taking off on a dribble and pulling a peacock out of his magician's hat or scoring a *golazo* from distance ... If he made a regular pass to his team-mates, they could close their eyes again for a while before hearing that special sound again. It was never too long afterwards..."

His legacy to football would also be difficult to elucidate;

"There can only be an evolution because there will never be, can never be, a replacement for Messi. That club has always been the stage for the Gods of the game; Kubala, Cruyff, Stoichkov, Ronaldinho etc., so perhaps another star will be born approaching these legends, but Leo eclipsed all of them. And how! I don't think that there's a player in the world that doesn't watch Messi play and feel their soul banging on the rib cage screaming to be let out. He intoxicates us with the sublime range of skill, touch and vision.

It's nothing less than a divine connection of eyes to brain to feet. Watching him play, it seems like he's always experimenting with the game, operating on a different frequency to the rest. Listen, every player has a vision of what he dreams he could or should do, we can all see a 'starry, starry night,' but it takes a Van Gogh to capture it, and that's what Leo does. A Mozart amongst banjo players is the only way I can try and do him true justice. Immortal. The greatest ever. Incomparable on a multitude of levels and the player that circumscribed the essence of pure, undiluted footballing brilliance."

Again, things would get worse before they got better for Messi and Co. A magnificent performance at San Mamés in the cup deserved a better reward than Iñaki Williams glancing a header home at the death to win the match. Lightning evidently does strike twice in Bilbao. A win at Betis and another at home to Getafe, coupled with Real Madrid surprisingly dropping two points at home to Celta, brought Barça to within touching distance of *Los Blancos* with El Clásico on the horizon. Then came Leo's performance of the season to date, a four-goal salvo in the 5-0 demolition of Eibar.

While a 1-1 draw against Napoli in Italy looked a decent result, Barça's away form, particularly in Europe, had been poor for some

February 22, 2020: Leo celebrates one of his four Camp Nou goals as Barça beat Eibar 5-0. (© Shutterstock)

time and the performance gave credence to Messi's assertion, in an interview he gave given to *Mundo Deportivo* before the match, that Barça simply weren't good enough to win the competition that year: "If we want to win the Champions League we have to continue growing a lot [as a team] because I think that today we are not good enough to fight for the Champions League."

On top of his dispute with Abidal, and compounded by Sergio Busquets post-match lament, "We don't have a deep enough squad because that's how it was planned," Leo's comments had the effect of a grenade and were seized upon across the media.

Victory in the second Clásico would have sent Barça five points clear, but they were struggling. So were Real, and in one of their poorest meetings in years, Messi failed to score – the 11th time in 15 games – in a fixture he had once dominated and was seen limping at times, prompting fears that his injury was deteriorating. Piqué and ter Stegen were the only exceptions to Barça's mediocrity. Goals by Vinicius Jr and Mariano Díaz gave Zinedine Zidane's side a deserved win – their first in five league meetings against Barça at the Santiago Bernabéu.

Barça reclaimed top spot the following week with a hard-fought win over Real Sociedad coupled with Madrid's surprise defeat at Betis, but it was the last football they played for months as Covid-19 forced a shutdown.

20

'Barçagate' and the Burofax

The End is Near

"I told the club, including the president, that I wanted to go. I've been telling him that all year. I believed it was time to step aside."

La Liga remained in suspension until June 2020, but lockdown did nothing to ease the club's off-field problems. Six directors had resigned in early April after Bartomeu asked four to resign as part of a restructuring of the board. Emili Rousaud left along with Enrique Tombas, Maria Teixidor, Silvio Elias, Jordi Clasamiglia and Josep Pont, offering a devastating parting shot that someone – the inference being Bartomeu – had their 'hands in the till'. The club quickly confirmed that they would be taking legal action against Rousand, however, with the board ousted by the end of the year, this never came to pass.

On May 23, 2020, Bartomeu's visit to Barça's training facility, ostensibly to reconnect with the first team and take a photo opportunity, had as its main mission a request for a collective cut of €10m in salaries. While looking to cut costs on one side of the club's balance sheet, just before the post-lockdown restart came the launch of the Barça TV+ streaming service offering fans more than 1,000 hours of content which sought to generate additional income.

Still, the relief when a spectatorless league season eventually returned was palpable. The Seville derby reopened the 2019-20 campaign on Thursday, June 11, and Barça returned on Saturday 13 at Mallorca, with substitutes spread out across empty stands, wearing masks and gloves. They had looked sharp in training, with Messi, despite a potential muscular issue, unplayable in the small-sided games. They'd carried that sharpness into the match and were a goal to the good from Arturo Vidal's sumptuous diving header after only 65 seconds. Martin Braithwaite added his first for Barça, followed by second half goals from Jordi Alba and Messi. Add in Leo's two assists, and it was a typical day's work for him. That injury-time fourth was his 20th of the season, making him the first player in La Liga history to score at least 20 goals in 12 consecutive seasons.

Leo's penalty in the win over Leganés moved him closer to his 700th professional goal, but it would take a while to arrive as a sequence of drawn matches hampered Barça's title bid. It finally came in the 2-2 draw against Atlético, a Panenka-style penalty which had 'keeper Jan Oblak almost sat down by the time it struck the net. It was a fitting way to reach that milestone, following on from the 500th – a last minute winner against Real Madrid – and 600th – a free-kick against Liverpool in the Champions League.

It was around this point that news broke that Leo had stalled his contract talks. Radio station *Cadena Ser* reported that, allegedly tired of leaks emanating from the club and disappointed to see another season dwindling in spite of his efforts, Messi would leave at the end of his existing contract in 2021.

For the first time it seemed possible Messi would actually leave Barça for another club rather than through retirement at the end of his career. Further pressure piled on the beleaguered Bartomeu, target for most *culé* ire. Messi maintained his habitual dignified silence, expressing himself with assists for Suárez and Griezmann against Villareal.

The title went to one of the worst Real sides in years who, unlike Barça, had still had enough about them to dig in and get the job done. Complaints from some Barça fans about 'a VAR-assisted title' said more about their lack of class and detachment from reality. Messi, however, had no illusions, saying:

"We didn't expect or want it to end in this way, but it's a reflection of our season. [We've been] an inconsistent, weak team that has been beaten in intensity and desire. It has been easy to score goals against us. Madrid did what they had to do. They haven't lost a game since the restart, which deserves credit, but we have helped them by dropping points we should not have dropped. We must be self-critical, starting with the players, but across the whole club. We are Barcelona and we're obliged to win every game. We have to look at ourselves, not the opposition, and the performances in recent games have left a lot to be desired."

"I have said before," he added, "that if we continued playing as we were it would be difficult to win the Champions League and now it's clear it wasn't even enough to win La Liga. We have to change a lot because if we don't, we will lose against Napoli as well. We need a little time to clear our heads and then to think about the Champions League, which starts from zero. The fans are angry with all that's gone on this season and it's normal, we are also angry. It's normal that they feel like this and that, after the defeats against Roma and Liverpool, they are losing patience because we're not giving them anything."

He looked and sounded angry, many interpreting the words as a dig at the board. Only the Champions League remained as a possible means of redemption and Messi was still up for the fight, scoring while almost lying on the floor, having another disallowed for handball by VAR and winning a penalty which completed the 3-1 victory over Napoli that sent Barça through to the quarter-finals against old foes Bayern. The Germans had not lost in 2020 and had 23 wins and a draw from their previous 24 matches, conceding only 17 goals. Barça looked relaxed and confident during training and the build-up, but the match rapidly showed that the ghosts of Roma and Liverpool were still living inside their heads. Once Thomas Müller gave Bayern the lead, the signs were ominous as their movement caused Barça huge problems. David Alaba's own goal for the equaliser drew only a rueful smile from the player himself. He knew which way the tide was flowing.

Normal, relentless, service was quickly resumed. Bayern were out of sight at 4-1 by half-time, and Barça's second from Luis Suárez was quickly countered by Bayern's fifth from Joshua Kimmich. The final, bitter insult was Philippe Coutinho, a Barça player on loan to Bayern, setting up Robert Lewandowski for a sixth before adding two late goals himself to complete an astonishing 8-2 defeat – the first time Barça had conceded eight in 74 years. Messi played his part in a deplorable display with TV coverage showing him just standing and watching the late goals fly in, making no attempt whatsoever to track back and, at times, even walking back upfield as his defence battled to stem the flow.

'Shame' and 'Humiliation' were screamed in the following morning's papers as they reported a battering that had been on the cards for months. It brought to mind the words of former president, Joan Laporta, and his warning that Josep Maria Bartomeu et al would all but abandon La Masia, with the intention of bringing in big name players at big money. The manner of the Bayern defeat brought everything crashing down and in its immediate aftermath, Gerard

Piqué suggested he would move aside if it meant the club would progress.

"We have hit rock bottom," he said to reporters. "You can't compete like that. You can't do that in Europe. And it's not the first time, or the second, or the third. It's very tough. I hope it serves for something. Now we all need to think. The club needs changes. Nobody is indispensable, and I'll be the first to offer to leave if we need new blood. I'll be the first to go. We all need to reflect internally and work out what's best for the club." Setién and sporting director, Eric Abidal were gone within a few days, but any successors would have to clear up the biggest mess in decades and convince Messi that this was a project worth staying for.

Former Barça 'Dream Team' member, Ronald Koeman, who had turned down the job in January, was appointed and told Barça TV+ of his pride at joining 'his' club, and how he felt he was coming home and was going to enjoy coaching Messi.

He also spoke of being straight and direct in communication and within a couple of days had told Luis Suárez and Sergio Busquets they wouldn't have as big a role to play as previously. Whether or not these were good decisions, they certainly showed the firm leadership Barça had enjoyed under Guardiola and Enrique, and which was needed again now. They, and Koeman, all former Barça players, knew that it sometimes needed an iron fist to corral the players into a cohesive, united team, and, ultimately, taking a harder line won respect.

Even so, leaks suggested that Koeman's meeting with Messi didn't go according to plan. Although understood to have been respectful on both sides, it was alleged that Leo took umbrage at the Dutchman's apparent suggestion that his captain would no longer have any freedom to roam as he pleased and would have to work for the benefit of the team.

Whatever happened, it quickly become clear that Messi hadn't been convinced by Koeman – at all. On August 25, 2020, he sent a burofax (a service used to send documents which require proof of delivery to third parties) to the club to tell them that he wanted out. He added that he believed that he would be able to leave unilaterally, per the terms of his contract, and therefore for free.

Whilst his most recent contract had a clause allowing him to leave for free at the end of every season, it required him to let the club know of his intentions by June 10 of each year. He argued that because the season had been extended by three months due to the

August 25, 2020: A copy of the famous burofax sent by Lionel Messi to FC Barcelona president, Josep Maria Bartomeu.

August 25, 2020: 'Goodbye by Burofax' – Leo sent shockwaves through the football world after sending a burofax to FC Barcelona president, Josep Maria Bartomeu, informing him that he wished to sever all ties with the club. (© AS)

pandemic, this clause was still active. Barça's board replied that the original date still applied and anyone wanting to buy him would have to pay his €700m release clause.

The news rocked the world of football to its core. In Barcelona crowds gathered at Camp Nou demanding Josep Maria Bartomeu's departure. Within days Bartomeu offered his resignation, but only on the basis that Leo came out in public to announce he would stay at Barça – a gambit showing that his problem was not with the club but the president. As leak was followed by counter-leak it was hard to see a way back for Messi, who had yet to make any public comment himself or deny the consistent rumours of a potential reunion with Pep at Manchester City.

Barça's board were convinced of the strength of their legal position but, while still hoping to keep Messi, for the first-time there was tacit acceptance behind the scenes that he could well be leaving. Even at this stage there were internal divisions. Some saw a fee of around

$100m, together with getting Leo's colossal salary off the books, as their best chance of keeping the club solvent, a serious consideration under the club's rules requiring directors to pay deficits out of their own pockets if the books do not balance at the end of a season.

Man City were reported to be ready to offer players, plus cash, and it was apparent that some members of the board were, privately, hoping he would go, even if their public faces said exactly the opposite. They could strengthen the squad in key areas and release a hefty financial burden in return for a player who was probably only a couple of seasons away from retirement. The private jousting between board members played out in public through multiple social media and traditional media channels. Depending on your news outlet of choice, there was the opportunity of round-the-clock updates. *Culés* couldn't switch on a TV or radio channel, pick up a paper or look at their smartphones without seeing some snippet of Messi news. The wall-to-wall coverage dominated the news and the noise was deafening.

Jorge Messi travelled from Rosario to Barcelona to meet Bartomeu on Wednesday, September 3. "Difficult"was all he would say about Leo's chances of staying, while admitting he had yet to speak to any other club.

Details of the meeting, reported as 'cordial' leaked on the Wednesday night, with the twist that there was now a 90% chance of Leo remaining for at least one more season. Jorge had been accompanied by Leo's brother, Rodrigo, and the family lawyer, Jorge Pecourt, while Bartomeu was joined by Barça's football director, Javier Bordas. The absence of any club lawyer underlined their view that it was a football rather than legal matter.

Jorge Messi opened by stating his son's request to walk away for free, but found Bartomeu was in no mood for negotiation, saying he could only leave for €700m. The club president, instead, made a counter-offer of a two-year renewal with the option of leaving at the end of each season. While this would tie him in for at least another year, he could then walk out with his head high and no hard feelings having, in the meantime, had the chance to score the 10 goals he needed to overtake Pelé's all-time one-club scoring record of 643 for Santos. The meeting ended without agreement, and the 'doomsday' scenario of the dispute going to court.

In order to leave, Leo would have to ask FIFA for a provisional transfer, which would force Barça to begin a civil court action against him and the club he joined, as well as reporting him to FIFA. This would lead to any transfee fee being fixed by a judge, a risk that not even Man City were prepared to take. In the end, not wanting to have to drag the dispute through the courts – where the only winners would be the lawyers – Messi stayed. However, in an interview with *Goal.com* he made his reluctance and frustration clear, accusing Bartomeu of breaking promises to him.

Goal: Why did it take you time to break your silence and go out to speak?

Messi: "First, because after the defeat in Lisbon it was very hard. We knew Bayern Munich were a very difficult opponent, but not that we were going to end that way, giving such a poor image for the city and the club of Barcelona. We gave a very bad image. It was wrong, I didn't feel like doing anything. I wanted time to pass and then go out to clarify everything."

Goal: Why did you tell Barça that you wanted to go?

Messi: "I told the club, including the president, that I wanted to go. I've been telling him that all year. I believed it was time to step aside. I believed that the club needed more young players, new players and I thought my time in Barcelona was over. I felt very sorry because I always said that I wanted to finish my career here. It was a very difficult year, I suffered a lot in training, in games and in the dressing room. Everything became very difficult for me and there came a time when I considered looking for new ambitions. It did not come because of the Champions League result against Bayern, no – I had been thinking about the decision for a long time. I told the president and, well, the president always said that at the end of the season I could decide if I wanted to go or if I wanted to stay and in the end he did not keep his word."

Goal: Have you ever felt lonely?

Messi: "No... I didn't feel alone. Not alone. There are those who have always been by my side. That is enough for me and strengthens me. But I did feel hurt by things that I heard from people, from journalists, from people questioning my commitment to Barcelona and saying things that I think I didn't deserve. It also helped me to see the truth in people. This world of soccer is very difficult and there are many fake people. This happening has helped me to recognise many fake people. It hurt me when my love for this club was questioned. No matter how much I go or stay, my love for Barça will never change."

Goal: Everything has been talked about. The money factor, your friends. What has hurt the most after 20 years defending the Barça shirt?

Messi: "A bit of everything, my friends, money... many things that have been said have hurt. I always put the club before anything else. I had the possibility of leaving Barça many times. The money? Every year I could have left and earned more money than at Barcelona. I always said that this was my home and it was what I felt and feel. To decide there was somewhere better than here was difficult. I felt that I needed a change and new goals, new things."

Goal: In the end it is very difficult to give up 20 years, a whole life, a family that is in Barcelona, a city... and that is what weighs more when making a decision. Because I understand that in the end, you are staying in Barcelona. You are still at Barcelona.

Messi: "Of course I had a hard time deciding. It does not come from the Bayern result, it comes from many things. I always said I wanted to end here and I always said I wanted to stay here. That I wanted a winning project and to win titles with the club, to continue expanding the legend of Barcelona. And the truth is that there has been no project or anything for a long time, they juggle and cover holes as things go by. As I said before, I always thought about the welfare of my family and the club."

Goal: What happened when you told your family that you can leave Barcelona?

Messi: "When I communicated my wish to leave to my wife and children, it was a brutal drama. The whole family began crying, my children did not want to leave Barcelona, nor did they want to change schools. I looked further afield and I want to compete at the highest level, win titles, compete in the Champions League. You can win or lose in it, because it is very difficult, but you have to compete. At least compete and let us not fall apart in Rome, Liverpool, Lisbon. All that led me to think about that decision that I wanted to carry out. As I said, I thought and was sure that I was free to leave, the president always said that at the end of the season I could decide if I stayed or not.

Now they cling to the fact that I did not say it before June 10, when it turns out that on June 10 we were competing for La Liga in the middle of this awful coronavirus and this disease altered all the season. And this is the reason why I am going to continue in the club. Now I am going to continue in the club because the president told me that the only way to leave was to pay the €700 million clause, and that this is impossible. There was another way and it was to go to trial. I would never go to court against Barça because it is the club that I love, which gave me everything since I arrived, it is the club of my life, I have made my life here. Barça gave me everything and I gave it everything. I know that it never crossed my mind to take Barça to court."

Goal: Is that what has hurt you the most, that there are people who think you could have hurt Barça? You have been defending the club for years and being the flag of FC Barcelona. Has it hurt you that they doubt your commitment?

Messi: "It has hurt me a lot that things are published against me and above all, that false things are published. Or that they came to think that I could go to trial against Barça in order to benefit myself. I would never do such a thing. I repeat, I wanted to go and it was entirely my right, because the contract said that I could be released. And it is not, 'I'm leaving and that's it'. I was leaving and it cost me a lot. I wanted to go because I thought about living my last years of football happily. Lately I have not found happiness within the club."

Goal: That is vital, to be happy. You are a born winner. You are in a team that fights for titles and in recent seasons Barça has not competed in Europe. You are going to continue leading the team at Barca. But something will have to change at Barça, right? Something will have to change at the sporting level, right?

Messi: "I will continue at Barça and my attitude will not change no matter how much I have wanted to go. I will do my best. I always want to win, I'm competitive and I don't like to lose anything. I always want the best for the club, for the dressing room and for myself. I said it at the time that we were not given the support to win the Champions League. Actually, now I don't know what will happen. There is a new coach and new ideas. That's good, but then we have to see how the team responds and whether or not it will allow us to compete at the top level. What I can say is that I'm staying and I'm going to give my best for Barcelona."

Goal: What was the first thing you thought when there were people who said that you could leave and that you really didn't care about Barcelona? What was the first thing you thought? Feelings of rage?

Messi: "I felt a lot of pain that my commitment to Barcelona was doubted, with how grateful I am to this club. I love Barcelona and I'm not going to find a better place than here anywhere. Still I have the right to decide. I was going to look for new goals and new challenges. And tomorrow I could go back, because here in Barcelona I have everything. My son, my family, they grew up here and are from here. There was nothing wrong with wanting to leave. I needed it, the club needed it and it was good for everyone."

Goal: Family is something very important in your life. Your father has had a bad time, your wife too, your children. What have they asked of you? What did they tell you? They must have told you, 'Dad, this, dad, that'. Did they watch the news on TV and ask you something?

Messi: "All this time it has been hard for everyone. I was clear about what I wanted, I have said what I felt I wanted. My wife, with all the pain of her soul, supported and accompanied me..."

Goal: But the most important member of the family is Mateo.

Messi: [Laughter] "Yes, Mateo is still little and he doesn't realise what it means to go somewhere else and make your life a few years elsewhere. Thiago yes, he is older. He heard something on TV and found out something and asked. I didn't want him to know anything about being forced to leave, to have to live in a new school, or make new friends. He cried to me and said, 'Let's not go'. I repeat that it was hard, really. It was understandable. It happened to me. It is very difficult to make a decision."

Goal: And for anyone. Of course, it's 20 years, that's a lifetime. You came to Barcelona at the age of your children now. That's hard. There are two fundamental things that people would like to know... you will stay at Barça, you will lead the team again. Is that an optimistic message for Barça fans for the future?

Messi: "As usual, I am going to give my best, I will do my best to fight for all the objectives and hopefully I can dedicate myself to the people who have had a bad time. I had a bad time this year, but it is hypocritical to say that if you compare it with people who have really had a bad time with the coronavirus, with people who have lost relatives and who have lost many things. Hopefully I can give my best and dedicate victories to all those people who accompany us and their families, to be able to dedicate the best to those people who are having a bad time and that once and for all we can overcome this virus and return to normality."

Goal: The famous burofax. There has been a lot of talk about Messi being badly advised by the decision to communicate that you wanted to leave by burofax. Why did you decide to send that burofax? What did you want to demonstrate? What was your position?

Messi: "The burofax was to make it official in some way. Throughout the year I had been telling the president that I wanted to leave, that the time had come to seek new goals and new directions in my career. He told me all the time: 'We'll talk, not now, this and that', but nothing. The president did not give me a clue at what he was really saying. Sending the burofax was making it official that I wanted to go and that I was free and the optional year – I was not going to use it and I wanted to go. It was not to make a mess, or to go against the club, but the way to make it official because my decision had been made."

Goal: So if you hadn't sent the burofax, maybe everything would have been forgotten and no one would have listened to you?

Messi: "Clearly. If I don't send the burofax, it's like nothing happens, I have the optional year I had to have continued all year. What they say is that I did not say it before June 10 – but I repeat, we were in the middle of all the competitions and it was not the moment. But apart from that, the president always told me, 'When the season is over, you decide if you stay or leave', he never set a date, and well, it was simply to make to the club official that he was not following his word, but not to get into a fight because I did not want to fight with the club."

Within a few days Messi joined up with his team-mates for his first training sessions of pre-season, and looked to be in good form, particularly in the second of the three fixtures, against Girona. Having already beaten Gimnàstic 3-1, Barça beat their near neighbours by the same score. Resplendent in their new pink and green third kit, Leo's first goal, on the turn before slamming home a right-footed howitzer in off the post, told us all we needed to know about his mindset. His second took a wicked deflection but was a reward for his industry. On the day, he was outshone by young American star, Konrad de la Fuente, who was certainly making the most of his opportunity with the first team.

A 1-0 win in the Gamper Trophy against Elche was uninspiring, bar Antoine Griezmann's early goal, and before the 2020-21 league opener against Villarreal a week later, there was still time for Leo to fire another broadside at the board. In the space of two days, the club sold Arturo Vidal to Internazionale, Nélson Semedo to Wolverhampton Wanderers and Luis Suárez to Atlético Madrid. The Uruguayan's hastily arranged final press conference wasn't befitting a player who was Barça's third highest-ever scorer, and someone who had been an unqualified success since his move in 2014. Suárez refused to have a final photo with Bartomeu, and a day later Leo took to Instagram. "You deserved to depart like what you are: one of the most important players in the club's history. Not for them to kick you out like they have. But the truth is that nothing surprises me anymore." This certainly wasn't the ideal way for Leo to begin, potentially, his final season at the club.

21

Beating Pelé's Record

History Maker Against Valladolid

"The club are in a difficult situation. It's difficult for everyone. It's going to be very hard to be where we once were."

In September 2020, a *moció de censura* (vote of no confidence) was instigated against Bartomeu. Securing the 16,250 signatures legally required for a formal vote was a huge challenge amid the pandemic, but the extent of fan discontent at the way the club was being run – with the Catalan police alleging corruption – was shown by the total of 20,687 signatures obtained. The campaign against Bartomeu was also given fresh impetus when Gerard Piqué spoke to *La Vanguardia* the day before the first Clásico of the season.

"My relationship with the president could be cordial," Piqué said, "but it's an absolute disgrace that the club has spent substantial sums of money criticising us. He [Jaume Masferrer, one of Bartomeu's executives alledged to be behind the scandal] is still a club employee and that hurts."

Piqué weighed in further, on attempts to reduce player salaries and the sacking of Ernesto Valverde: "The club's way of handling this [salary reduction] is far from ideal and we're all not happy with this manner of doing things. It didn't seem coherent either to sack a coach halfway through the season being top of the table and having won the last two leagues."

Nor did he finish there: "One is obliged to come to an arrangement with a player who has spent 16 years at the club. What has forced the best player in history to send a burofax to the club as he feels he's not being listened to. It's a shocking level to reach." Piqué's frankness signalled open warfare as stage two of the no-confidence process began.

There had been mixed fortunes on the field as the league campaign began. Wins over Villarreal (4-0), Celta (0-3 at Balaídos) and a 1-1 draw against an impressive Sevilla side gave everyone a reason to be hopeful. Leo led from the front in each game and Barça looked re-energised, but a 1-0 loss at Getafe was followed by a 1-3 home defeat by Real Madrid, blamed by many *culés* on the penalty given after Clément Lenglet's challenge on Sergio Ramos was referred to VAR. Barça's league position was noticeably lower than expected, but this was easily explainable due to the games in hand over the teams above them. Ferencváros had been comfortably dispatched 5-1 in the opening Champions League group stage match, so there seemed little to worry about.

Perhaps the main concern was that Leo hadn't yet scored in open play, though he'd certainly made himself busy in all of his games, never more so than when he tracked right back to his own corner flag to dispossess Vinicius Junior who was looking threatening for *Los Blancos*. Champions League wins against Dynamo Kyiv and an under-par Juventus had put Barça in total control of their group, but don't tell the whole story.

Juventus, though outplayed, were not fully dispatched until Leo's injury-time penalty, whilst Kyiv could count themselves incredibly unlucky to leave Camp Nou without a point. Another Messi penalty had sent Barça on their way after just five minutes, but it would take another hour before Gerard Piqué doubled the lead. Even then, the Ukrainians pulled one back and could have grabbed an equaliser. Perhaps the 1-1 draw from another disappointing 90 minutes at Alavés was a better guide to Barça's standing under Koeman, whilst a sparkling 5-2 win over Betis, including Leo's first from open play, lightened the mood before a trip to Atléti's Wanda Metropolitano.

There was no reunion with Luis Suárez, who'd been ruled out after testing positive for coronavirus, but Atléti's other players were more than good enough for Barça, claiming the points when Yannick Carrasco shot into an empty net with ter Stegen stranded outside the box.

Two 4-0 wins followed, one with Leo and one without. Dynamo Kyiv were rolled over with ease and Osasuna beaten in a match marked by the tributes to Diego Maradona, who had recently died aged 60. Messi paid his own special tribute after smashing home Barça's fourth. Taking off his shirt, he revealed a top that Maradona once wore whilst playing for Newell's Old Boys, the Argentinian team

November 29, 2020: 'Messi, a 10' - Leo's iconic tribute to the recently passed Diego Maradona after slamming home Barça's fourth goal against Osasuna. (© MARCA)

they had in common. Not even being booked and then fined according to football's inflexible procedures could detract from another iconic celebration destined for the game's collective consciousness.

The next day, former club president, Joan Laporta, announced his candidacy for the January elections. He cited the need to restore La Masia to its former glory and to do whatever was necessary to keep Leo at the club: "I'm running for elections because I love the club. We have the preparation, experience and determination necessary for the changes that the club need. We have a plan. The plan is to work. I want to unite all Barça fans. This is not the time to reproach or look back. In the Barça that we propose, everyone fits. Our plan is to bring back happiness to the people. It's not a simple election promise. It's an ethical, civic, moral, social and united commitment."

While yet to speak to Messi, Laporta continued: "We appreciate each other and we respect each other. He has time to decide – I am waiting to have the confidence of the *socios*. Messi loves Barça and I'm sure that the club can give him an opportunity. I see myself capable of, at the right moment, having a conversation with him. I know we can give each other some margin, anything can happen in life."

With the date of the presidential elections set for January 24, Laporta, Víctor Font, Jordi Farre, Toni Freixa, Lluis Fernandez Ala, Agustí Benedito, Pere Riera and former vice president and 'Barçagate' whistleblower, Emili Rousad, were all expected to stand. On the same day the club, doubtless spotting a good opportunity to bury bad news, announced player salary cuts amounting to €190m: "The managing commission would like to publicly thank the footballers, coaches and employees for their understanding, their commitment and their help to the organisation to make possible this fundamental agreement to guarantee the club's immediate sustainability. The managing commission considers this to be a great step on the road to dealing with the extraordinary circumstances in which the organisation finds itself due to the global pandemic which has affected everyone since March of this year," the statement read.

Another Champions League victory over Ferencváros, the second group game without Messi, made it five from five, but Barça continued to struggle on the road in La Liga. Cádiz, back in the top division after a 14 year hiatus, were too good for a clueless, defensively inept Barça. Although Koeman's job wasn't exactly hanging by a thread, it didn't go unnoticed that he'd already lost more games in less that half a season than Quique Setién during his entire Barça tenure.

Koeman soon lost another when Juventus deservedly snatched top spot in the Champions League group with a 3-0 win at Camp Nou with, somewhat inevitably, Cristiano Ronaldo stealing the show with two goals. Presidential candidate Víctor Font's statement that Koeman wouldn't remain as coach if he won the election didn't help his cause and the Juve defeat saw *culés* demanding a change of manager. He was done for, and so were Barça. Out of contention for the league and with minimal chance in the Champions League, only the Copa del Rey stood between them and consecutive trophyless seasons, something unheard of in the Messi era.

The *Blaugranes* went unbeaten through the rest of December, although their inability to beat Eibar – the club from a Basque town whose entire population could fit into Camp Nou and leave 60,000 seats free – rather summed up the year.

Messi, who watched Eibar claim their first ever point at Camp Nou from the stands after spending Christmas in Argentina, had accomplished another of his targets in the final match, against Valladolid, before the winter break. His 644th goal for Barça took him past Pelé's long-standing one-club record. Of all his records, this is likely to be the hardest to break. Scoring an average of 43 goals a season for 15 years is a tough ask, but to remain at one club long enough to achieve that record is highly unlikely in modern football.

Then came an extensive and candid Messi interview. Given to *La Sexta*'s Jordi Evole, it felt like no previous Messi interview. He was completely at ease, speaking with a frankness and eloquence that did not appear forced at any time. Nor, for once, was any topic off limits. It began innocently enough with his memories of childhood Christmases, before getting down to his relationship with Barça: "When I was little, I always asked for something football related. A jersey, a ball, boots ... My parents did everything to make me happy. I even remember receiving a ball that was very expensive, the official ball of the league. My father and mother always did their best ... This [Barcelona] shirt means everything for me, my love for the club, the city, my kids were born here. Barça gave me everything. I've lived here for longer than in Argentina ... I learned everything here. The club formed me as a player and as a person ... The club are in a difficult situation. It's difficult for everyone. It's going to be very hard to be where we once were ... I'm good now and the episode of the summer is behind me ... the club is having a rough time and is in bad shape but I'm full of enthusiasm ... Playing in empty stadiums is horrible ... it's cold ... strange and different ... I think that may have something to do with strange results that we're seeing with home advantage being less important."

He continued in the same direct vein when asked about Maradona's death, his feud with Bartomeu, whether he really wanted to leave the club and potential future plans: "I was here at my house and I got a message from my dad [about Maradona]. I turned the TV on right away, and I started to find out about everything. The tribute to Maradona? The people of Newell's gave the shirt to me. That day I knew that I had to score a goal and it was strange. In a play out of nowhere, when I least looked for it, the goal appeared ... Yes, it was a manner of making a point and expressing my feelings. It was me telling the club that I wanted to leave. It was far from easy for me to say I wanted to leave the club and the city ... the family wanted to stay here, this is their home but I genuinely felt it was time to go. Luis Suárez's departure had nothing to do with the decision, but I felt it was crazy the way his exit was handled and that Barcelona let him go to a direct rival ... Yes, that bothered me ... I felt I'd completed a cycle and it was time to leave the club that had given me so much. I wanted to win titles and battle for the Champions League and felt it was time for change. The president then started to filter this and that to paint a negative picture of me.

"I am not sure if I'll vote in the forthcoming presidential elections. Whoever comes in will find the club in a tricky state and will have to work hard to put the club back where it was. As yet none of the candidates have called me ... I would like to play in the United States and experience life and the league there ... but ultimately come back to Barcelona in some capacity. I'm not thinking too far ahead in the short term and just want to see how the season finishes. I will not negotiate with other clubs. I will wait for the season to end and in June I will decide. If I leave, I would like to leave in the best way and later return to contribute to the club. Barcelona is bigger than any player. After retirement? I would like to be involved in football, not as a coach, I don't see myself coaching, but maybe as a sporting director."

The implications were clear. If he was going to leave, it would be to the United States – it looked very much as if he already made his decision. Man City were still waiting in the wings, Pep Guardiola wouldn't say no to a reunion even if his preference was for Messi to stay at Barça, and City would not only offer the competitive squad that Leo desired, but a pathway to Major League Soccer (MLS) via their arrangement with New York City FC. Barça fans had a feeling they needed to make the most of the five months they had left to enjoy his talents.

The New Year opened well with wins in Bilbao and Granada with the teenager Pedri showing himself as a true successor to

January 6, 2021: Leo celebrates with Pedri after the No. 16 had played an exquisite back heel pass to the Argentinian, allowing him to score against Athletic Club in a match that Barça would go on to win 3-2. (© Shutterstock)

the best Barça traditions, when he combined with Messi in an exquisite passage of play at San Mamés. His backheeled pass to Leo who, with a broad grin on his face, rifled the ball home, was one to match the ball from Guti to Karim Benzema for Real Madrid which is often called La Liga's best-ever assist, and ter Stegen's heroics secured victory on penalties over Real Sociedad in the Spanish Super Cup.

Laporta won the first stage of the presidential elections comfortably, with only Font and Freixa getting enough votes to qualify for the final run-off, but with voters confined to their home districts by Covid protocols, the poll was postponed until March 7.

While Messi remained impeccably neutral, Laporta emphasised their connection, and his chances of persuading him to stay, at every opportunity: "I see him as being more and more happy, he's enjoying himself. Against Real Sociedad it was a great football match. I know that he wants to stay, and I know that he will do everything in his power to stay as long as the club can offer him something that suits him," was one of his many soundbites.

Messi was far from happy after the Spanish Super Cup final on January 17. Barça led Athletic Club 2-1, from an Antonie Griezmann double, with just 40 seconds left when Jordi Alba ducked instead of blocking an Athletic free-kick which led to the equaliser. Gutted at losing their grip on the cup in the last minute, the Barça players lost heart and Athletic Club went on to lift the trophy.

For once, Leo's frustrations boiled over. Barça had been moribund as an attacking force in extra-time but in the final minute, the left side of the pitch opened for one of his trademark runs ready for the pull-back. Athletic's Asier Villalibre had other ideas and deliberately blocked him. An attempted right hook which ended up as more of a slap downed Villalibre, and it was immediately clear what was

Joan Laporta. (© Shutterstock)

coming next. Sure enough, after a VAR review, Leo was handed the first red card of his Barça career.

His body language spoke volumes. Barça had failed him again. A cup that had been there for the taking had been gifted to Athletic on a plate. It was only Athletic's second trophy in three decades, both Super Cup wins over Barça, but where – in 2015 – Athletic had beaten a Barça team en route to a treble, the 2021 edition was shaping up for a second consecutive trophyless year. Hardly a record to tempt Leo to stay.

His 650th goal for Barça, a magnificent free-kick, provided revenge of sorts over Athletic Club at the end of January and followed on from Copa del Rey wins at Cornellà and Rayo Vallecano and a league victory at Elche, but it was overshadowed by details of his contract being leaked. Believed to eminate from unfriendly elements within the club, the leak clearly unsettled Leo.

El Mundo reported that the four-year deal signed in 2017 was worth €555,237,619 (£492m) – £123m per season. The club denounced

January 31, 2021: 'The mammoth contract of Messi that ruins Barça' - Details of Messi's incredible FC Barcelona contract, signed in 2017, are leaked to the press. (© El Mundo)

the leak, while not denying the detail: "FC Barcelona categorically denies any responsibility for the publication of this document and will take appropriate legal action against the newspaper *El Mundo*, for any damage that may be caused as a result of this publication," a statement read. "FC Barcelona expresses its absolute support for Lionel Messi, especially in the face of any attempt to discredit his image, and to damage his relationship with the entity where he has worked to become the best player in the world and in football history."

Joan Laporta phoned Messi to reiterate his promise to do everything in his power to keep him at Barça, but the final decision remained with the player, and nobody yet had any idea how that would play out.

22

Laporta's Promise

False Hopes and New Beginnings

"We cannot even grasp and understand the magnitude of his achievements and contributions because something which is totally extraordinary has become the new normal."

February brought unmistakable reminders of the toughest opponent of the lot – age – and an impending change of generations. Kylian Mbappé hat-trick for PSG ejected Messi and Barça from the Champions League, whilst Erling Haaland was among the goals for Borussia Dortmund against Sevilla. New footballing royalty was emerging to dethrone the old.

Sevilla hoped that a 2-0 win in the first leg of the Copa del Rey semi-final signalled an end to their persecution by Messi, but found him back in his usual form with an assist and a goal in their league meeting. It the *Blaugranes* best display of the season, the goal was Leo's 30th against Sevilla in La Liga, and the 38th in all competitions.

In the return Copa del Rey tie, Sevilla were to be thwarted again as Barça dominated but still trailed on aggregate until the 94th minute when Gerard Piqué made it 2-0 – from a corner taken by Messi – and unleashed wild celebrations. Martin Braithwaite's extra-time goal confirmed Barça's place in their 10th Copa del Rey final in 13 seasons.

Success on the pitch contrasted to the turmoil off it as the first four arrests over 'Barçagate' were made. While the Catalan police refused to name those in custody, it was widely reported that former president, Josep Maria Bartomeu, as well as the club's chief executive, Oscar Grau, head of legal, Roman Gomez Ponti, and Jaume Masferrer – said to be Bartomeu's former right-hand man – were the four detained on charges concerning unfair administration, corruption between individuals and money laundering within the club's finance, legal and compliance departments. A *Mossos* press release stated: "Today, members of the Central Economic Crimes Area of the DIC [Criminal Investigation Division] have carried out actions under an investigation into alleged crimes related to property and socio-economic order. These actions have resulted in 4 arrests and 5 entries and searches in different locations, both companies and individuals, in search of useful material for the investigation. One of these entries has been made in some specific departments of the FC Barcelona offices. From the Generalitat Police – *Mossos d'Esquadra* – we want to highlight the attitude and collaboration of FC Barcelona in the records that have been made today and during the course of the investigation. The investigation, which has been going on for almost a year, is still ongoing."

The presidential candidates, aware of the damage being done to the club, were reticent about the arrests. Laporta was duly returned with 54% of the vote and chose to emphasise Messi in his first speech after results were declared: "Special thanks to our players, many of them have come to participate in these elections and they are proud. Also, a thank you to people closely linked to us who are no longer here like Johan Cruyff. He inspires us in many things, this was a Cruyffista and Barcelonista candidacy. Seeing the best player in history come to vote with his son and take part in this FC Barcelona election, shows that Leo loves Barça. We are a great family and hopefully this will serve to encourage him to continue at Barça."

The new presidency had a decent on-field start with a 1-1 draw against PSG in Paris. Messi scored with a thunderbolt, but failed with a penalty after Kylian Mbappé had equalised, and journalists seeking hints to his eventual destination made an enormous amount of his brief, respectful embrace of fellow-Argentinian Mauricio Pocchetino as the teams left the field. Before the week was out, Marcelo Bechler, who had broken the Neymar story and the news that Messi wanted to leave Barça, took to Twitter to announce that PSG were absolutely confident that Messi would indeed be signing for them on a free transfer in the summer.

At that point in, mid-March, nobody other than close family could have known his true intentions, and there were good arguments for and against him staying. Whether or not Barça cared to admit it, his departure would be a financial godsend, as well as moving them on from 'Messi-dependence'. Nonetheless, Leo attended Laporta's first official address, streamed live from Camp Nou, unable to hide a smile behind the mask worn in order to adhere to Covid protocols.

Leo's record-breaking 768th appearance for the club, passing Xavi's total, came at Reale Arena, the new name for Real Sociedad's Estadio de Anoeta – Barça's bogey ground on the Basque coast. He'd lost there on five previous occasions to *La Real*, but this would be very different. Unbeaten in 17 matches, Barça knew a win would keep up pressure on leaders Atlético Madrid, and sealed the win with a barrage of four goals in 20 minutes either side of half-time. Griezmann scored against his old side, Sergiño Dest claimed his first two league goals – the first from a sublime Messi assist – and Leo marked his own record with a goal, completing the 6-1 rout by finishing Barça's best move of the day in the 89th minute as title momentum shifted towards the *Blaugranes.*

A wildy celebrated late winner from Ousmane Dembélé against Valladolid took Barça into something new in the way of El Clásico encounters, played in a biblical deluge at the Estadio Alfredo di Stéfano, Castilla's ground at *Los Blancos'* Valdebebas training complex. The weather was no excuse for Barça's mainly lacklustre showing as Leo was again marked out of the biggest game of the season and two lapses of concentration in the first half gave Real an ultimately decisive 2-0 half time lead. Barça's superiority in the second half was to no avail, bringing only a single goal from Óscar Mingueza. It was no way to prepare for the Copa del Rey final at La Cartuja stadium in Seville, but the match against Athletic Club turned into a procession for Barça, with Messi – in his 10th final – right at the heart of the victory.

Goalless at half-time, even though statistics had at one point showed Barça enjoying 97% of possession, four goals in 12 minutes settled it. Frenkie de Jong set up the first for Griezmann, scored himself and then supplied the pass for Messi to score a goal similar to the one he had scored in the 2015 final. Leo's second goal, following a 60-metre, work-of-art passing masterclass, crowned a triumphant victory, more emphatic than the 5-0 thumping of Sevilla in 2018.

With Jorge Messi spotted watching Barça B's victory that Sunday, and believed to be in town to discuss a new contract for Leo, it had become a celebratory weekend for *culés* – at least until just before midnight when news broke of their involvement in the projected European Super League. Barça's supporters were as vocal as any of their counterparts at the other clubs, but the financial element of the deal – rumoured to be in the hundreds of millions of Euros – undoubtedly explained why the club remained interested in the project and refused to rule themselves out as others quit, within hours, under intense pressue.

Two days later, after most of the ESL founder members had already backed out, it was clear the project was dead. The recent transition of power enabled Laporta to blame Bartomeu, whose final act had been to commit Barça to the project. A belated statement was issued directly before the match against Getafe that attempted to justify the initial decision but then provide the get-out clause to save face.

"The FC Barcelona Board of Directors accepted, as a matter of immediate urgency, the offer to form part, as the founding member, of the Super League, a competition designed to improve the quality and attractiveness of the product offered to the football fans and, at the same time, and as one of FC Barcelona's most inalienable principles, seek new formulas for solidarity with the football family as a whole," the statement read, before confirming, "Given the public reaction that the aforementioned project has generated in many and various spheres, there is no question that FC Barcelona appreciates that a much more in-depth analysis is required into the reasons that have caused this reaction in order to reconsider, if necessary, and to the required extent, the proposal as originally formulated and resolve all those issues, always for the good of the general interest of the football world. Such in-depth analysis needs time and the necessary composure to avoid taking any rash action."

Not for the first time, Messi offered a fine distraction from the misadventures of Barça's leaders, with two goals and an assist in a 5-2 victory. The title chase was still on and a win at Villareal, while both Real and Atléti faltered, put Barça in charge, only for them to promptly go down 2-1 at home to Granada, losers on their 24 previous visits to Camp Nou. The following game, a trip to Valencia, brought Messi's 50th goal of the season, from a free-kick, settling a 3-2 thriller in Barça's favour.

It was feats like this which guaranteed the admiration of defeated presidential candidate Víctor Font, now fully behind the new regime. He told me:

"Leo is the best ever in sport. I still remember when we signed Maradona. I was 10 but I remember very vividly going to the stadium and watching Maradona play. He was obviously also a spectacular player, but Messi does what Maradona used to do with one main difference. He does it every game, for pretty much 80 or 90% of the games, and for the time being, 15 or 16 years already. This [Messi's longevity] is definitely his biggest achievement. We cannot even grasp and understand the magnitude of his achievements and contributions because something which is totally extraordinary has become the new normal – for many, many years – and that's why, once he's not with us, we will fully realise what he's done. Just like in the cup final [against Athletic], and it's amazing – but kind of normal. Romario once promised 30 goals in a season and we all thought 'what is this guy doing?!' and when he achieved that, it was like 'wow, what an achievement'. Turning extraordinary things into normal ones is Messi's legacy."

Font also confirmed how close Leo had come to leaving the club the previous summer:

"Unfortunately, or fortunately, I don't know, I had first-hand information and insights that told me that this was not just an over-reaction or something that could be easily managed. He was serious about it, and really reached that decision after a very difficult thought process. Therefore, I knew that it was going to be very hard to turn things around. I had mixed feelings and mixed emotions – a mixture of anger, disappointment and disbelief – I couldn't believe it to be honest. It was probably the true bottom point of where the club could go. I mean, I thought that the defeat in Lisbon meant that we had reached the bottom, but the Messi event last August took us even further down. In the sense that the defeat in the Champions League, an historical 8-2, showed to the world what we were. More than the result it was the way in which we played and our inability to compete. The Messi event proved to all of us and to everyone else that the mess wasn't only sporting related but also institutional."

Each candidate had known he would need a plan for keeping Messi and Font knew it would take something special for him to even enter negotiations:

"For us, the solution was to offer him, first and foremost besides any contractual proposal, a sports project which was convincing, and that convinced him it would be a project capable of allowing us to compete at the very top. That for me was a pre-requisite and priority number one. And then, in terms of how to translate this into a contractual relationship – a contract for life. Ensuring that we could tie Messi's involvement in the club, the partnership between Messi and Barça, Barça and Messi, for the rest of his days or up until the time he decided to finish. Because, again, having the best player of all time in the club, and this player being a one-club man, that was of tremendous value to us – huge. We needed to think commercially of course, we wanted to talk about money, but that probably wasn't his number one priority. The opportunity to build a win-win proposition was there, however, because the amount of potential commercial value we could generate, even after he retired ... just look at Maradona. That guy, with all the problems he had, with the lack of association to a top club, without even being properly advised or managed, and still the amount of expectation everywhere he went ... that's the type of vision that I believe Barça needed to have with Leo and then translate that into a win-win proposition."

At the time of the interview, Barça were chasing the title and Font considered the suggestion that Koeman, though not his choice, had played an important part in this:

"From what we have seen with the change in Koeman, he's the coach that managed to change Messi for the better, when he was at rock bottom wanting to leave. We'll see what Messi decides [Leo still hadn't communicated a decision to stay or leave at the time this interview was conducted], but he seems much happier now. So Koeman is, for sure, one of the contributors to this change. How much of a contribution he's made, I don't know. Whether he's at the level of other coaches too in terms of ability to convince the players, and especially Messi, of having a winning plan and so on ... someone like Guardiola for example, maybe he's not at that level but it's difficult to say from the outside. When you talk about how Leo can be managed effectively ... I think that Guardiola said it best one day ... Messi, because of his full attention and dedication to football, wants to win. He's a competitive beast. He wants to win every day, even in training, so the best way to manage him is to have a coach that is convincing. Convincing in the sense that Leo is told 'if you're going to do this, we're going to win' – and then he does it because he wants to win. When there is no proper leadership and lack of convincing arguments, then that's when things get complicated. Xavi was our pitch at the elections because it's a natural evolution. Johan, Pep, Xavi. It's clear at some point that's where things need to go.

With Leo, it's not that there's 'Messi-dependence' either, but there's so much of a difference when he's not there. Obviously it's not going to be the same. The good thing is that there's no other Messi's. It's not that without Messi you are not competitive, but you miss one of the things that gives you an edge, particularly if the team isn't coached in the best possible way or the team isn't at a level where it needs to be. That's what Messi gives you, and without him you lose that advantage. He's irreplaceable. There's no one that will replace Messi, but as I said, with Messi there is only one and without Messi, we are closer to the rest. Therefore, we can definitely continue competing and aspiring to be the best team in the world, even when Messi leaves. We need to ensure that we are very consistent and that we make the best possible decisions, because now when a mistake is made, the fact that we have Messi allows us to compensate for those mistakes. Without Messi we won't have the opportunity to compensate such mistakes.

Leo is an ultra-professional guy, and he lives for football. He doesn't have distractions that other top players in history have had, that didn't allow them to reach their optimum level on a sustained basis. The sustainability of his performances is because of his full focus and dedication to football. I would say to someone who plays PlayStation very well, Messi is like the very best player on PlayStation – but for real. He can do whatever you want. Besides goalkeeper – because we've not seen him play in that position – he could play anywhere. His ability to know what he's going to do even before things happen, his intuition, the broader view he has of the pitch and the game itself ... it's just phenomenal and that's why he's been able to play as a forward, on one side, in the centre, in midfield, even going back into defence and taking the ball there to almost play as a centre-back that starts the build-up ... he's just phenomenal. Obviously, we know also that professionals in football do not need to be training like swimmers or gymnasts. There is time that he can use, which he does, to serve the community and to make an impact in the world. I think that that's time very well spent. It makes his actions consistent with the type of person or individual that Leo is."

Messi fully justified those words when Barça entertained Atléti. Only Jan Oblak's outstretched fingertips kept him off of the scoresheet, and the 'keeper stopped everything else in a 0-0 draw that Barça desperately needed to win. With three matches remaining there was still hope, but it was rapidly extinguished when the *Blaugranes* blew a 2-0 lead at Levante then lost at home to Celta, leaving Atlético to win their 11th title.

The disappointing end to the season meant questions rapidly turned to when, rather than if, Koeman would be sacked. Laporta had told the Dutchman's representatives that he would give himself a couple of weeks to seek a better alternative, but if he could not find one he would stick with Koeman for one more season until his contract ran out.

Koeman's agents were understandably furious. A tweet from Rob Jansen left no room for conjecture: "Imagine: I want to marry you, but I have doubts. Give me two weeks to find a better partner ... If I can't find the right person, we will get married anyway!"

Messi was happily distanced from all of this, in Argentina preparing for the Copa América. While he focussed on the tournament, the football world speculated on his future at club level. Laporta had suggested that things were coming together nicely, but the contract still had not been signed, sealed and delivered. Surely it wasn't going to be the end of the story ... was it?

The Copa América began with no further news on the part of Messi's contract, but movement in the transfer market with the signings of Leo's Argentine compatriot, Sergio Agüero, and defender, Eric García, both from Manchester City, as well as Emerson Royal, who was brought back from Real Betis, and Memphis Depay on a free after his contract with Lyon expired. Koeman also survived the cull as Joan Laporta got his business done early, but it would take a little longer to start clearing out the dead wood.

Leo started the tournament in fine form. A vintage long-range free-kick deserved to win Argentina's opener against Chile, but their inability to hold onto a lead meant that Eduardo Vargas' leveller was enough for the spoils to be shared. He then delivered a man-of-the-match showing against Uruguay in *La Albiceleste*'s next game which included a superb assist for Guido Rodríguez to power home an early header that, on this occasion, was enough for the win.

Another early goal, this time from Papu Gómez, gave Argentina the victory over Paraguay, before the 'Messi show' against Bolivia. An insane assist for Papu, as well as a brace for himself, helped the side to a deserved 4-1 win. The reward was a quarter-final berth against an Ecuador side that finished second bottom of Group B without winning a game. Speculation remained rife as to Messi's renewal with Barça, and a widely circulated image on social media that had clearly come from the club's content management system indicated that good news would soon be in the public domain.

Ecuador were dispatched 3-0 in the quarter-final, with Leo again at the hub of everything, and the penalty win over Colombia in the semis was notable for the way in which he taunted former Barça team-mate, Yerry Mina, after Mina's penalty had been saved by Emi Martínez. "*Baila, ahora*" ("dance now") Leo repeatedly screamed at the top of his lungs – a visceral eruption of distain and relief – as Mina made his way, head bowed, back to the centre circle. It was in reference to the jig that the Colombian had performed in the quarter-final penalty shoot-out, against Uruguay.

The Copa América final saw Leo facing his friend and former team-mate Neymar, with much of the pre-match media and social media talk focusing on just how corrupt the officials might be in terms of doing all within their powers to ensure that Brazil walked away with the trophy again.

The cavernous bowl that is the Estadio Maracanã had a smattering of supporters from both sides, at opposite ends of the stadium, who made themselves heard. After a sterile tournament in terms of no fans being allowed inside the various stadia, it made a welcome change to the atmosphere, which was highly charged by kick-off.

Brazil, with Ederson, Danilo, Marquinhos, Thiago Silva, Renan Lodi, Lucas Paquetá, Casemiro, Fred, Everton, Richarlison and Neymar appeared to have the stronger team when compared to the Argentine line-up of Emi Martínez, Montiel, Romero, Otamendi, Acuña, Di María, De Paul, Paredes, Lo Celso, Lautaro Martínez and Messi. In addition, there was the knowledge that the *Seleção* had never lost to *La Albiceleste* in a competitve game at the Maracanã, and had only ever been beaten there once in their entire history, and that was way back in 1950 against Uruguay. If history was going to repeat itself and end 28 years of hurt for Argentina, it was going to take a monumental effort from Messi and his team-mates.

The way the game started certainly set the tone. For the first 20 minutes it was an uber-aggressive war of attrition, with both sides going at each other with real menace. Tackles were flying in all over

July 11, 2021: Leo is given the 'bumps' as Argentina finally win a major trophy after a 28-year wait. The Copa América final against Brazil was won by a solitary goal from Ángel Di María. (© Shutterstock)

the pitch, and it's a wonder that referee, Esteban Ostojich, was able to keep a measure of control. Not until the 22nd minute did we see the first moment of real skill, as firstly Rodrigo De Paul pinged an inch-perfect 50-yard pass to Ángel Di María's feet, before the latter expertly controlled the ball and then lobbed an outcoming Ederson to open the scoring. It would prove to be the match-winning moment on the back of an incredibly disciplined performance from the Argentines. Brazil, by contrast, became more ragged the longer the game went on. Neymar wasn't given the time he craves in possession, and as a result his petulance, which had been well hidden in the tournament to this point, came to the fore.

Brazil's manager, Tite, hadn't lost a single Copa América fixture during his tenure and only five games in total, but whatever he tried just wasn't paying off on an evening that would end in glory for Leo. Even the introductions of Emerson, Vinícius Júnior, Roberto Firmino and Gabriel 'Gabigol' Barbosa, as the hosts went for broke, had little effect. A Richarlison offside goal and a couple of half chances notwithstanding, Lionel Scaloni's side were beating the Seleção at their own game and in their own backyard.

July 11, 2021: Messi leads the Argentina squad in celebration with their fans after the Copa América final victory against Brazil. (© Shutterstock)

Another 'Maracanazo' soon appeared to be a formality despite a smattering of yellow cards which forced Scaloni to change some personnel before they were red carded. As the full-time whistle was blown, Messi sank to his knees and was quickly joined by his teammates in an exhibition of unbridled joy. They all knew, everyone knew, just how much this title meant to him. The celebrations, which included throwing Leo into the air, were sustained, emotional and beautiful to behold, and in stark contrast to the Brazil players who looked stunned and exhausted.

Neymar was completely bereft, the TV cameras capturing him sobbing his heart out for a good few minutes as he sought to make sense of what had just occurred. To his credit, he eventually sought out Messi for a congratulatory hug. Despite ending on the losing side, his greeting was warm and genuine, and reciprocated by Leo in what will become one of the final's most enduring images.

Before lifting the trophy aloft, and sending a nation into rapture in the process, Leo first had to accept the man-of-the-tournament trophy as well as the Golden Boot for being its top scorer. This brought the pre-tournament questions, as to whether he still has the skill and fight to win an international competition, into very sharp focus. The 2021 Copa América was Messi's tournament from start to finish, without a shadow of a doubt, and underlined, yet again, that he was head and shoulders above his contemporaries.

Thanks to fellow journalists, Marirro Varela and Sergio Levinsky, a post-tournament interview with Argentina manager, Lionel Scaloni, was secured for this book. It was easy to understand, when listening to Scaloni, why this time it was different for *La Albiceleste*:

"I believe that a team in a championship must be dependent on certain players. In this case we're talking about Leo, but it could be others, and the virtues of all of the players – Paredes, De Paul, Lautaro etc. – needed to be exploited. If we extract and take advantage of their characteristics, we'll get the best out of the team, and in Messi's case, it was even more important for us to get the best out of him. To do that, his team-mates had to not stop contributing and they understood that perfectly. I'm clear why we were champions. It was because of the way we understood and 'felt' the responsibility of wearing the shirt, and the fact that we prioritised team-mates and the group over the individual. Each player understood that they could contribute a grain of sand in the time that they had to play in each game. The one who played 20 minutes contributed the same as the one who played in every game. These players got it into their heads that this title was going to be won by everyone – both those who played a little and those who played a lot. That sacrifice led them to a long-awaited Copa América, and proof of this is that I was able to use every outfield player in the tournament, something that's not often the case in this type of competition."

Given that Argentina had previously come so close to breaking Messi's international duck in terms of a tournament win, Scaloni had another very simple explanation for the victory in the final.

"I think the only difference is that in this final against Brazil, the ball went in. The previous squads got to finals but just couldn't score in normal time or in extra- time, and they lost on penalties. That line is a very fine one because those squads also deserved to win the Copa América. We were able to score through Di María, and that allowed us to play with greater peace of mind. That was our advantage. I don't think there were any footballing differences between us or the other Argentina squads, since those teams also had clear lines of play and ideas. If we look at the final of the 2014 World Cup in

Brazil against Germany, Argentina deserved to be champions, the only thing missing was putting the ball in the net. That's football. As unfair as it is beautiful."

Coaching Messi had been a pleasure rather than a chore for Scaloni, given the little time that they generally had to work together.

"I don't have any difficulties. On the contrary – it's a privilege to train him and even see how proud his team-mates are to play alongside him. For us he is important, and there's no coach in the world that wouldn't want him on their side. As a set of coaching staff, we feel more than fortunate to be able to count on him. When we talk with him, we never refer to what has happened before, we always concentrate on the present. What we want, how we can generate it and the way in which he will contribute alongside his team-mates. We were convinced that this generation of players had a great sense of companionship which would make him feel comfortable, and for us it was key that Messi connected with the current group.

Messi is a winner who is at his happiest on the pitch. He is a midfielder/forward who assists and scores goals, knows when to press and when to hold back. In some matches we can modify things based on the opponent, but I think his role with us is quite clear, and he'll always play in the position that is the most profitable for the team. He was born to play football and it's on the field where we see the happiest version of Lionel. It's what he does best and what gives him the most joy. Off the pitch, he takes everything that happens around him very naturally."

Looking forward, not back, is clearly a big part of Scaloni's way of working, but looking too far ahead would be a mistake.

"We have to qualify for the World Cup first. It would be illogical to think about that now and even more so about being a world champion. We are very far from that. You have to go step by step and the time will come to think about other goals. We need to solve the first one which is to qualify from the South American group which is always difficult. It would be a big mistake to project any further than that at the moment. We've met our objectives so far, and today the national team has young players that will continue to bring joy for a long time. There's still room for improvement and it's our idea to continue refreshing the team and try to ensure that no one rests on their laurels. Those who perform well will continue to represent the shirt, whilst being aware that other players with a great desire will be pushing to get a place. I'd like my legacy to be that I was part of a group and project that had the idea of reaching a goal or a World Cup, and we did our bit to achieve it. The best thing is that I know the players come to a place where there is harmony and comfort, which allows them to develop and do their bit to hopefully bring success. I hope that everyone understands that, and I think that's happening now."

For once, the newspapers worldwide were all in agreement - the G.O.A.T. (Greatest of All Time) debate had been settled in that final, and Leo had also become one of only a few footballers in history to win a major tournament whilst not being attached to any club, given that his contract with Barça had still not been settled despite everyone's best efforts. By the time he was due back for pre-season training, the club had still not managed to get him to sign on the dotted line either. Laporta was having a terrible summer trying to shift on players who just didn't want to leave. Junior Firpo, Jean-Clair Todibo and Carles Aleña were sold and Trincão had been sent on loan to Wolves, but their transfer fees wouldn't make a dent in club's massive debts. If Laporta couldn't pull a rabbit out of the hat quickly, not only would Messi not be able to be re-signed, but Agüero, Depay, García and Emerson couldn't be registered either. As it turned out, no one was prepared for what happened next, not even Leo.

Chatting with Xavi Gamper, the grandson of FC Barcelona's founder, Joan Gamper, on August 5, when neither of us had any inkling of the news that was about the break, he spoke about the situation at the club, telling me;

"Laporta has some experience as you know, but is he the right president at this time? I don't really want to answer that, it's too soon, but what I will say is that the last president didn't do a good job. Laporta has found a black hole financially. Everyone can see that Bartomeu made decisions that no one agrees with. Dembélé, Coutinho and Griezmann ... Liverpool knew Barça had plenty of money and took advantage. Coutinho? There's no way Barça should've paid so much money for him – 50 or 60 million euros maybe but €160m? Pffff"

With no official news on Messi's deal, Xavier was, nevertheless, looking forward to watching him again during the upcoming season.

> "For me he's the best player I have ever seen in a stadium. I have to recognise that I haven't seen Pelé or Maradona, but Messi has had a long career. If you compare him to all of the fantastic players, he has had the longest career of any player I know. As a goalscorer and assister, he has been incredible too – eyes in the back of his head. The recognition of space that he has, the pitch dimensions, he knows everything."

Just a couple of hours later, the bombshell dropped. Not only was there to be no signing announcement, but Barça were unable to afford to re-sign Leo because of the mixture of financial constraints being placed upon them by La Liga in terms of Financial Fair Play, and the inability to make room in club coffers because shifting anyone else had become hugely problematic. The party line from the club was that, in simple terms, no other players appeared to be willing to leave, meaning that Barça were unable to underwrite Messi's salary. Spanish football rules state that salaries should make up 70% or less of club income. However, had Messi's new deal somehow been signed off, it would have seen salaries at an impossible 110% of Barça's income. Even without it salaries were still taking up 95% of income, so whilst it appeared scarcely believable that Barça's best-ever player wasn't going to be finishing his career in *Blaugrana* after all, Joan Laporta attempted to explain the legitimate reasons why the unthinkable had become a reality at a press conference the following day.

He reiterated that there was a deal in place for Leo and that both parties had effectively 'shaken hands' on it. He wanted to stay at Barça, and Barça wanted him to stay, however, when the numbers were crunched properly, Laporta just couldn't make it work. "He did everything he could to stay. His wish to stay was the first step in ensuring we could find the right way. We must thank everyone who has been negotiating between the club and the player. Leo deserves everything. He has demonstrated his love for the club. First, we reached a two-year agreement to be paid in five years. Leo agreed to it. He always wanted to stay and tried to make it easier. We thought it was in line with fair play, but the 'cash' criterion here wouldn't accept it. "Then we agreed to a five-year contract, and he agreed to that as well, but La Liga studied it and didn't accept it either. There was a moment when La Liga insinuated to us that the proposed contract could suffice, but after a technical analysis by its financial commission, they then informed us that wouldn't fully suffice either. If I could make a personal assessment, I am sad, but we have done the best thing for the club. I would love to have appeared here with Leo beside me to announce that he is staying. That's what everyone at Barça was dreaming of. I would have loved to have signed his final contract and Leo has done everything and more to make that happen. There is nothing to resent."

Given that supporters were still reeling from the shock, many were looking for the merest hint of the possibility that Messi could stay. Some read between the lines of Laporta's answers and took them to mean that if Javier Tebas and La Liga could massage the fair play rules somehow, Leo would continue. Reporters asked some pointed questions in much the same way.

Some even hinted that Laporta had hung Messi out to dry in order that the club could press ahead with Barça's participation in the Super League. Indeed, the president had even met with Florentino Pérez and Andrea Agnelli in Barcelona just two days after making the announcement about Messi. Could it be that he knew all along that Leo wouldn't be able to continue and had done a magnificent job of covering up the truth until the point where doing so became impossible? Was Leo, in fact, betrayed? It was certainly on many minds in those following few days.

Once the reactions of his team-mates started to filter through onto social media later that Thursday evening, the penny finally dropped and all the hope the *culés* possessed was gone. It really was goodbye. Gerard Piqué was the first to break cover on Instagram. "Nothing will be the same anymore. Neither Camp Nou, nor Barcelona, nor ourselves," he wrote. "After 20 years at the club, you will no longer be wearing the Barça shirt. The truth sometimes hurts. We met in 2000, we were 13 years old with our careers before us. What a career! Wow! We couldn't have designed it better. Bloody crazy! In my first season, after coming back to FC Barcelona, we won the treble and you became the best player of all time. From Rosario to touch the heavens in Rome. That's where the legend started. What followed was history. What fun we had. Now you are leaving but I know you will be back one day. There are still things to do. Have fun, wherever you go and keep winning the way only you know. We'll miss you here. I love you Leo."

The messages of goodwill and good luck just kept on coming.

Xavi: "As a *culé*, team-mate and friend I can only thank you for everything you have done for us over all these years. Whatever you do, I wish you the best."

Carles Puyol: "Thank you very much for everything, Leo. I can never be thankful enough for everything you've given us. I wish you all the best."

Luis Suárez: "Young man, I know there are no words to describe the history you wrote at FC Barcelona. The club watched you grow, the club you love so much and where you won so many titles and became the best player in history. I will always be grateful for the way you welcomed me and for being the great person you are. Proud to have shared thousands of wonderful moments at FC Barcelona and to have been fortunate enough to play with you. I wish with all my heart that whatever happens in the future will be the best for you and your family. I love you loads."

Sergio Busquets: "I'm still trying to take it all in and knowing how difficult it will be, I just want to say thank you for everything you have done for the club and for those you have been with these years and specifically myself. You came as a child and you are leaving as the best player of all time, having made this club grow to the size it deserves and making individual and team history. I will always be able to say that I played and shared moments with you, most of them very good and I had the chance to grow and enjoy football at your side for 13 seasons. Aside from all that, I also have the person and our friendship, I will miss you a lot. I can only wish you and your family the best because you deserve it. We will miss you very much."

Sergi Roberto: "When I was small my dream was to play in the Barça first team. But to do so beside the best footballer of all time is something I never imagined. Thank you for all the moments you have given me and all Barça fans, all the joys, all the goals you've scored, all the titles we've celebrated, to take this club to the very top, for making people dream with your football and especially for doing it with this shirt. I wish you and your family all the best. We love you and we will miss you very much. In eternal gratitude."

Jordi Alba: "What a privilege to have spent these nine seasons together. Such nice experiences together and we have overcome such difficult situations. I was lucky enough to be there to see your first goal against Albacete at Camp Nou in 2005 and I never imagined we would come to have such an understanding with just a single glance. We have had such fun on the pitch with your running passes and my passes back that have come off so well for us. I'm going to miss it so much! Not just because you're the best player in football history but because you're an exceptional human. Friend, thank you from the heart for what you've done for the club, for your friendship, for your support on grey days, for the great moments we've lived that will always stay in our memories. I wish you and your family all the best on your new adventure. A big hug, I love you brother."

Marc-André ter Stegen: "Leo, it has been a pleasure to play with you for these years and to have such great moments in terms of moments and titles. Although we didn't always share the same opinion, we were always looking in the same direction and every one of us grew as a person whether we won or lost. Thank you! You made history at your lifelong club and you will leave as a true football legend, and achievement that no other player will get close to. You changed football. I wish you and your family all the best for what's ahead. A big hug from Dani and Ben too."

Antoine Griezmann: "The only thing me and everyone who loves football can say is THANK YOU! Thank you for everything you have done for Barcelona. For the city, the club ... you changed everything! I am sure this not a goodbye but a see you later and that your path will cross with FC Barcelona again. I wish you all the best and for you and your family to be happy wherever you go. Very few know what it means to be Messi and you always set an example in every sense."

Ansu Fati: "All the kids that come to La Masia dream of playing by you and I feel fortunate that my dream came true. I want to thank you for these two years, for your gestures towards me and for everything I learned. My family and I shall always be eternally grateful, I wish you and your loved ones all the best."

To a man, every message carried genuine warmth and the same theme of thanks, and best wishes for the future. They may have provided Leo with some comfort as he addressed the media in Camp Nou's Auditori 1899 at midday on August 8, a day when he should have been playing against Juventus in the annual Gamper Trophy match. With hundreds of thousands also watching online, he couldn't stop the tears from flowing as he took to the stage and could barely muster a sentence as the gravitas of the situation finally got the better of him. He was in pieces, with pain etched across his face. Little wonder. Thankfully Antonella was on hand with a handkerchief, and with his family, team-mates and assorted dignitaries in attendance along with the media, the time had come for him to cut ties with a club that had given him everything in a footballing sense. To his credit, he eventually composed himself enough to answer every question directly and honestly, knowing that he would still leave the club through the front door so to speak, and with his head held high.

"Over the last few days, I have been thinking about what I was going to say, what I could say. The truth is that I am stuck, it's really difficult for me after so many years, a whole life. I was not prepared. I was convinced I was staying, at home, that's what we wanted. We always placed our own happiness first, being at home, enjoying life in Barcelona on a sporting and personal level ... It's time to say goodbye to Barça. It has been a long time, all my life. I can't be more proud of what I have done and experienced in the city and I know that after a few years away I will be back – that I have promised to my kids also ... It's really difficult to leave after so many years. After spending most of my life here, I was convinced I could continue here at home. I was not prepared. Last year I was, I was convinced about leaving but this year no ... I want to thank all my team-mates and former team-mates. I have always tried to behave with humility and respect, and I hope that is what stays here with people, as well as everything I had to fortune to give to the club ... I would also like to thank the people for their affection towards me, I would have liked to say goodbye in a different way. To be able to do it out there on the field, hear my last ovation, have them close, hear the cheering ... I leave the club without having seen them for a year and a half. I have always been up front with the members and fans, what was important for me was to tell the truth to the people who gave me so much, as I did for them. We have grown up and had fun together.

"We have had lots of memorable moments, also painful ones but the affection has always been the same. I have felt the recognition and the love that I also feel for the club. Let's hope I can return at some point and help as best I can because this cub is still the best in the world ... It's very difficult to just think of one moment. There have been many good ones and some bad but perhaps the moment that stays with me is when I made my debut, which was the start of my dream coming true ... Everything was agreed and then at the last moment, because of the issue with La Liga, it could not be done. I did all I could to stay, that's what I wanted but it could not be done. ... This is the most difficult moment of my sporting career. I have had a few difficult moments, many defeats but nothing like this. There is no coming back, it's the end at this club and now a new story begins ... Barça is the biggest team in the world, and they have a great squad. The club is more important than anything and people will get used to that. At first it will be strange, but they will come around ... It's very sad and tough but we are taking it in as we can. When I leave here it will be even worse, but I will be accompanied by my family and I will keep on playing football which is what I like best. The people at Barça know me and they know I am a winner that wants to remain competitive."

It was far from the ending that Barça's finest player deserved, and certainly not in-keeping with his legendary status. The standing ovation he received spoke volumes. What should have been a glorious celebration of a magnificent career in *Blaugrana* was anything but. At times, the undeniably awkward press conference felt almost funereal and it was uncomfortable to watch. Not just for the fact that Leo didn't look at Joan Laporta once, and barely referred to him at all if he could help it. There was very definitely something in the air, though nothing was said to give the media vultures something else to feed on. For once, they too seemed to understand that this was neither the time nor the place to inflict more pain on a man in total turmoil. Even when they asked their questions, one could sense their sadness, and all were respectful.

With media duties taken care of, it was time to pose for a few photos alongside his trophy haul and say his goodbyes to team-mates and staff. That there was no hanging around thereafter spoke volumes. Not even one last stroll out onto the Camp Nou pitch, or a backward glance. As he attempted to drive away with his family for the last time, his white Range Rover was mobbed by adoring *culés* desperate for one last picture and image with their hero – the man that made them believe anything was possible when he was in the team. After slowly winding his way through a heaving mass of bodies he was gone, and 21 years had passed by in a flash. As he sped off into the distance, the Lionel Messi era at FC Barcelona was over.

Epilogue

With the Gamper Trophy match against Juventus being played on the same day as Messi's press conference, and crowds allowed back inside stadiums for the first time in 18 months, it was the first chance for *culés* to publicly voice their displeasure at the situation that the club had found itself in.

However, a comfortable 3-0 victory over the Old Lady and no attempt to ignore what had happened with Leo thanks to speeches from Busquets and Koeman, who specifically referenced his importance, took the wind out of the crowd's sails somewhat. Samuel Umtiti bore the brunt of any ire, booed every time he touched the ball on the night. Clearly rattled, the Frenchman walked straight down the tunnel of the Johan Cruyff Arena at full-time, rather than staying on the pitch with his team-mates.

Laporta's popularity had plummeted, and not just because further reports were suggesting that the president knew well before the announcement that he couldn't keep Messi. His unhealthy obsession with the Super League concept alienated him further, as did standing right behind Florentino Pérez in his attempt to sue La Liga. Both clubs were fiercely opposed to a deal with private equity firm CVC, to whom La Liga chief, Javier Tebas, had proposed to sell a 10% share in the league's future television rights for €2.7bn (£2.3bn). Getting into bed with Barça's eternal rivals was never a good look. Particularly when Laporta's major concern had to be how he was going to steer Barça through the stormiest of waters and back to the pinnacle of European football. A place they'd inhabited just over a decade earlier. Laporta's decision to then go on holiday before the new players had been registered was an incredibly poorly judged move too.

It wouldn't be until the day before Barça opened their 2021-22 campaign against Real Sociedad that Memphis Depay, Eric García and Rey Manaj were finally eligible for league action. Even then, that had only come about because Gerard Piqué had taken a 'substantial' pay cut according to FC Barcelona's official site. Thirty thousand fans inside Camp Nou provided a beautiful soundtrack to a brilliant performance, which ended in a 4-2 home win. Aside from Messi chants on 10 minutes, and again 10 minutes after half-time, this was a game which evidenced that Barça had much to be excited about moving forward. Piqué's opener, Memphis' hard-working debut, Pedri's brilliance, Martin Braithwaite's industry, and Antoine Griezmann's incredible skills. All that and more showed that however tough the divorce had been, there was more than enough quality left in the squad to still remain competitive.

Josep Maria Bartomeu then had the brass neck to send a highly critical letter to Laporta, also making it public. Laporta was so incensed he took the former president apart, point by point, in a press conference on the Monday after that match. "The end of the financial year of the '20-'21 season will bring losses of €481 million. This has been audited by Ernst & Young, and presented to the league. The impact of the pandemic is €91 million. The wage bill represents 103% of income (€617 million), 25-30% above our competitors. The club's worth is minus €451 million, this is very delicate. It has been necessary to come up with a strategic plan to make sure we have a functioning business and enjoy the confidence of our creditors. The club's debt is €1,350 million ... Invoices were split up in the case of I3 Ventures, the Espai Barça ... the debt invoked was split up to be less than 10% of income so as not to have pass through the Assembly."

Laporta didn't waste any time either when articulating what an "appalling" sports project the club had under Bartomeu's stewardship, and continued to pull apart the many 'lies' that he believed were in the letter. When asked again about Leo, given that a short time had passed since his departure, Laporta, for the first time, indicated that it was a decision he had made, suggesting it was "sad, but necessary." It may not have won him any more friends, but at least he was dealing with things head on and acting like a president, something Gerard Piqué had made reference to in a live Twitch broadcast after the Real Sociedad match.

The club's perilous financial situation wasn't going away anytime soon, and any commercial opportunities – including those with potential new sponsors – were going to be much harder to come by. Although Messi was one of the most highly paid players in the world, his popularity ensured that he effectively paid for himself. Within two days of saying goodbye to the Catalans, he had passed a medical with Paris Saint-Germain, and within 48 hours of his official announcement, somewhere in the region of 150,000 PSG shirts

As the move became inevitable, France Football published a mocked-up image of Leo in a PSG shirt. It was a day that broke the hearts of Barça fans around the world. (© France Football)

adorned with Messi's name and the number 30 were believed to have been sold. They were already reaping the rewards of what Barça had sown. Oddly enough, the club shop at Camp Nou was still selling the new season's shirt with Messi's name and number on even after he'd been pictured at the Parc des Princes – and it was selling well.

Evidently, fans didn't want to give up on their hero worship just yet, even if the feeling of disbelief was common amongst the Barça fraternity. The pain was still raw and they were hurting. More so when they saw and heard *their* No.10 telling the world how happy he was to be in Paris. What a sickener. With his press conference duties, interviews and unveiling taken care of, his job was done. Now it was time to get match fit and ready to play. Only time will tell if Messi's presence in the French capital will help PSG win their longed-for Champions League title, but under fellow countryman, Mauricio Pochettino, and with Ramos, Wijnaldum, Di María and others alongside Leo, the French giants certainly have their best chance ever of reigning supreme in the premier European competition.

PSG's gain was Barça's pain, but it was time to move on: time for his former team-mates to step up; time to stop talking about 'Messi-dependence'; and time for the new signings to show the Camp Nou faithful exactly why they were signed in the first place. It was also time for the La Masia graduates to give the supporters something to dream about again. It was time to show that there really was life after Messi.

Index

Lionel Messi Career Statistics

(to 5 August 2021)

1. FC Barcelona

Season	Games	Minutes	Goals	Assists	G+A per 90 min	Free Kick Goals	Hat-tricks+	Braces
2004-05	9	238	1	0	0,38	0	0	0
2005-06	25	1414	8	3	0,70	0	0	1
2006-07	36	2763	17	3	0,65	0	1	4
2007-08	40	2954	16	13	0,88	0	0	3
2008-09	51	3890	38	17	1,27	1	1	7
2009-10	53	4402	47	11	1,19	2	4	10
2010-11	55	4579	53	23	1,49	1	4	12
2011-12	60	5221	73	29	1,76	3	10	12
2012-13	50	4070	60	15	1,66	4	2	18
2013-14	46	3742	41	14	1,32	3	4	7
2014-15	57	5060	58	27	1,51	2	6	11
2015-16	49	4229	41	23	1,36	7	3	7
2016-17	52	4452	54	16	1,42	4	2	14
2017-18	54	4468	45	18	1,27	7	4	7
2018-19	50	4023	51	19	1,57	8	4	11
2019-20	44	3810	31	25	1,32	5	3	3
2020-21	47	4192	38	11	1,05	3	0	10
TOTAL	778	63507	672	267	1,33	50	48	137

2. Argentina

Season	Games	Minutes	Goals	Assists	G+A per 90 min	Free Kick Goals	Hat-tricks+	Braces
2004-05	0	0	0	0	0,00	0	0	0
2005-06	10	432	2	3	1,04	0	0	0
2006-07	10	784	4	2	0,69	0	0	1
2007-08	10	840	3	3	0,64	0	0	0
2008-09	9	807	3	2	0,56	0	0	0
2009-10	11	979	1	1	0,18	0	0	0
2010-11	11	986	4	6	0,91	0	0	0
2011-12	9	810	9	4	1,44	0	2	0
2012-13	12	942	9	3	1,15	2	1	1
2013-14	11	996	7	2	0,81	1	0	2
2014-15	10	826	4	5	0,98	0	0	1
2015-16	10	735	9	4	1,59	2	1	1
2016-17	5	450	3	2	1,00	1	0	0
2017-18	10	900	7	3	1,00	0	2	0
2018-19	8	621	3	1	0,58	0	0	1
2019-20	2	180	2	1	1,50	0	0	0
2020-21	13	1170	6	5	0,85	2	0	1
TOTAL	151	12458	76	47	0,89	8	6	8

3. Club & Country

Season	Games	Minutes	Goals	Assists	G+A per 90 min	Free Kick Goals	Hat-tricks+	Braces
2004-05	9	238	1	0	0,38	0	0	0
2005-06	35	1846	10	6	0,78	0	0	1
2006-07	46	3547	21	5	0,66	0	1	5
2007-08	50	3794	19	16	0,83	0	0	3
2008-09	60	4697	41	19	1,15	1	1	7
2009-10	64	5381	48	12	1,00	2	4	10
2010-11	66	5565	57	29	1,39	1	4	12
2011-12	69	6031	82	33	1,72	3	12	12
2012-13	62	5012	69	18	1,56	6	3	19
2013-14	57	4738	48	16	1,22	4	4	9
2014-15	67	5886	62	32	1,44	2	6	12
2015-16	59	4964	50	27	1,40	9	4	8
2016-17	57	4902	57	18	1,38	5	2	14
2017-18	64	5368	52	21	1,22	7	6	7
2018-19	58	4644	54	20	1,43	8	4	12
2019-20	46	3990	33	26	1,33	5	3	3
2020-21	60	5362	44	16	1,01	5	0	11
TOTAL	929	75965	748	314	1,26	58	54	145

259

4. Senior Team Trophies

Season	Number	Trophies
2004-05	1	La Liga
2005-06	3	La Liga + Champions League + Supercopa
2006-07	1	Supercopa
2007-08	0	
2008-09	3	La Liga + Champions League + Copa del Rey
2009-10	4	La Liga + UEFA Supercup + Club World Cup + Supercopa
2010-11	3	La Liga + Champions League + Supercopa
2011-12	4	Copa del Rey + UEFA Supercup + Club World Cup + Supercopa
2012-13	1	La Liga
2013-14	1	Supercopa
2014-15	3	La Liga + Champions League + Copa del Rey
2015-16	4	La Liga + Copa del Rey + UEFA Supercup + Club World Cup
2016-17	2	Copa del Rey + Supercopa
2017-18	2	La Liga + Copa del Rey
2018-19	2	La Liga + Supercopa
2019-20	0	
2020-21	2	Copa del Rey + Copa América
TOTAL	36	

5. By Competition

Season	Games	Minutes	Goals	Assists	G+A per 90 min	Free Kick Goals	Hat-tricks+	Braces	Titles
La Liga	520	42142	474	192	1,42	39	36	97	10
Champions League	149	12332	120	35	1,13	5	8	25	4
Copa del Rey	80	6512	56	32	1,22	3	3	11	7
Supercopa	20	1674	14	5	1,02	1	1	2	8
UEFA Supercup	4	420	3	2	1,07	2	0	1	3
Club World Cup	5	427	5	1	1,26	0	0	1	3
Copa América	34	2907	13	17	0,93	4	1	1	1
World Cup	19	1625	6	5	0,61	1	0	1	0
WC Qualifiers	51	4315	23	10	0,69	3	1	2	-
International Friendlies	47	3611	34	15	1,22	0	4	4	-
TOTAL	929	75965	748	314	1,26	58	54	145	36

6. By Manager

Manager	Games	Wins	Draws	Losses	Goals	Assists	Trophies
Frank Rijkaard	110	70	22	18	42	19	5
Pep Guardiola	219	159	43	17	211	80	14
Tito Vilanova	50	34	9	7	60	15	1
Tata Martino	66	42	16	8	54	23	1
Luis Enrique	158	121	18	19	153	66	9
Ernesto Valverde	124	85	28	11	112	46	4
Quique Setién	24	15	4	5	15	16	0
Ronald Koeman	47	29	7	11	38	11	1
José Pékerman	10	6	1	3	2	3	0
Alfio Basile	24	12	6	6	8	6	0
Diego Maradona	16	10	0	6	3	2	0
Sergio Batista	11	6	4	1	4	6	0
Alejandro Sabella	32	22	8	2	25	9	0
Edgardo Bauza	4	3	0	1	3	2	0
Jorge Sampaoli	11	5	4	2	7	3	0
Lionel Scaloni	23	13	7	3	11	7	1
TOTAL	929	632	177	120	748	314	36

7. Favourite League Opponents

Opponent	Goals	Assists	Goals + Assists
Sevilla	38	17	55
Valencia	31	12	43
Levante	24	19	43
Athletic Club	29	11	40
Real Madrid	26	14	40
Atlético Madrid	32	5	37
Real Betis	26	10	36
Espanyol	25	11	36
Getafe	21	14	35
Osasuna	25	8	33

8. Favourite Stadiums

Stadium	Goals	Assists	Goals + Assists
Camp Nou	396	134	530
Santiago Bernabéu	15	9	24
Sánchez Pizjuán	13	8	21
Ciudad de Valencia	11	9	20
Vicente Calderón	15	4	19
Mestalla	12	7	19
Riazor	13	5	18
Benito Villamarín	10	7	17
El Monumental	8	9	17

9. Notable Records

9.1 World Records

- Most Ballon d'Or awards: 6
- Most European Golden Shoe awards: 6
- Most official goals in a calendar year: 91 goals in 2012
- Most official goals for a single club: 672 goals for FC Barcelona
- Most official trophies won for a single club: 35 trophies for FC Barcelona
- Most goals scored in finals: 31
- Most goals scored in a domestic league: 474 goals in La Liga
- Most goals scored in a single season of a domestic league: 50 goals in La Liga 2011-12
- Most consecutive league games scored in: 21 games in La Liga 2012-13
- Most Champions League goals for a single club: 120
- Most Champions League opponents scored against: 36
- Most consecutive Champions League seasons scored in: 16

9.2 Spanish Records

- Most Pichichi awards: 8
- Most league games scored in: 300
- Most goals scored in La Liga history: 474
- Most goals scored in Supercopa history: 14
- Most hat-tricks in La Liga history: 36
- Most La Liga wins: 383
- Most Spanish titles won: 25
- Most Supercopa titles: 8
- Most Copa del Rey titles: 7
- Most goals in Copa del Rey finals: 8
- Most goals in El Clásico history: 26
- Most assists in El Clásico history: 14
- Most La Liga stadiums scored in: 38
- Most La Liga teams scored against: 38

9.3 FC Barcelona Records

- Most appearances in Barça's history: 778
- Most goals in Barça's history: 672
- Most wins in Barça's history: 542
- Most trophies in Barça's history: 35
- Most games played at Camp Nou: 381

9.4 Argentina Records

- Most appearances for Argentina: 151
- Most goals for Argentina: 76
- Most goals in a calendar year: 12 goals in 2012
- Most hat-tricks for Argentina: 6

St David's Press

Also by Jason Pettigrove

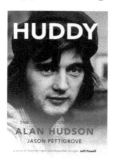

'A story of dizzying highs and desperate troughs'

Jeff Powell

'A total one-off footballer. There's never been anyone quite like him, in his ability and what he was able to do with a football.'

Malcolm McDonald

'I was fortunate enough to play with a few great players and Alan was up there with the very best.'

Denis Smith

'Alan was a top quality, gifted player.'

Gordon Taylor

One of the finest players football has ever seen, Alan Hudson is still revered at Chelsea, Stoke City, Arsenal and Seattle Sounders, and yet his professional success was dogged by injuries and enormous personal challenges. His love of the glitzy 'footballer lifestyle', dominated by hard-drinking and glamorous women, saw Alan descend into rampant alcoholism, depression, and frequent brushes with authority.

Huddy - his official biography - reveals for the first time, the full story of the real Alan Hudson, the man behind the lurid newspaper headlines and booze-fuelled anecdotes. A straight-speaker who doesn't suffer fools gladly, he has as many enemies as close friends. Speak to either and you'll get a vastly differing perspective on just who the man is. Even his team-mates were evenly split; they either loved or loathed him. The one thing that couldn't be taken away from him, however, was his talent for the beautiful game.

pb - 978 1 902719 573 - £13.99
pb - 978 1 902719 870 - £13.99